Taking the IB Diploma Programme Forward

Edited by
Mary Hayden and Jeff Thompson

John Catt Educational Ltd

First Published 2011

by John Catt Educational Ltd,
12 Deben Mill Business Centre, Old Maltings Approach,
Melton, Woodbridge IP12 1BL

Tel: +44 (0) 1394 389850 Fax: +44 (0) 1394 386893
Email: enquiries@johncatt.com
Website: www.johncatt.com

© 2011 John Catt Educational Ltd

All rights reserved.

No part of this publication may be reproduced, stored in a retrieval system, transmitted in any form or by any means, electronic, mechanical, photocopying, recording, or otherwise, without the prior permission of the publishers.

Opinions expressed in this publication are those of the contributors and are not necessarily those of the publishers or the editors. We cannot accept responsibility for any errors or omissions.

ISBN: 978 1 908095 19 0

eISBN: 978 1 908095 20 6

Set and designed by John Catt Educational Limited
Printed and bound in Great Britain by Bell & Bain, Glasgow, Scotland

Acknowledgements and notes

The authors, editors and publishers are grateful to the International Baccalaureate Organization for permission to reproduce its intellecutal property, specifically the IB learner profile and the current DP model.

In 2008 the IB dropped the 'O' from their acronym – IBO became IB. The latter style has been used throughout.

Contents

About the contributors 5

Foreword, *Mary Hayden and Jeff Thompson* 9

Part A: The Diploma Curriculum

1. The IB Diploma Programme, *Mary Hayden and Jeff Thompson* ... 15

2. The identity of the IB Diploma Programme core, *Nick Alchin* 24

3. A question of balance, *Neil Richards* 42

4. Moving on from the 1960s: a new model of diploma
   for our global citizens, *James MacDonald* 52

5. The IB Diploma Programme as pedagogic
   discourse, *James Cambridge* 65

6. The IB diploma in a national education system:
   a case study of curriculum convergence in Turkey, *Jale Onur* 77

7. Extending access to the Diploma Programme:
   IB courses online, *Keith Allen* 91

8. Schools' contributions to curriculum innovation in the
   IB diploma: a case study of the world studies extended essay,
   David Wilkinson, Cyrus Vakil and Veronica Wilkinson 105

9. Supporting the school and the IB diploma community
   through the school library, *Anthony Tilke* 117

Part B: Aspects of Growth and Development

10. The 'growth' of the IB diploma: critical perspectives on balance,
    depth and 'development', *Tristan Bunnell* 131

11. Growth of the international school market in China and its potential implications for the IB, *Barry Drake* 142

12. Assessment in the IB diploma: the role and potential of e-marking, *Keith Allen* 161

Part C: Contexts for the IB Diploma

13. Taking forward the IB diploma in India: context and challenges, *Gillian Ashworth* 179

14. The internationalisation of Dutch secondary education: the IB DP and the Dutch international secondary schools, *Boris Prickarts and Theo Brok* 197

15. Higher education and the IB diploma: a UK perspective, *Leslie Currie* 206

16. Promoting understanding and tolerance in a post-conflict society: the role of the IB diploma at the United World College in Mostar, *Paul Regan* 217

Taking the IB Diploma Programme Forward

About the contributors

Nick Alchin has taught in IB schools since 1995, first teaching ToK and mathematics at the United World College of South East Asia in Singapore and subsequently at the International School of Geneva in Switzerland. After working as director of IB at Sevenoaks School, UK, he is currently dean of studies at the Aga Khan Academy in Mombasa, Kenya. He was chief assessor for ToK from 2005 to 2010 and is currently vice chair of the IB Examining Board.

Keith Allen taught in British comprehensive schools for ten years before 23 years in IB schools, including senior administrative roles in four DP schools. He currently has two posts: academic manager for Oxford Study Courses (OSC) and training officer for the IB Schools & Colleges Association of the UK and Ireland (IBSCA). Both in and beyond these jobs, he is passionate about widening access to high quality education systems such as the IB.

Gillian Ashworth was MYP coordinator at The International School of Azerbaijan before moving to Mumbai to become head of secondary at Ecole Mondiale World School. Her IB roles include being a face-to-face regional and in-school workshop leader for both DP and MYP, an online workshop mentor, MYP consultant and school visits team leader, and she is both an examiner for DP language A literature and a moderator for MYP English A.

Theo Brok has been working as an administrator in Dutch education for more than 30 years. In 1989 he introduced bilingual education into Dutch secondary schools and in the 1990s he implemented the IB Middle Years Programme in a Dutch secondary bilingual school. Theo is Director General of Alberdingk Thijm Schools Association (approximately 6500 students) and he chairs the Dutch International Secondary Schools Association. He is also a church historian.

Dr Tristan Bunnell has been teaching IBDP economics since 1990. He has held a post at the Copenhagen International School since 2004 and prior to this he taught for 14 years at the International School of London. He was awarded a doctorate from the University of Southampton in 2003 and has since published papers about the growth and development of the IB in 15 different journals. He is also a presenter on the topic at international conferences.

Dr James Cambridge is an international education consultant. Formerly head of research projects with the IB Research Unit and a visiting research fellow at the University of Bath, he has worked in Britain, the Middle East and Southern Africa in posts including science teaching, assessment, curriculum development, initial teacher education and continuing professional development. His research interests include inquiry into international curriculum, international schools, evaluation and intergenerational service learning.

About the contributors

Leslie Currie studied mediaeval and modern history at the University of Glasgow and then worked in international banking for ten years, in Cyprus, Bahrain, Hong Kong and the UK. From 1988 to 2007 he worked at the University of Bath, first setting up and directing the International Office and then as head of undergraduate admissions and UK/EU recruitment. He now works for Supporting Professionalism in Admissions (SPA), a national programme promoting good practice in UK admissions to higher education.

Dr Barry Drake is currently an independent educational consultant and a senior associate with an international teacher recruitment organisation. He has over 40 years of teaching and leadership experience in the field of international education and international schools, incorporating periods in Africa, the Middle East, South East and East Asia, and including 17 years in Hong Kong. Barry was involved with the IB programmes for 20 years as a teacher, workshop leader, examiner and moderator.

Dr Mary Hayden is Director of the Centre for the study of Education in an International Context (CEIC) at the University of Bath, and editor of the *Journal of Research in International Education*. Her teaching, publishing and research supervision focus particularly on international schools and international education. For nine years she held the posts of IB mathematics and science subject officer and head of research. She is a trustee of the Alliance for International Education, and a member of the Curriculum Advisory Board for the International Primary Curriculum and International Middle Years Curriculum.

James MacDonald is currently Head of School at Yokohama International School in Japan, having previously worked in Canada and Singapore. He has held a number of teaching and leadership positions over his career, including those of DP teacher and DP coordinator. James has published a number of journal articles on international education, and is a regular conference presenter. He is also a member of the IB Asia Pacific Heads Council.

Dr Jale Onur is Assistant General Director of the Koç School in Istanbul, where she previously taught English. She holds degrees from Istanbul University and from The School for International Training in Vermont, USA, and subsequently gained her doctorate from the University of Bath, England. She is an executive board member of the Turkish Private Schools Association. Her research interests are centred on bringing together theory and practice in education.

Boris Prickarts is founding Headmaster of the Amsterdam International Community School (AICS). Previously he was a history teacher and junior administrator at the International School of The Hague (ISH). He has also taught in the UK and in Australia, and has both written and edited history school books in Dutch and English. He is a member of the board of the Dutch International Secondary Schools (DISS), and is currently researching Dutch international education policy at the University of Bath.

About the contributors

Paul Regan. After graduating in Russian, and working initially as a translator and tutor, Paul taught modern languages after obtaining his initial teacher education qualification from the University of Nottingham, UK. He has held the post of Headteacher in five schools in the UK, Africa, the Balkans, India and the Ukraine. In three of them he was the founding Head. He is currently Head at the Oaktree International School in Kolkata, India.

Neil Richards has held headships at international schools in Lesotho, Japan and the United Kingdom. His involvement with the International Baccalaureate diploma began over 25 years ago when he was the senior administrator responsible for its introduction and implementation at the British International School, Cairo; he has been involved in the teaching of theory of knowledge almost continuously since that time. He is a trustee of the 21st Century Learning Initiative.

Professor Jeff Thompson teaches, supervises, researches and publishes through the CEIC at the University of Bath in areas relating specifically to international schools and international education. He has worked closely for many years with the IB, having held posts, *inter alia*, of Chair of the DP Examining Board, Director of Research, and Academic Director. Currently, he is Chair of the Curriculum Advisory Board for the International Primary Curriculum and International Middle Years Curriculum. He was founding editor for the *Journal of Research in International Education*.

Dr Anthony Tilke is head of library at the International School of Amsterdam; he previously worked in three international schools in Asia, and has been involved with IB programmes for 12 years as librarian, ToK teacher and workshop leader. He developed a major library building project at Oakham School, UK, and was school library advisor with the professional organisation for librarians. His doctoral research concerned the impact of an international school library on the Diploma Programme.

Dr Cyrus Vakil has been Academic Head at UWC Mahindra, India, since 2000 and deputy head of college since 2005, and has taught British and colonial history at Yale and Wesleyan universities. His interest in interdisciplinary study goes back to his 1995 Yale PhD dissertation – at the interface of history, literature and political economy. Bringing the critical and interdisciplinary spirit of a liberal arts college education to DP students is his longstanding passion.

Dr David Wilkinson was appointed Head of a college in Lesotho after a number of years in teaching and research. Whilst in Southern Africa he was Government representative for Lesotho on the IB Council of Foundation and Governing Council. He was also co-founder of the first association of non-racial schools in Southern Africa. He was the founding Head of two United World Colleges, in Hong Kong and in India, and is currently working as an educational consultant.

About the contributors

Dr Veronica Wilkinson began teaching at the Li Po Chun United World College of Hong Kong, since when she has worked for the United World College movement and the International Baccalaureate (IB). Since 2001, she has been an IB examiner of English and is currently a Deputy Chief Examiner. She works for the Pestalozzi Overseas Children's Trust, and has experience of examining, teacher training and teaching in India, Italy, Singapore, Lesotho, Hong Kong and Thailand.

Foreword

We were delighted when we received an invitation from John Catt Educational to act as editors for a book about the International Baccalaureate Diploma Programme. We readily agreed to do so for two principal reasons. Firstly, we had previously edited the book entitled *Taking the MYP Forward* for the same publishers, and our role in the process was as professionally satisfying as it was personally enjoyable, working – as we did – with a group of writers who were prepared to share their experience and expertise with the wider constituency of those with responsibility for designing and implementing the programme in schools throughout the world. The prospect of engaging with yet another group in a similar way, for the International Baccalaureate (IB) Diploma Programme (DP), was difficult to resist! The second reason we were attracted to the task was more personal. We have both been involved in teaching and researching in the field of international education, particularly as it relates to international curricula and international schools, throughout a significant proportion of our academic work to date. The IBDP has featured majorly in our research over many years and we have had the privilege of working in partnership with colleagues from wide geographical and educational contexts in enquiring into the range of factors involved in its successful implementation in schools. Additionally each of us, in various ways, with differing roles and at different times, has been involved directly in working for the IB.

The IBDP is the longest standing programme of its kind in the world, owing its creation and initial realisation in practice to the inspiration and selfless commitment of a dedicated group of far-sighted educators from the middle of the last century. That the overall programme design, and its major features, remain essentially the same as those conceived nearly 50 years ago is a point that has been debated vigorously in recent times. There are those who believe that the Diploma Programme's original design has proved fit for purpose in the wide range of contexts in which it has been introduced during that time and that it has represented, from a politically independent standpoint, an exemplar for the development of other curricula – in national and international systems – throughout the world. Others believe that experience to date suggests that the current model is in need of a more radical review, if it is to serve validly as an appropriate response to IB policy for widening access and greater inclusivity.

Against that background, all the contributors to this book shared a similar brief, which we, as editors, were responsible for generating. Writing from their own experiences with the IBDP, every contributor was given the opportunity to identify issues arising from current practice and to indicate how those issues would need to be addressed, in the context of the topic chosen, as part of the implementation of the policy for future growth that the IB has recently adopted. Thus, we were concerned primarily with generating a range of ideas and suggestions, based upon a constructive analysis of current practice and arising from the personal experience of the authors, which could be offered to the IB as an independent contribution to the debate about the future development of the programme.

We entertained a variety of ways in which the rich sources of material received from the authors could be represented. In the end we have chosen to organise the chapters in three distinct, though clearly related, parts. It seemed to us that, given the challenges currently experienced by the long-established programme, it would be appropriate to bring together contributions from those who have offered their thoughts about the ways in which consideration may be given to the development of the curriculum model itself. Thus, Part A: The Diploma Curriculum, opens with a chapter written by the editors that is intended to provide – for those readers who may not be so familiar with the IBDP as are others, and as a general context for the book as a whole – background information about the programme and the ways in which it has arrived in its current form. The core of the IBDP curriculum, represented in the familiar hexagon model, is often credited with being the most important, and indeed unique, feature of the programme – but what does it represent in educational terms? Nick Alchin explores the basis of the identity of this central aspect of the curriculum. The ways in which the programme and its certification could be reviewed in order to encompass and to acknowledge the much wider range of student achievement than is currently represented within the formal structure of the diploma are explored through the respective experiences of Neil Richards and James MacDonald in effecting change in schools. James Cambridge offers us a lens through which to review the programme in thinking about its comparison with other curricula and its own future development.

Many teachers face reconciling the IBDP with national requirements, and Jale Onur has shared with us her own research on the convergence of the curricular and pedagogic demands of the Turkish national system with those of the IBDP, as an encouragement to others faced with a similar challenge. Against the backdrop of extending access to the programme that is an explicit target for the IB, Keith Allen describes the work that has been undertaken in offering IBDP courses online, and considers some of the future challenges associated with its extension. Teachers and administrators have contributed to the introduction and revision of new programmes within the Diploma Programme from the outset and continue to do so; that has been seen as a great strength of the organisation, and David Wilkinson and colleagues share with readers their experience of attempting to introduce a new programme into the IBDP. Although it is not possible to include examples of all the valuable contributions made in school to the successful running of the IBDP by professional colleagues who offer a wide range of support for teachers and students, one such example is Anthony Tilke's chapter describing the role of the librarian and the outcomes of his own research in the area.

In Part B: Aspects of Growth and Development, we invited contributions from three colleagues on different aspects of this fundamental tenet of IB policy.

Tristan Bunnell, who has written widely on this and other aspects of IB, shares his perspectives on issues of balance and depth in the programme as affected by the pursuit of growth and development as major aims of the organisation. Some of these issues are also explored by Barry Drake as he illustrates the challenges faced in the context of China, whilst Keith Allen offers a way forward through a consideration of the role of e-marking in addressing the large increase in candidature for the diploma examinations arising from the huge anticipated growth.

Part C: Contexts for the IB diploma comprises four contributions from individuals who have experience of the introduction of the IBDP in differing educational environments. We are aware that each specific geographical context has its own characteristics and lessons to be learned from them, and we could have chosen a much wider range of exemplars to illustrate how changing context demands unique responses. That would have been to extend the book beyond a reasonable size – especially in publishers' terms! We decided instead to highlight the introduction of the programme in what is commonly regarded as one of the fastest growth areas for the IBDP, by drawing upon Gillian Ashworth's perspectives on its introduction and growth in India. An account of the ways in which the IBDP contributed to partnership in The Netherlands context is provided by Boris Prickarts and Theo Brok. For many students, success in the diploma opens up entry pathways to the higher education sector worldwide. Leslie Currie, experienced in university administration, raises a number of issues relating to the process of university admission in a UK context. The potential role of the Diploma Programme in facilitating the process of student integration in post-conflict societies is illustrated through Paul Regan's account of his experience in Bosnia and Herzegovina, as founding Head of the United World College in Mostar.

We owe a tremendous debt of gratitude to our authors, all of whom have responded positively to the quite unreasonable time and textual demands of these editors. In spite of the high professional loads each one of them bears, they have been willing to share with us – and therefore with our readers – their views based upon years of experience in practising, and reflecting upon their practice of, the IBDP as it currently exists and the implications of their analyses for the future development of the programme. We once again wish to acknowledge the support we have received from colleagues at John Catt who have not only given freely of their advice but have done so in a way that has been a valuable learning experience for us as editors.

As the production of this book neared completion, we learned of the death of Ruth Bonner. Among the relatively small group of those charged with the responsibility for translating the ideals and ideas for an international curriculum into practice in the very first days of the IBDP, Ruth was a dominant figure over the first two decades of the programme's existence. Her expertise, inspiration, dedication and motivation, together with her ability to accomplish

Foreword

administrative tasks of huge proportions (by both personal example and coercion of others!) were crucial factors in the building of a foundation from which the IBDP grew, and from which it will surely progress in the future.

Mary Hayden
Jeff Thompson

Part A

The Diploma Curriculum

14

Chapter 1

The IB Diploma Programme

Mary Hayden and Jeff Thompson

The 1960s was a remarkable decade on many counts. In the context of education, it was a time of great innovation. With the memories of two horrific World Wars still live in many minds, and the early stages of what might now be described as globalisation evident in increasing international mobility, technological developments and awareness of the interdependence of humankind, came growing realisation that education need no longer be constrained by national borders.

Early international schools had been in existence for some time (including the International School of Geneva and Yokohama International School since 1924 and, according to Sylvester (2002), since at least 50 years earlier), and support for that growing network was emerging in the form of organisations including the International Schools Association, established in 1951 (Peterson, 1987), and the European Council of International Schools (ECIS), founded in 1965. European Schools (providing education for children of employees of the then European Community) had existed since 1956, with a mission encouraging students to become good European citizens, while 1962 saw the founding in South Wales of Atlantic College (later the United World College of the Atlantic), the first of what are now 13 United World Colleges worldwide (UWC, 2011). Spearheaded by the vision of Kurt Hahn, a German of Jewish origin who was committed post World War II to creating an environment in which young people from many national and cultural backgrounds could live and study together, with a view to the breaking down of barriers of prejudice and ignorance and the promotion of world peace, Atlantic College offered a form of education that could be described as a mix of pragmatic (preparing young people for what even then was clearly likely to be an increasingly global future) and ideological (encouraging international-mindedness, respect for others from different backgrounds and commitment to promoting greater global understanding).

Against this backdrop, of global mobility, awareness of growing global interdependence, and increasing numbers of school age students being educated away from their home environments and national education systems, the need for a form of education other than the many existing separate national programmes was all too clear. Indeed, Peterson (1987) points out that in 1925, a year after its founding, the Board of Governors of the International School of Geneva had discussed the need for an international version of the Swiss *maturité* to be developed as an international school-leaving examination tentatively described as a *maturité internationale*. Though the idea did not bear fruit at that time, by the 1960s the need for such a development was abundantly clear to schools such as Atlantic College, which struggled with educating young people from many national backgrounds through the national A level system (with its then heavy emphasis on, for instance, British history, and language examinations that focused on translation into and out of English). International schools such as the International School of Geneva were similarly struggling with preparing young people from many backgrounds, in common teaching groups, for university entrance examinations of different national systems. That a clear need exists for something, however, does not mean that its introduction and development will be straightforward or even possible. And, indeed, the pathway from the need for an international pre-university programme and qualification having been identified to the International Baccalaureate Diploma coming into existence was not a smooth one. The progress made by those pioneering individuals and schools – including the International School of Geneva, Atlantic College and the United Nations International School New York, as well as other organisations including Oxford University Department of Educational Studies, the College Board in Princeton, and various national ministries and funding agencies – has been well documented, *inter alia*, by Alec Peterson (1987), Elizabeth Fox (1998) and Ian Hill (2010). A reading of these accounts makes clear just what a slippery path it was, with the existence of the new creation threatened on a number of occasions by lack of funds and questions of recognition and credibility.

The 1960s was also a period of wider curriculum innovation, and the new programme grew up against a backdrop of work on both sides of the Atlantic by, amongst others, Phenix in the USA (1964) and Hirst and Peters in the UK (1970) who promoted, respectively, the notions of 'realms of meaning' and 'modes of experience' that have echoes in the IB diploma structure developed then and still, in essence, in place half a century later. Research interests of the Department of Educational Studies at Oxford University, then led by Alec Peterson (later to become the IB's first Director General), were similarly influential in the development of the IB Diploma Programme.

After a set of trial examinations, the first 'real' (Peterson, 1987) IB diploma session took place in May 1970 as the beginning of a six year experiment, with a structure arising from much debate about the most appropriate form of education at pre-university level in terms of breadth vs specialisation, the place of language, coherence, encyclopaedic knowledge vs 'learning to learn' – and how to ensure university recognition of the end product. For some years the structure of the diploma was described in various documents in text only. The diagrammatic representation, with which many are now so familiar, emerged only in the 1980s when Jeff Thompson conceptualised a model of the DP requirements in the form of a hexagon (Figure 1) that was the precursor to the model widely recognised today.

The IB Diploma Programme

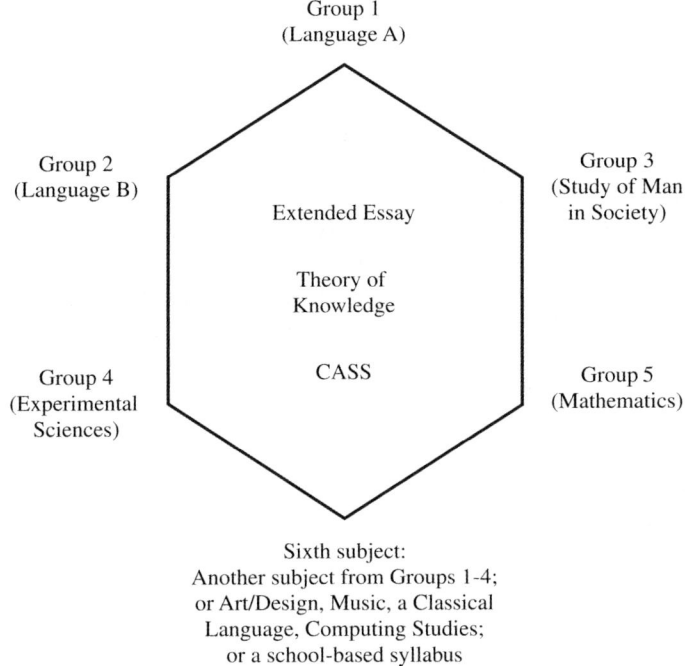

Figure 1: Jeff Thompson's original Diploma Programme hexagon

In Ian Hill's words:

> The Diploma Programme was first depicted as a hexagon by Professor Jeff Thompson, at the time chief examiner for chemistry and physical science. It occurred during a conference of the Fondazione Cine in Venice, 9-11 December 1983 where he spoke about the IB Diploma Programme and presented it on an overhead projector transparency (Renaud, 2001). Jeff is well known for his propensity to visualise ideas. His geometrical shape corresponded to the six groups of subjects with the extended essay, theory of knowledge and CASS (creative and aesthetic activity, and social service), as it was at the time, in the middle. CASS became CAS (creativity, action, service) in 1989.
>
> Renaud had been present at the meeting in Venice and liked the visual representation. In a paper on the theory of knowledge, Renaud (1986) refers to the way in which Thompson's schema showed the coherence of the IB programme through the hexagonal structure.
>
> Thompson used the hexagon again at a major IB conference at the University of London in 1988 (Hayden *et al*, 1995: 131-2). However, it was not until 1993 that the hexagonal representation of the Diploma Programme first appeared officially in IBO documents, notably in a number of subject guides printed that year (Hill, 2007).

The fact that Thompson was a chemist by academic discipline led him to use the benzene ring as the basis for the model. It is interesting to note that, as part of a 1990s review, he proposed a naphthalene ring model to accommodate growing interest in vocational dimensions of the IB diploma, which proved to be a molecule too far! Other systems of education have also found the model helpful in thinking about national curriculum reform; the Finnish experience in remodelling their vocational system is one example. In that connection, it is interesting to note the recent introduction of the IB career-related certificate (IBCC) (IB, 2011c).

The development of the Diploma Programme in its first 50 years has not always been smooth or without controversy. In terms of take-up by schools, recognition by universities and an increasingly high profile, however, it has clearly been successful, with numbers of schools offering the diploma at the time of writing standing at 2311 in 139 different countries (IB, 2011a).

The IB context

The case for an international curriculum having been made and its benefits experienced by schools and students worldwide, it was perhaps only a matter of time before the question would be asked as to why such a concept should be restricted to the 16-19 age range. After some 30 years as an only child, the DP was joined by two new siblings: the IB Middle Years Programme (MYP) in 1994 and the IB Primary Years Programme (PYP) in 1997. Described as the IB 'continuum', the three programmes taken together cover the age range 3-19, and share a common mission that aims to develop inquiring, knowledgeable and caring young people who demonstrate intercultural understanding and respect, and who become active, compassionate and lifelong learners (IB, 2011b).

Common, too, to all three programmes is a set of standards and practices translated into programme-specific requirements for each programme's implementation (IB, 2010), as well as a set of attributes it is expected will be exemplified in those emerging from any of the IB programmes, described as the IB learner profile. Details can be found in Appendix 1. In summary, IB learners strive to be:

Inquirers	Knowledgeable
Thinkers	Communicators
Principled	Open-minded
Caring	Risk-takers
Balanced	Reflective

(IB, 2008)

Schools may only offer any of the IB programmes if they have been authorised by the IB organisation to do so, at which point they become known as an 'IB World School'. Though increasing numbers of schools now offer all the IB programmes, the majority offer only one or two of the three. As a not-for-profit organisation, administration of the IB is organised through a network of offices and staff members based in Geneva (headquarters), Cardiff and the Hague (curriculum and assessment centre), and further offices in Singapore, Bethesda Maryland, Vancouver and Buenos Aires. With the Director General based in Geneva, IB governance consists of a Board of Governors including representation from schools and examiners.

The Diploma Programme structure

The IB diploma hexagon today represents the programme's requirements as shown in Figure 2.

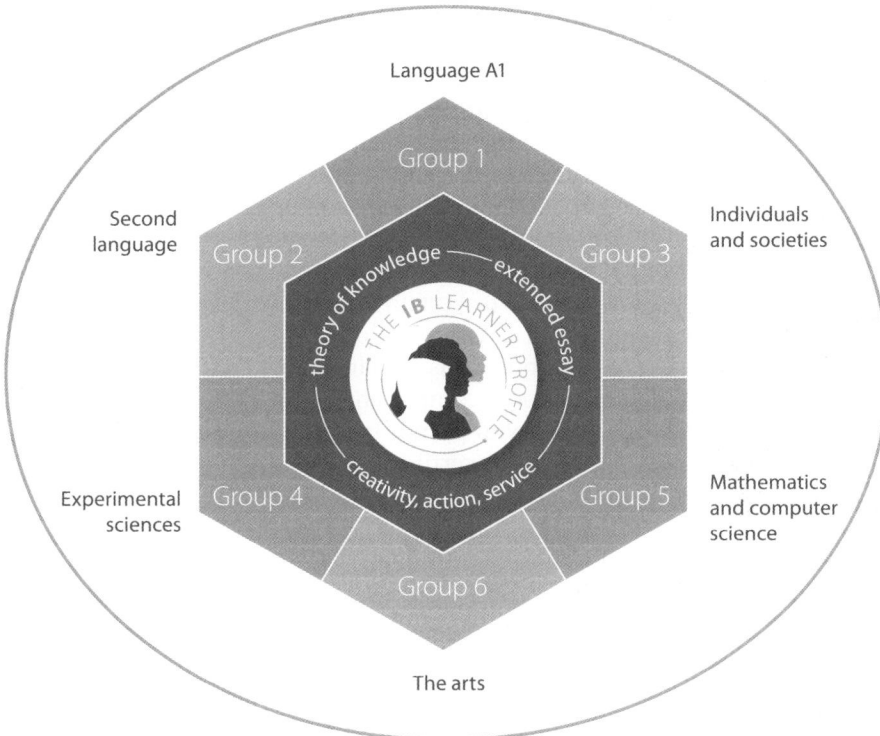

Figure 2: The IB Diploma Programme hexagon today

Full details of the requirements leading to the award of the IB diploma are best accessed by referring to IB documentation (IB, 2011d). In essence, students must study one course from each of groups 1-5. A sixth subject must be chosen either from group 6, or as a second subject from one of the other five groups. Normally, three subjects are offered at higher level (requiring 240 hours of teaching time), and three at standard level (requiring 150 hours of teaching time). As an alternative to one subject from groups 2 to 6, a school may be authorised to develop a school-based syllabus in response to its own needs and teaching resources. In addition to six subjects, students must successfully complete the three elements of the diploma 'core': an extended essay (EE) of around 4000 words, a course in the theory of knowledge (ToK), and a programme of activities entitled creativity, action, service (CAS).

The IB diploma has three working languages: English (through which the majority of students study and are examined), French and Spanish. The student's work is essentially externally examined (though with internally assessed elements in many cases). CAS is not examined, but schools are required to monitor and attest to students' participation in that programme of activities. The majority of students complete their examinations in the May examination session. Some schools, mainly those following a southern hemisphere timetable, enter their students in the smaller, November, examination session. Though most students complete all examinations in one session, it is possible, with certain restrictions, for either one or two subjects to be 'anticipated' after the first year of the two year programme. It is also possible to 'retake' an examination in the hope of improving the grade. Grades are awarded for each of the six subjects on a scale of 1 (lowest) to 7 (highest); up to three further points can be awarded for the combined results of ToK and the EE. The maximum number of points that a DP student can be awarded is therefore 45. The diploma is awarded to those who achieve at least 24 points, subject to certain minimum levels of performance across the whole programme and satisfactory completion of CAS. Under certain circumstances (relating to combinations of languages studied and languages through which the different diploma components are completed), a bilingual IB diploma may be awarded. Those who do not meet the conditions for the award of the IB diploma may be awarded certificates indicating achievement in the different elements of the programme.

Summary

The IB diploma is now not only well recognised by universities worldwide but, having been created principally to cater for globally mobile students in international schools, is also increasingly well-regarded within national schools in many contexts. Whether for its academic rigour, its international dimension in a context where national education systems are increasingly recognising the imperative of preparing young people for a global future, or its social cachet for those who aspire to a competitive edge for their child over peers in the national education context, it is undoubtedly the case that the IB diploma has now moved beyond the educational niche from which it emerged. Though still catering for the globally mobile international school student for whom it was initially developed, the diploma is now increasingly seen as an option of choice for those in independent and state schools of national systems who may have no particular international aspirations in terms of future lifestyle or career. Indeed, it is currently the case that more than half of all IB World Schools are schools in state systems (IB, 2011e).

The environment in which the IBDP is to be found 50 years on is markedly different in many other ways too, as the effects of globalisation and increasingly sophisticated technology place ever-greater demands on it from the many constituencies with expectations of how it might meet their particular needs. Undoubtedly still leading the field as an international programme for the pre-university level, the IBDP has been followed as an international programme not only by its own MYP, PYP and IBCC stable-mates, but also by non-IB programmes including the International GCSE (IGCSE), International Primary Curriculum (IPC) and International Middle Years Curriculum (IMYC), as well as international elements or versions of programmes including the Cambridge Pre-U, A level, and the College Board's Advanced Placement. The IB diploma is thus no longer the novelty it once was, nor quite the source of wonder it perhaps ought to be that such a thing as an international curriculum actually negotiated the slippery path of creation, development and recognition as it did – a testament to the power of motivated practitioners to move educational mountains if ever there was one. Rather it is now so well-established and well-recognised that expectations of it from all quarters are high.

As research about IB programmes (though still largely small-scale and unfunded) increases, and as the body of literature pertaining to IB issues extends, so is it clear just how broad are the issues engendering current debate. Now asked of the IB are questions relating to the provenance of its international credentials, its essentially western liberal philosophy, its working languages, and its Euro-centric underpinnings (see, *eg*, Drake, 2004; Van Oord, 2007; Walker, 2010). And as the programme is taken up by a wider range of constituencies, so too are questions asked as to how it can satisfy all those constituencies without some feeling overshadowed by others. Nor are these questions only being asked from outside the IB organisation; those centrally involved in its administration and delivery in schools are similarly raising such issues, as can be seen in the recently-published collection of writings by a number of those closely involved in IB and edited by George Walker, emeritus IB Director General (Walker, 2011).

The IBDP is thus an increasingly high profile contributor to the debate on globalisation and the role of education in the changing world of the 21st century. That debate and discussion about the role of the IBDP in that world is ongoing and challenging is healthy. This collection of chapters asking questions about aspects of the IBDP, offering suggestions for its development, raising issues about its implementation in different contexts and highlighting challenges facing it, is offered as a contribution to that healthy debate. We hope the contribution will be seen as a positive one to the next phase of development of this innovative programme.

References

Drake, B (2004): International Education and IB Programmes: worldwide expansion and potential cultural dissonance, in *Journal of Research in International Education*, 3 (2) pp189-205.

Fox, E (1998): The Emergence of the International Baccalaureate as an Impetus for Curriculum Reform, in M C Hayden and J J Thompson (eds), *International Education: principles and practice*. London: Kogan Page, pp65-76.

Hayden, M C, Richards, P N and Thompson, J J (1995): Validity and reliability issues in International Baccalaureate examinations, in T Kellaghan (ed), *Admission to Higher Education: issues and practice*. Princeton: International Association of Educational Assessment, pp131-141.

Hill, I (2007): Early stirrings in international education Part XII: marketing the IB Diploma Programme to ministries of education, government and examining bodies, in *International Schools Journal*, XXVII, 2, pp76-84.

Hill, I (2010): in M Hayden (ed), *The International Baccalaureate: pioneering in education, The International Schools Journal Compendium Volume IV*, Woodbridge: John Catt Educational.

Hirst P H and Peters R S (1970): *The Logic of Education*. London: Routledge and Kegan Paul.

IB (2008): *Learner Profile booklet*. Cardiff: International Baccalaureate.

IB (2010): *Programme Standards and Practices*. Cardiff: International Baccalaureate.

IB (2011a): Online: www.ibo.org/facts/schoolstats/progsbycountry.cfm (last accessed 4 September 2011).

IB (2011b): Online: www.ibo.org/mission/ (last accessed 4 September 2011).

IB (2011c): Online: www.ibo.org/ibcc/ (last accessed 4 September 2011).

IB (2011d): Online: www.ibo.org/diploma/ (last accessed 4 September 2011).

IB (2011e): Online: www.ibo.org/history/ (last accessed 4 September 2011).

Peterson, A D C (1987): *Schools Across Frontiers: the story of the International Baccalaureate and the United World Colleges*. La Salle IL: Open Court.

Phenix, P H (1964): *Realms of Meaning*. New York: McGraw Hill.

Renaud, G (1986): *La Théorie de la Connaissance*. 18 November, Geneva: IB archives.

Renaud, G (2001): Conversation with Ian Hill, 14 June, Geneva

Sylvester, B (2002): The 'first' international school, in M C Hayden, J J Thompson and G R Walker (eds), *International Education in Practice: dimensions for national & international schools*. London: Kogan Page, pp3-17.

UWC – United World Colleges (2011): Online: www.uwc.org (last accessed 4 September 2011).

Van Oord, L (2007): To Westernize the Nations? An analysis of the International Baccalaureate's philosophy of education, in *Cambridge Journal of Education*, 37 (3) pp375-390.

Walker, G R (2010): *East is East and West is West*. IB position paper, Geneva: International Baccalaureate.

Walker, G R (ed) (2011): *The Changing Face of International Education: challenges for the IB*. Cardiff: International Baccalaureate.

Appendix 1: The IB learner profile

The aim of all IB programmes is to develop internationally minded people who, recognizing their common humanity and shared guardianship of the planet, help to create a better and more peaceful world.

IB learners strive to be:

Inquirers	They develop their natural curiosity. They acquire the skills necessary to conduct inquiry and research and show independence in learning. They actively enjoy learning and this love of learning will be sustained throughout their lives.
Knowledgeable	They explore concepts, ideas and issues that have local and global significance. In so doing, they acquire in-depth knowledge and develop understanding across a broad and balanced range of disciplines.
Thinkers	They exercise initiative in applying thinking skills critically and creatively to recognize and approach complex problems, and make reasoned, ethical decisions.
Communicators	They understand and express ideas and information confidently and creatively in more than one language and in a variety of modes of communication. They work effectively and willingly in collaboration with others.
Principled	They act with integrity and honesty, with a strong sense of fairness, justice and respect for the dignity of the individual, groups and communities. They take responsibility for their own actions and the consequences that accompany them.
Open-minded	They understand and appreciate their own cultures and personal histories, and are open to the perspectives, values and traditions of other individuals and communities. They are accustomed to seeking and evaluating a range of points of view, and are willing to grow from the experience.
Caring	They show empathy, compassion and respect towards the needs and feelings of others. They have a personal commitment to service, and act to make a positive difference to the lives of others and to the environment.
Risk-takers	They approach unfamiliar situations and uncertainty with courage and forethought, and have the independence of spirit to explore new roles, ideas and strategies. They are brave and articulate in defending their beliefs.
Balanced	They understand the importance of intellectual, physical and emotional balance to achieve personal well-being for themselves and others.
Reflective	They give thoughtful consideration to their own learning and experience. They are able to assess and understand their strengths and limitations in order to support their learning and personal development.

Used with permission from the IB learner profile booklet © *International Baccalaureate Organization.*

Chapter 2

The identity of the IB Diploma Programme core

Nick Alchin

Introduction

Much of the IB Diploma Programme (DP) consists of well-known subjects – mathematics, history, art and so on. The three elements of the core of the DP, by contrast – theory of knowledge (ToK), extended essay (EE) and creativity, action, service (CAS) – are far less familiar to most people. Parents, students and educators are, perhaps for this reason, often very interested in these elements, and when making presentations about the core I have often begun by stepping back from the details of the DP hexagon model and asked the audience to consider broader issues, such as the purpose of education, lifelong learning, learning to learn, international-mindedness, critical thinking, active learning or skills for the 21st century. These important and fascinating areas, rich in possibility and promise, then form the backdrop for an exploration of the core, which I always find to be intimately and profoundly linked to important themes in these areas. My presentation explores these links, and I try to call on present or former DP students to ground the ideas in specific examples from their experience. The presentation then ends with the claim that the essential nature of the core is based in this or that broad theme, that the core therefore provides something special that cannot be found elsewhere, and that it is the unique selling point of the DP and is therefore of immense value.

I do believe that the core has great value, and I am happy making a claim to that effect. I am, however, sometimes troubled that this value seems to reside in whatever concept I turn to. Is it really the case that the essence of the core is such a chameleon that it can blend in with whatever thoughts or ideas are in the surrounding educational landscape? Given the precisely articulated IB mission and values, it would be strange indeed if the central aspects of the DP were so malleable, and in this chapter I hope to suggest that, while there are several possible interpretations of the core, and while these have evolved over time, there is a bedrock aspect about the core that underlies these different perspectives but that is articulated in different ways according to the current spirit of the age.

What is the core?

The core is made up of three elements; the extended essay (EE), theory of knowledge (ToK) and creativity, action, service (CAS), all of which must be successfully completed for the award of the IB diploma. The assessment of ToK and EE is criterion-referenced, on the basis of which students may be awarded up to a total of three core points. Extremely poor performance in ToK/EE may lead to non-award of the diploma (see IB, 2006: 42 for full details).

The EE is a piece of writing of up to 4000 words – probably the longest single piece of writing a diploma candidate undertakes over the two years of the programme. The essay is not a general overview of a broad area but is instead a focused critical examination of a narrowly-defined topic, generally within a DP subject. Its purpose is not to deepen subject knowledge, but rather to ensure that students have an authentic experience of the research process, and the essay is expected to include the formal elements of a research piece normally found at university level study (such as, for example, abstract, research question, referencing and bibliography). In assessing the EE, examiners focus on how well the student has structured and communicated ideas and information, and the extent to which the essay is a logical and coherent whole, appropriate to the subject chosen. Students are expected to spend a maximum of 40 hours on their EE, and to have up to four hours of contact time with an academic supervisor (who must be a teacher in the school), working independently for the remainder of the time. The work is typically undertaken over a period of several months, often with the bulk being completed over the break between the first and second years of the programme, and can involve an optional viva voce at the end of the process. Some examples of EE titles are included in Figure 1.

Example Extended Essay Titles	
English	The depiction of violence in Anthony Burgess' *A Clockwork Orange* and Chuck Palahnuik's *Fight Club*.
Economics	Does the internet make market structures more perfect?
Philosophy	Is happiness a necessary condition for a fulfilling life?
History	How far was Salvador Allende responsible for the demise of Communism in Chile?
Chemistry	Does stirring affect the rate of a chemical reaction?
Geography	Environmental quality in central Mumbai.
Physics	What is the effect of air resistance on the distance travelled by a variety of sports balls?
Visual Arts	To what extent is the functionality of the Pompidou Centre secondary to the aesthetic intentions?
French	La langue française, est elle menacée par la langue anglaise?
Mathematics	Geometric consequences of trigonometry on a sphere of imaginary radius.
Italian	Que impacto tuvo el muso Guggenheim en Bilbao?
Politics	To what extent can Belarus gain energy security?

Figure 1: Examples of extended essay titles

Students are also required to study ToK over the two DP years for a recommended 100 hours. The course considers the nature of knowledge, four 'ways of knowing' (reason, sense perception, language and emotion) and six 'areas of knowledge' (the arts, the human sciences, mathematics, ethics, history and the natural sciences). Students are required to make comparisons across these categories; asking questions about, for example, the extent to which reason operates similarly in mathematics, history and ethics, or about the differences between natural sciences and social sciences. The course is assessed through a combination of a 1200-1600 word essay based on a prescribed title, and a presentation based on a real-life situation of the student's own choice. Figure 2 includes examples of ToK essay titles, published annually in the *Handbook of Procedures for the Diploma Programme* and through the online curriculum centre.

Example ToK essay titles

- Evaluate the strengths and weaknesses of reason as a way of knowing.
- 'Seek simplicity, and distrust it' (Alfred North Whitehead). Is this always good advice for a knower?
- 'Context is all' (Margaret Atwood). Does this mean there is no such thing as truth?
- 'What separates science from all other human activities is its belief in the provisional nature of all conclusions.' Critically evaluate this way of distinguishing the sciences from other areas of knowledge.
- '…we will always learn more about human life and human personality from novels than from scientific psychology' (Noam Chomsky). To what extent would you agree?
- 'Moral wisdom seems to be as little connected to knowledge of ethical theory as playing good tennis is to knowledge of physics.' To what extent should our actions be guided by our theories in ethics and elsewhere?
- Are reason and emotion equally necessary in justifying moral decisions?

Figure 2: Examples of theory of knowledge essay titles

CAS involves students in a range of activities – more traditionally called extracurricular or co-curricular activities – alongside their regular academic studies. Students are required to spend at least 150 hours over the two years of their DP on CAS activities, which should be both challenging and enjoyable, and which are aligned with the CAS learning outcomes. The IB currently defines the three CAS elements as shown in Figure 3 (IB, 2008a):

> Creativity: Arts, and other experiences that involve creative thinking.
>
> Action: Physical exertion contributing to a healthy lifestyle, complementing academic work elsewhere in the Diploma Programme.
>
> Service: An unpaid and voluntary exchange that has a learning benefit for the student. The rights, dignity and autonomy of all those involved are respected.
>
> IB states specific CAS learning outcomes; that students have, by the end of the programme:
>
> • increased their awareness of their own strengths and areas for growth
> • undertaken new challenges
> • planned and initiated activities
> • worked collaboratively with others
> • shown perseverance and commitment in their activities
> • engaged with issues of global importance
> • considered the ethical implications of their actions
> • developed new skills

Figure 3: CAS elements and learning outcomes

What do students think about the DP core at its best?

The gap between the written and experienced curriculum can be a chasm. In seeking to locate and better understand the essential nature of the core, therefore, it is worth asking students what they think. No part of the DP elicits as strong a reaction from students as does the core, and it is instructive to consider a few student comments. Of course it is hard to generalise, and in my experience the quality of ToK and the EE is more variable than is the case for other DP elements (given their ambitious and, for schools, unusually broad and deep remits, perhaps this is not surprising): while some students love ToK and EE, some hate them. But if we are really to understand what the core is, or at least what it can and should be, we need to look to students who have had highly rewarding experiences, and bear their remarks in mind when we seek commonalities to the three elements.

The matter is surely worth a detailed empirical study, but the comments from students note some important overlapping features. For me, these remarks (and many consistent conversations with students, ex-students and parents over the years) paint a clear picture; that at its best the core has great cognitive value, has great affective value, can help students find qualities in themselves they did not know they had, provides excellent university preparation, and has a lasting effect on students' lives and values. But this does not, in itself, shed light on the unity, or otherwise, of the DP core. So what is it, beyond the simple facts recounted above? Below are quotations from recent IBDP students about different aspects of the core (quoted with their permission).

About the extended essay
No part of the Diploma Programme gives you the taste of university life as well as the extended essay does. The process can be frustrating: you have to research a very specific question, you are faced with a deluge of data and you are left to manage it all in your own time. However, the process is incredibly rewarding: not only can you work on your own topic but also you gain the satisfaction of putting together a 4000-word paper after many hours of work. (Marta Szczerba)

About creativity, action, service
CAS… is one aspect of the diploma that gives the individual a chance to give back to the community by helping people realize their dreams. This is a new part of my personality that I have discovered since coming here to this school. I have realized that a little help goes a long way because I went as far as working with [a local charity] as an intern giving back not only to the school community but also to other communities outside Mombasa. Now that I have come to the end of my two years here, I look back and see myself a changed person. I am not the same student I was when I first arrived. (Stephen Kimanzi)

About theory of knowledge
ToK is the IB's greatest asset… as I gained an understanding of how knowledge 'works' in various fields, it became much easier for me to recognise fallacies in the opinions or the material that teachers, other people or the media would have me believe were truth, and more importantly I was able to confidently demonstrate these inconsistencies. The lessons were truly stimulating. (Olalere Williams)

About theory of knowledge and extended essay
I am only seven weeks into my first year at university now but I have this urge to write to you about my academic experience. Going to lectures and tutorials and especially writing my first important paper now, I am so grateful for all these things we hated so much while doing the IB! All this preparing for scientific research and work, philosophy classes *etc* we do here now seem like kindergarten practice, especially after ToK and the extended essay! Maybe you hear this a lot, but I just wanted to share my joy about this with you! (Chrissie Moeller)

Does the core have a coherent identity?

In *Pierre Menard, Author of the Quixote*, Jorge Luis Borges (1989) tells of Menard, a man who sets out to write Cervantes' 15th century *Don Quixote* – not by copying it, but by literally re-creating it independently. Remarkably, he succeeds. Now, suspending our disbelief momentarily, what are we to make of a 20th century man writing *Don Quixote*? How do we interpret what he has written?

Borges argues that 'Cervantes' text and Menard's are verbally identical, but the second is almost infinitely richer' as it must be considered in light of all the philosophy and events since Cervantes lived. That is, we can attribute links and references to Menard's text, and ascribe to him a richness of reference that we know was not available to Cervantes. We can therefore far more easily ascribe current interests and understandings to Menard's text – and thus see in it things we do not see in the original. Borges writes:

> It is a revelation to compare Menard's *Don Quixote* with Cervantes'. The latter, for example, wrote (part one, chapter nine): '… truth, whose mother is history, rival of time, depository of deeds, witness of the past, exemplar and adviser to the present, and the future's counselor.'
>
> Written in the seventeenth century, written by the 'lay genius' Cervantes, this enumeration is a mere rhetorical praise of history. Menard, on the other hand, writes: '… truth, whose mother is history, rival of time, depository of deeds, witness of the past, exemplar and adviser to the present, and the future's counselor.'
>
> History, the *mother* of truth: the idea is astounding. Menard, a contemporary of William James, does not define history as an inquiry into reality but as its origin. Historical truth, for him, is not what has happened; it is what we judge to have happened. The final phrases – *exemplar and adviser to the present, and the future's counselor* – are brazenly pragmatic.

The point here is not that we interpret the texts differently because they are written by different people, but that we bring different conceptual lenses to bear, depending on our broader understanding of a situation. Underneath Borges' playful banter is the idea that we can view events using these different ideas and see different things that are *only there in the light of our ideas*. This relatively straightforward observation has a less obvious implication – namely, that what is 'really there' depends on what categories we use; that we are *constructing* what we see as much as finding it. Physicist Werner Heisenberg (1958) said much the same thing when he claimed that 'what we observe is not nature itself, but nature exposed to our method of questioning'.

So when we ask if the core has a coherent identity, we have to understand that we will be constructing what we see on the basis of what we are now, and that what has happened in the world – educationally and beyond – since the IB was created some 40 years ago offers us radically different ways of interpreting the core. So we are asking less about what the core *really is*, and more about what we *want it to be*. There is an element of invention here, and if the core does have a coherent identity, it's partly because we want it to. And what we want largely reflects broader socio-cultural issues that tell us as much about our current dreams and aspirations for future generations of students as it does about what is in the core. This is only right and proper, as identity is indeed a construction that allows individuals and organizations to draw on the past and project themselves into the future. The question of the identity of the core is, therefore, a deeply political question, and the answers will be at least partly politically determined.

Historically, there has been little emphasis on commonalities between core elements, let alone a central core identity, though the value of individual components has rarely been questioned. Gellar (2002) recalls Alec Peterson – then Director General of the IB – claiming in 1980 that ToK (not the whole core) is the lynchpin of the whole programme, and it has been argued that – in Kurt Hahn's founding DP vision – CAS, while absolutely vital, was seen less as coherently linked to other academic areas than as a chance to *escape* the academic, at least temporarily.

The question in hand – *does the core have a coherent identity?* – should therefore be seen in light of other IB developments. The articulation of a PYP-MYP-DP continuum, of the cross-programme learner profile (IB, 2008b and 2009) and the inclusion of core details in all DP subject guides, for example, all speak to the move towards increased coherence between and within programmes. This move towards coherence and perhaps even unification may be inevitable given the explosive growth of the IB and the resulting scrutiny and external pressure on the organisation, from schools and from various national regulators, and it is no surprise to see the core subject to the same scrutiny. So given that we can (retrospectively if nothing else) impose some coherence, we need to examine possible roots where this coherence can be found. I offer three suggestions that seem to me to be reasonable possibilities given wider socio-cultural trends:

- coherence rooted in *thinking skills*;
- coherence rooted in an emancipatory *global outlook*; and
- coherence rooted in *self-awareness* and *identity*.

These suggestions overlap considerably, but are all rooted in a notion that we are rationally seeking an underlying set of principles on which the three elements are based. This approach is not entirely unproblematic, and while lack of space prevents more than a passing remark, we note Broadfoot's (1999) argument that this rational approach is itself a hallmark of 'the rationality that underpins advanced industrial society'. If this is correct, then perhaps seeking coherence is already value-laden in a way that some educators would find troublesome. To impose such a coherence might, then, undermine any lofty vision for the core, and a more radical re-think might be necessary.

Coherence rooted in thinking skills?

'Many educators believe that specific knowledge will not be as important to tomorrow's workers and citizens as the ability to learn and to make sense of new information.' (Gough, 1991)

While the need for students to be able to think has been forcefully articulated at least as far back as Socrates, there is no doubt that the emergence of the 'knowledge economy' and the general rate of technological and social change have given renewed focus to thinking skills as a vital part of education. The prevalence of terms such as critical thinking, independent learners, and lifelong learners speaks to the fact that we are no longer interested in simply imparting 'truths' to passive students to regurgitate in examinations. Instead we need students to develop flexible capacities to deal with, and process, large volumes of information in an intelligent and active manner. At the same time, the concept of 'thinking' has itself been subject to a renewed scrutiny, and the very concept of rationality has expanded so that it is no longer tenable to conceive the ability to think critically as a purely cognitive skill. From the natural sciences, Anthony Damasio has demonstrated (2006) that rational thought has an affective basis; from the human sciences Daniel Goleman has argued (1996) that emotional intelligence (EQ) is as important as IQ in working and personal life (did we really need a scientist to tell us that?); from history Stephen Toulmin has shown (1992, 2003) that recent forms of rationality are narrow and (he hopes) a temporary deviation from a more human approach; from philosophy, Martha Nussbaum has shown (2001) that emotions are 'suffused with intelligence and discernment, and thus a source of deep awareness and understanding'.

As a result, there has emerged a general consensus that thinking needs to encompass affective and emotional aspects as well as purely cognitive aspects. The ability to relate well to others, to work in teams, to read the emotions of others, to empathise and respond appropriately, to understand and regulate one's own emotional state – all these now legitimately fall under the term 'thinking skills'. (This is in stark contrast to some *critical thinking* courses, which concentrate solely on matters of logical deduction and inference, without reference to affective matters.)

In this wider social context, the increased IB emphasis on a constructivist, child-centred pedagogy is not surprising, and it sits well with the idea that, more than anything else, we need to teach students how to think in intellectually robust and emotionally appropriate ways. This idea provides a powerful possibility for uniting the core. The cognitive, intellectual requirements of the EE and ToK are very much focused on independent research and thought, on the analysis and synthesis of ideas, and on communication. Students are neither taught nor assessed according to *how much* they know, but according to *what they can find out or create* and *what they can do* with this information. The affective, emotional components of thinking skills are similarly thoroughly addressed in the core. Their most obvious location is in CAS, where students are required to work collaboratively with others, identify their own strengths and weaknesses, and show perseverance and initiative. These affective elements are also interwoven through ToK, where students examine and extend their own attitudes to ethical judgements and judgements about cultures, and where they are also encouraged to develop certain dispositions such as a willingness to challenge their own deeply-held convictions, a willingness to hold themselves to the same standards to which they hold others, and a willingness to entertain opposing views charitably. In the EE too, a certain strength of character is developed by most students when they undertake what is a lengthy (and, let us be frank, at least initially often very unattractive) project over several months. Much more could be written here, but readers will recognise the overall theme.

The 'thinking skills' approach does, therefore, have merit as a potentially unifying theme of the core, and echoes of this theme are clear in all of the above remarks from students. I agree with Leat (1999) when he claims that 'thinking skills programmes ... seem to provide an antidote for teachers to the instrumentalism of prescribed curricula as they address more general aims of education'. Coherence through thinking skills, broadly understood as described, would offer close alignment with the IB mission, and offer in a central place proof that progressive values and academic rigour can go hand in hand. They should serve to counter the danger of producing highly educated but unbalanced or amoral IB graduates, thus aligning with Ginott's (1972) report from an anonymous Principal in a letter to new teachers: 'I am suspicious of education. My request is: help your children to become humane. Your efforts must never produce learned monsters, skilled psychopaths, educated Eichmanns.' Socrates claimed that if we truly understood what we were doing then we would never do anything immoral; this may be going too far, but there is more than a grain of truth in the idea. We should have confidence that *thinking skills* – properly and broadly understood – can result in better ethical thinking, and such a theme for the core offers significant promise to build on existing practice and bridge any real or perceived gap between cognitive and affective aspects of the diploma.

Despite the attractiveness of this idea, the relatively recent focus on thinking skills is one narrow manifestation of a wider phenomenon – the need to locate one's own thinking in relation to the thinking of others. The broadest application here would involve a global outlook; and a direct focus on this would be a more natural focus, and one which could still encompass thinking skills.

Coherence rooted in an emancipatory global outlook?

'We as educators have an urgent responsibility to alert young people to new realities that result from globalization and to encourage their wholehearted search for solutions.' (Lewis, 2006)

While the IB mission speaks of creating a 'better, more peaceful world', the core of the programme for its most mature students does not appear to explicitly reflect, or perhaps even recognise, this phrase. Paulo Freire (1990) argues that 'there is no such thing as a neutral education process' and that education is always about either maintaining or challenging the current social and political *status quo*. Perhaps, then, an obvious identity for the core as a central element would be one with a more explicit, moral focus on the 'better, more peaceful world'.

The idea that the *thinking skills* focus can be generalised into *thinking with a global outlook* has its mirror in the way that being *open-minded* has in recent times been generalised into *international-mindedness*. The dimension of otherness present in thinking skills is being transformed into the global other, and there is an increasing expectation that thinking skills are exercised in the direction of, or at least in the context of, a global outlook. The field is emergent, and even the terminology is not settled, but the IB theme of *Sharing our Humanity*, the emergence and development of concepts such as international-mindedness, global consciousness and global competence, the trialling of world studies EEs (more on this below, and elsewhere in this volume), and interest in IB curriculum groups in inter-school projects all suggest that this transformation is underway. The 'I' in IB no longer means simply 'present in lots of countries', if it ever did. As this is a development that resonates with the dominant discourse of globalization (see, for example, Beck and Cronin, 2006) it would not, in my view, be surprising if coherence through this concept were to be sought. This is a potentially very exciting change; it fits well with the IB mission and into a well-established tradition of *critical pedagogy*, which argues that the curriculum should be written so as to enable actions that 'identify and unmask those human beliefs and practices which limit freedom, justice and democracy' (Scott, 2006). A link between global citizenship and critical pedagogy is nothing new – since Freire's *Pedagogy of the Oppressed* (1990) many have sought explicitly to link education with an understanding of the dynamics of power and oppression, arguing that 'becoming fully human' necessarily involves students coming to a consciousness of the world around them. More recently Byers (2005), quoted in Roberts (2009), exhorted us to 'talk frankly about how and where power vests and is wielded in today's world... and about the hypocrisies and hollowness of less rigorous or more benevolent conceptions of global citizenship'. Given how closely these ideas echo the IB mission, it could be argued that moving the core in this direction would be a natural development.

Such a move, while unashamedly political, would build on aspects of the core that are already present. ToK, with its emphasis on identifying hidden assumptions, understanding the perspectives of others and locating one's own views in a broader context, has clear links to notions of a global outlook. One of the CAS learning outcomes requires that students 'engage with issues of global significance' (IB, 2008a) even if in a local context (environmental concerns, or visiting the elderly, are cited as global issues that can be acted on locally). The current world studies EE, under trial at the time of writing, requires students to use a local case study to engage with global issues. This EE is worth closer examination; as a recent development it offers an insight not into how the DP core was envisaged, but into the direction that curriculum planners are currently taking. A central aim of the world studies EE is to deepen understanding of students' 'global consciousness', which is defined as 'the capacity and the inclination to place people, objects, situations… and the self within the broader matrix of our contemporary world. An individual exhibits global consciousness when she… can place such encounters in a broader narrative or explanatory framework of contemporary global processes' (Boix-Mansilla and Gardner, 2007). That consideration is being given to how to extend these ideas across all EEs speaks to an already existing leaning in this direction, and is a strong indicator that this is currently a favoured conceptualization of the core.

There are, of course, concerns with developments of this sort, and if the core were to be further developed in this direction (which would be the inevitable result of seeking coherence this way) the narrow 'will the new curriculum be as good as the last one?' question will arise. Though a detailed and contingent question, it is one that cannot easily be brushed aside. The recent success of the DP has been as much, if not more, about its academic merit relative to alternatives than about its ideological approach, and it will be vital that idealism is tempered by pragmatism here. There is also the more serious worry that this approach replaces a fairly implicit ideology with another far more explicit one, and any move toward an overtly political agenda may not do the IB any favours with some individual students, teachers, parents and even states around the world. However, given the ideological nature of the IB mission, this may not be an insurmountable obstacle. To my mind, a more fundamental critique is the argument that the core is already predicated on critical pedagogy in a properly constructivist fashion; it already seeks to equip students with tools rather than furnish them with finished products, and therefore already does, albeit obliquely, what proponents of a global agenda want to do. I believe that the nature of the core is such that when it is done well, students are likely to develop naturally the sort of ethical and pluralistic dispositions that will lead to them being good global citizens; with a good CAS experience, students will encounter, empathise and better understand the situations of others; with good EE and ToK experiences students will have opportunity and incentives to engage in genuinely critical examination of not just ideas, but of whole perspectives and paradigms. The core thus provides the tools and encourages the dispositions with which to de- and maybe even re-construct for themselves notions such as *globalization*. Any development that focuses more explicitly on global citizenship within the core therefore needs to be wary of replacing the currently open and critical core approach with a more closed model of learning, which pre-supposes that the answers are known and that profound and difficult ideas of truth, justice and freedom can be better *taught to* students rather than *constructed by* students with appropriate scaffolding.

If this is correct, then any unifying theme for the core will need to be more open and less restrictive than can be managed by a *global outlook* approach. The unifying theme needs to encourage understandings, approaches and dispositions that are consistent with and conducive to a global outlook, but which remain open to a richer set of possibilities.

Coherence rooted in the idea of self-awareness and identity?

'Ideally, at the end of the IB experience, students should know themselves better than when they started, while acknowledging that others can be right in being different.' (Peel, 1997)

My most memorable teaching moments have been those where students have realised that an experience, claim or argument is more than just 'something that happened at school', but has implications for them as young individuals discovering and creating their places in the world. Finding, in EE supervisions, that students have stepped up to a level beyond their expectations in answering, over several months, questions of their own writing, and have really enjoyed the experience, is a delightful thing to behold – not because of the academic attainment, but because something has changed for those students forever. Seeing, in a ToK lesson, a student realising that something that seemed so obvious is actually, when seen from another perspective, absurd (or *vice versa*) is the moment that you know that he has made a profound discovery – not about the issue, but about himself. And hearing from a student, in a CAS activity, about her reflection on her reaction to a situation tells you that she has developed the ability to see herself from (at least a small) distance; a rare and important skill.

In each case we find that experiences in the core afford opportunities for students to become more aware of their identities, to self-consciously develop these identities, and hence to become the people that they want to be. The opportunities also appear elsewhere, of course, but it seems to me that students take them up far more frequently in the core than elsewhere. This is largely due to the nature of the elements themselves, which are more self-driven and reflexive than are other diploma elements (and of course with fewer diploma points riding on the core, there is also more freedom for invention and creativity than elsewhere). CAS is largely about the learning that results from reflecting on interactions with other people; EE is about students constructing their own ideas as a result of engagement in depth with academic writings; ToK is about students measuring their own beliefs and views against the beliefs and views of others. CAS, EE and ToK are thus all about *conversations* of one form or another – conversations with people, with academic discourses and with the idea of knowledge itself. It is in the conversation that self-awareness and identity can be cultivated, and nowhere in the DP is the idea of conversation (properly understood) more applicable than in the core.

It is interesting to note that this view is entirely consistent with (perhaps even essential for) a global outlook. Michael Oakeshott, whose idea this is, writes that:

Education, properly speaking, is an initiation into the skill and partnership of this conversation in which we learn to recognize the voices, to distinguish the proper occasions of utterance, and in which we acquire the intellectual and moral habits appropriate to conversation… [conversation] is impossible in the absence of a diversity of voices: in it different universes of discourse meet, acknowledge each other and enjoy an oblique relationship which neither requires nor forecasts their being assimilated to one another. (Oakeshott, 1962)

The idea has been taken up elsewhere, and these days we are all acutely aware of these 'universes of discourse' that we cannot avoid, and which are so troubling when making judgements cross-culturally. We can, however, skirt the problem of relativism by promoting self-awareness of our own discourse and identities, so that these are as close to chosen, rather than received, as we can make them. Mackenzie (2000) writes that 'all of us are now part of a… discourse or narrative… there are two ways in which one can be part of a narrative, however: blindly, or self-consciously. If students are able to see themselves as part of a discourse or narrative, and to understand that what they consider obvious and natural (their "common sense") is the result of belonging to this tradition, then I for one would be happy'. So perhaps the core is best conceived as a tool with which to empower students to develop their own identities and hence to interpret everyday experience and make decisions. If so, it is a potentially profound and emancipatory element of the DP – one that can change the lives of the students in no small measure.

Note that the concepts of *identity* and *otherness* are elastic enough to meet the criticism that the DP – with its focus on individual achievement – is too western-oriented for a truly international curriculum. I have often heard it said that Asian or African traditions emphasise the individual in the context of his or her place in the community, and that the (western) IB approach does not suit this way of thinking. Whether or not this criticism is valid generally (it seems likely to me that the idea of monolithic Asian or African approaches is itself a western construct), focusing on students' self-awareness and identity is neutral in this respect. Using *conversation*, with its intrinsic focus on other-ness, allows the balance between individual and community to be struck as appropriate around the world. Identity might be more individually-focused in some parts of the world, and more community-focused elsewhere; local interpretation would offer no problems of principle. So the core, understood as a tri-partite course on identity, can be a truly cross-cultural aspect of the DP, as befits the central part of an international curriculum.

Which concept for the core?

Each of the three ideas considered – *thinking skills, global outlook, identity* – could be developed into a theme for the core. In this and the following section I argue that the concept of *identity*, properly understood, rooted in notions of *other-ness* and *conversation* as described above, is the most promising of the three for two reasons.

I warm to the ambitions of the *thinking skills* and *global outlook* approaches; they both seek to move students beyond a parochial outlook, to ask questions that are bigger, in some sense, than the traditional curriculum tends to ask. Their virtues, as described in the sections above, are considerable. I believe, though, that these approaches are both contemporary manifestations of the deeper and more profound human impulse, famously captured in the philosophical injunction inscribed above the Temple of Apollo at Delphi: 'Know thyself.' *Thinking skills* approaches seek to analyse and improve an individual's mental abilities; *global outlook* approaches seek to locate individuals in a broader context in order to come to deeper understanding of their own beliefs and capacities for action. Both are, ultimately, about the human condition or, perhaps more precisely, about self-awareness of the human condition; that is, they are both specific ways of talking about the general issue of *identity*.

The quest to explore self and the search for identity have been at the heart of philosophical, religious and literary inquiry for centuries, and the Delphic decree is echoed by many great traditions. The Islamic 'He who knows himself, knows God' (Prophet Muhammad, PBUH, in Suhrawardy, 2010) is echoed by the Taoist 'Knowing others is wisdom. Knowing oneself is enlightenment' (Lao Tze, *nd*). More recently, very different expressions of the idea have been found in existential philosophers such as Sartre (1958) who regarded self as an ongoing project of creation with other people, or Glover (1989) who examines the concept from a psychological standpoint. The point is not whether the exploration of identity is best done through religion, science, or philosophy, but rather that the theme recurs throughout the ages because each generation undertakes the search anew, from its own perspective, and in its own way. A focus on *thinking skills* sees identity as bound up with rationality and intellect; a focus on a *global outlook* sees identity as bound up in cultural perspectives. Neither is wrong, but both are simply recent and perhaps fleeting ways of expressing the more important, recurring, ongoing search for identity.

The importance of exploring identity is noted by Hindu scholar Radhika Sekar (2010) in a line that could almost have been designed for a ToK lesson: 'Knowledge of the natural sciences, of arts, crafts, literature, music, and every conceivable type of worldly knowledge do not bring peace or bliss, unless rooted in *Atma Jnana* – the knowledge of the Self.' *Identity* is not only the theme that can unify the core; it also has the potential to bridge cognitive, affective and personal domains, and to bring meaning and purpose to the *whole* DP in a way that is completely consistent with the broader IB mission. And it has a leaning towards action to make the world a better place too; as Spanish Jesuit Baltasar Gracián wrote (1647): 'Self-correction begins with self-knowledge.' That core elements can be bound by such a profound theme is, to me, an exciting prospect, and little short of an incredible affirmation of the DP. It's not just that the theme follows in such a venerable tradition (encouraging though that is); a second, more important reason is that the core brings the idea alive, in a developmentally appropriate way for students precisely when they are at an age when they need some way of navigating and articulating their identity and experiences. Recall Stephen Kimanzi's earlier comment in relation to CAS (see above), having worked with and helped others: 'I look back and see myself a changed person. I am not the same student I was when I first arrived.' He means he is a better, more self-aware person. He has developed his *identity*.

This chapter started by noting the chimeric nature of the core, and the reason for this is now clear – the core is best interpreted as being about identity and selfhood, and these ideas are extremely elusive and open to interpretation according to the spirit of the age. This makes an unambiguous affirmation of the theme problematic.

Conclusion

The aim of this chapter was to find some 'bedrock' for the core; some narrative that unites the three elements, and we have considered three options. I am of the belief that the notion of *identity* has the most promise, tapping into a deep vein of philosophical traditions and speaking powerfully to maturing DP students as it does. *Identity* is richer, broader and more resonant with the IB mission than either alternative, and it leaves open the possibility of being shaped to address either issue in locally and culturally relevant ways. That is, identity can be made to encompass *thinking skills* or a *global outlook* if so desired.

But perhaps the whole project of an overarching theme for the core is misguided. Instead of three aspects of the same central thing, maybe the core is better conceived along the lines of a triathlon consisting of swimming, cycling, and running. While it is true to say that all three elements are linked by involving movement, the strongest link is that they are all part of the triathlon, and the triathlon is none the worse for that. We need to be wary of forcing what is generally regarded as the strongest, and certainly the most distinctive, part of the DP into a strait-jacket. I am not sure we gain a great deal by taking three already successful and at times extraordinary elements of the core and pressing them into the service of one single idea. Incoherence is not necessarily a pejorative term!

In one sense the core is simply what it is – a set of three inter-related offerings that are defined centrally in the written curriculum by the IB, and then enacted and experienced by students and teachers in schools around the world. In a broader sense we can say, if we wish, that the core has a central narrative that we educators are continually constructing in the intersection of socio-cultural imperatives and educational aspirations. For better or worse, this narrative is manifested in a current evolution of focus away from cognitive and affective thinking skills towards international-mindedness and a global outlook. It could and should be broadened to address student self-awareness and identity in more general terms, but this need not be formalised. In any case, the core will evolve to reflect the changing nature of the IB itself, which has also been engaged in an ongoing construction of its own identity as it has, in recent years, self-consciously grown at a remarkable rate from a niche provider in the educational market to a global leader with great and increasingly realistic ambitions. Refocusing all core elements towards only the global may be counterproductive, and might unintentionally reinforce the dominant discourse of globalization. As this may be opposed to, or at least not aligned with, the IB mission, great care will be needed to avoid introducing unwanted tensions.

The DP is arguably the flagship IB programme, and the core is arguably the flagship of the DP. As an IB branding exercise alone, therefore, how we treat the identity of the core *matters*. But that's not to say that it needs nailing down; leaving it open to interpretation would allow stakeholders to construct their own meaning – within reasonable limits, as they currently do. If, as I have argued, the core is one of the reasons that the DP inspires students, teachers and parents, then it cannot be a bad thing to leave some freedom to schools to make the core their own, rather than simply make it another rigidly defined curriculum element. When Borges described Menard's *Quixote* as 'almost infinitely richer' than the original, he went on to say that it was 'more ambiguous… but ambiguity is richness'. That the core is open to many interpretations is not, to my mind, a problem. That there is something to be preserved in the core is beyond question. Retaining some ambiguity might, therefore, be good advice for curriculum planners, whatever the next step.

Acknowledgements

Thanks to colleagues who read an initial draft and shared their ideas: Ellie Alchin, Naheed Bardai, Aziz Batada, Joel Godiah, Alex Holland and Bulemi Mulama. Thanks also to current and ex-students who have shared their reflections on the core, and especially to those who have given me permission to print their thoughts here: Stephen Kimanzi, Chrissie Moeller, Marta Szczerba, Olalere Williams.

References

Beck, U and Cronin, C (2006): *Cosmopolitan Vision.* Cambridge: Polity Press.

Boix-Mansilla, V and Gardner, H (2007): From teaching globalization to nurturing global consciousness, in M M Suárez-Orozco (ed), *Learning in the global era: International perspectives on globalization and education.* Berkeley, CA: University of California Press.

Borges, J L (1989): Pierre Menard Author of the Quixote, in *Labyrinths.* London: Penguin Books Ltd.

Broadfoot, P (1999): Assessment and the Emergence of Modern Society, in R Moon and P Murphy (eds), *Curriculum in Context.* London: Paul Chapman.

Byers, M (2005): Are you a global citizen? Really? What does that mean? in *The Tyee*, 5 October 2005. Online: http://thetyee.ca/views/2005/10/05/globalcitizen

Damasio, A (2006): *Descartes' Error: Emotion, Reason and the Human Brain*. New York: Vintage Press.

Freire, P (1990): *Pedagogy of the Oppressed*. New York: Continuum.

Gellar, C (2002): International Education: a commitment to universal values, in M Hayden, J Thompson and G Walker (eds), *International Education in Practice: dimensions for national and international schools*. London: Kogan Page.

Ginott, H (1972): *Teacher and Child*. Bristol: Avon Books.

Glover, J (1989): *I: The Philosophy and Psychology of Personal Identity*. London: Penguin Books Ltd.

Goleman, D (1996): *Emotional Intelligence; why it can matter more than IQ*. London: Bloomsbury Publishing.

Gough, D (1991): *Thinking about Thinking*. Alexandria, VA: National Association of Elementary School Principals (ED 327 90).

Gracián, B (1647): *The Art of Worldly Wisdom*. (Maxim 69.)

Heisenberg, W (1958): *Physics and Philosophy: The Revolution in Modern Science*. London: Penguin Books Ltd.

IB (2006): *Theory of Knowledge Guide*. Cardiff: International Baccalaureate.

IB (2008a): *Creativity, Action, Service Guide*. Cardiff: International Baccalaureate.

IB (2008b): *Towards a continuum of international education*. Cardiff: International Baccalaureate.

IB (2009): *IB learner profile booklet*. Cardiff: International Baccalaureate.

Lao Tze, (nd): quoted in: *Ask The Religion Experts: How Important Is Knowledge?* Online: www.interfaithing.com/religion-experts-important-knowledge-319/ (last accessed 13 June 2011).

Leat, D (1999): Rolling the Stone Uphill; Teacher Development and the Implementation of Thinking Skills Programmes, in *Oxford Review of Education*, 25 (3), pp387-403.

Lewis, C (2006): International but not Global: How international school curricula fail to address global issues and how this must change, in *International Schools Journal*, XXV (2), pp51-67.

Mackenzie, J (2000): Curricular Interstices and the Theory of Knowledge, in M Hayden and J Thompson (eds), *International Schools and International Education*. London: Kogan Page.

Nussbaum, M (2001): *Upheavals of Thought: The Intelligence of Emotions*. Cambridge: Cambridge University Press.

Oakeshott, M (1962): *Rationalism in Politics and Other Essays*. London: Methuen.

Peel, R M (1997): *Education for Life*. Geneva: International Baccalaureate.

Peterson, A D C (1987): *Schools across Frontiers*. La Salle, Illinois: Open Court.

Roberts, B (2009): *Educating for Global Citizenship*. Cardiff: International Baccalaureate.

Sartre, J P (1958): *Being and Nothingness: An Essay on Phenomenological Ontology*, transl. Hazel E Barnes. London: Methuen,

Sekar, R, quoted in Delaine (2010): *Ask The Religion Experts: How Important Is Knowledge?* Online: www.interfaithing.com/religion-experts-important-knowledge-319/ (last accessed 13 June 2011).

Scott, D (2006): Six Curriculum Discourses, in A Moore (ed), *Schooling, Curriculum and Society*. Oxford: Routledge.

Suhrawardy, A (2010): *Sayings of Muhammad*. Whitefish, MT: Kessinger Publishing.

Toulmin, S (1992): *Cosmopolis: The Hidden Agenda of Modernity*. Chicago: University of Chicago Press.

Toulmin, S (2003): *Return to Reason*. Boston: Harvard University Press.

Chapter 3

A question of balance

Neil Richards

"Which bits can I leave out and still get a good grade?" asked Freddy, all those years ago, as examinations loomed.

Good question.

This is exactly how the brain seems to function: excising the irrelevant; seeking efficiency. And Freddy was very good at efficiency. We laughed in the staff room, but I wonder now if there was just a hint of nervousness as we mocked his approach to learning. After all, which bits did the syllabus itself leave out? Which bits did I as a teacher then leave out of the syllabus? Which bits did I emphasise because of my own preferences? Which bits did I dismiss as being irrelevant in my own push for good grades as examinations loomed? Which bits did I drill into innocent brains until the responses were as automatic and unthinking as the slimy drool from Pavlov's dogs?

The answer to Freddy's question has taxed the energies and resourcefulness of countless generations of students and teachers struggling with external examinations, as well as of the curriculum engineers themselves in their search for a balanced and rigorous programme that could facilitate objective discrimination as well as provide an appropriate foundation for subsequent higher education. Of course, lurking in the background of all formal state education systems has also been the need to mould responsible citizens (although 'compliant' would perhaps be a more appropriate adjective in many cases). And although the IB diploma struggles to free itself of national and cultural bias in a noble attempt to develop 'internationally minded people who, recognizing their common humanity and shared guardianship of the planet, help to create a better and more peaceful world' (IB, 2011a), it is still mired in the thick, loamy earth of its occidental genesis.

The vital elements

Assessment

Freddy's pragmatic approach to academic success, and his not-so-innocent question, has resonated somewhat uncomfortably throughout my career as a teacher and administrator in so-called international schools. In this one disingenuous question he nailed me, kicking and screaming, to that cross that all teachers have to bear. I refer, of course, to Assessment (and surely this hoary nemesis deserves to be capitalised).

Yet Assessment is the key. Without it we are doomed to flounder in an imprecise sea of banalities and self-serving interests. Individual progress has to be measured against some sort of metric, and the underlying requirement is that this metric is rigorous yet realistic, widely understood and consistently applied; in themselves these are the necessary prerequisites for trust. This is true in the classroom and for the daily functioning of our schools, as well as for the national and international systems in which our schools operate. However, our systems of assessment contain more than just a faint, sulphuric, Faustian whiff: in exchange for surety and the promise of riches beyond compare, we must follow an, essentially, predetermined path to a predetermined destination. Freddy, of course, intuitively understood that there must be a few shortcuts to this final destination, especially for the weary or flabby-brained; as did I, and so used them whenever expedient. With calibrator in hand I checked my students in, crossing the finishing line in one final, heaving, pulsating charge, while the crowds of stakeholders roared their approval in a welter of 'high-fives' and congratulatory back-slapping. You know what I mean.

This tension between learning and assessment is at the ambivalent heart of our educational systems. Of course, good grades and scores ought to be a consequence of learning, not the purpose, but the very act of constructing curricula and assessment objectives, of charting paths through our systems of knowledge, of ensuring the necessary rigour to provide reassurance, may be in themselves highly subjective, or at the very least culturally imbued, and are, perforce, exercises in limitation. It was a dilemma well understood by the founders of the IB diploma, who dared to look beyond the narrow confines of national curricula, but yet remained cognisant of the need to create a universally accepted university-entrance qualification. Their creation, the diploma, had to be both practically and philosophically driven, but there was no getting away from assessment, which provided the glue for this extraordinary enterprise and to a very large degree must remain a central consideration for diploma development. No matter what the future holds, whatever geometric configuration or insight grips the imagination, there will still be a need for a mechanism or an instrument to assess the learning that has taken place and this will continue to tax the energies and resources of the IB. And, of course, someone will always be there, with a lopsided grin and a loaded question.

The curriculum

Although the diploma was created as a vehicle for entry into higher education worldwide, and its remarkable growth is surely predicated upon this very fact, thankfully this is not it entirely; in fact, this is not *it* at all: this need opened the door of opportunity to a whole bunch of wide-eyed educational idealists, who were, I like to think, probably slightly mad (let's just call them risk-takers). But it is their unfolding vision and values that have since captured the imagination of teachers and parents from around the world. Through their pioneering vision the diploma offered hope for a better connected and more understandable world, and through the carefully constructed feedback mechanisms it has provided for professional inclusion and reflection; these are central values of the organisation and must remain so. And finally, to use the words of the IB itself, the diploma 'was developed as a deliberate compromise between the specialization required in some national systems and the breadth preferred in others, without bias towards any national system' (IB, 2002).

In education the word 'ownership' is overused – if not become trite – and may seem out of place in light of the rapid expansion of the IB, and more particularly throughout the last decade. But in the refreshing absence of state interference it is good to know that in matters of policy there is only us – the practitioners – and we are, and must continue to be, masters of our own destiny. As a consequence, however, the curriculum needs to be in a constant state of flux which, in a developing world, is exactly how it should be. But growth and development must be facilitated by a framework that is equally flexible and able to accommodate and respond to the increasing clamour for change and inclusion. In this rapidly evolving world, old notions of 'balance and breadth' may need to be revisited.

The challenge

Without abandoning the basic principles at the heart of the diploma, it must be acknowledged that there are some gathering storm clouds on the horizon. In the first place, the world has changed dramatically over the past 20 years, not least in our understanding of the complexity of the learning process and the functioning and plasticity of the human brain. In addition, the communication revolution has made the world, in all its myriad manifestations, more immediate, more connected and most certainly more intrusive, while the movement towards global economic integration and resource management – led in large part by multinational corporations, with or without the moderating influence of state control – has radically altered traditional political allegiances and social patterns. The democratisation of information demands a new interpretation of knowledge and expertise, not least in our schools, as well as highlighting a desperate need for improved skills of synthesis. And in this over-connected yet still fragmenting world many peoples, bewildered by the seemingly uncontrollable imposition of alien mores and values, have sought refuge in cultural and religious orthodoxy.

A number of years ago, a colleague well rehearsed in the principles of positive thinking (for me this has Orwellian overtones) knocked on my door and presented me with a list of her 'challenges'. She meant, of course, 'problems'. At least that is the uncharitable interpretation that I placed upon them, and her subsequent litany did little to persuade me otherwise. But she had a point. Even as she dropped her 'challenges' in my lap, she did so with a degree of hope, if not faith, that these could be met rather than be 'fixed'; there is a difference. The 'challenge' for the IB, for all the practitioners, is to *meet* the needs of a rapidly changing world, and not just to fix the problems that this world imposes upon the diploma. In short it is a creative rather than a reactive brief; ultimately, a matter for design and not just mechanics, and despite the alarming speed of technological innovation it most assuredly cannot be fixated upon the use of ever smarter and quicker tools to access information or process assessment.

The programme

Essentially, the diploma is constructed out of discrete, specialist subjects; the configuration of the hexagon reflects the subject 'areas' and within the specialised subjects there is a choice of level. In this way balance and breadth has been engineered, with the central core requirements acting as a bonding agent. The over-arching importance of this core has been recognised by its recent development as a course for those students who do fewer than the requisite number of courses to obtain the full diploma:

> The IB is pleased to announce that the core elements of the Diploma Programme – theory of knowledge (ToK), extended essay (EE), and creativity, action, service (CAS) – will be available as individually recognized stand-alone offerings for first teaching in 2012 (applied to first examination session 2014). Presently, students are able to take individual courses from the six groups of the Diploma Programme hexagon. Therefore, currently, it is only those students who take the entire diploma who benefit from and experience the unique elements at the core of the programme. The decision to allow Diploma Programme (DP) course students to experience these core elements of the diploma supports the IB's continued dedication to its access agenda and is fully supported by the academic committees of the IB. (IB, 2011b)

Two important observations arise out of this latter development: the first is that a major compromise has taken place through the acknowledgement that the carefully constructed integrity of the full diploma is no longer absolutely paramount – and this immediately poses a threat to the founding philosophy; the second, that we are not yet fully able to think out of the box (or in this case, the hexagon).

Incidentally, having long recognised the importance of the core elements, some schools already provide *all* their students with this opportunity, unconcerned about external moderation or validation. The United World Colleges (UWCs) are an obvious example, being founded upon the principle of service long before the advent of the IB diploma. As part of the attempt by the UWCs to create a new diploma model, ways are being explored to reflect and acknowledge the 'value-added' that each of the colleges provides over and above the IB diploma requirements. There are many other examples, too, where school requirements far exceed the expectations of the IB (see chapter 4, by James MacDonald, for instance).

A question of balance

The core

Over 25 years ago, when I first started teaching IB diploma courses, my first thought was to discover the standard text(s) that would prepare my students for the final examination. I am not sure if I was reassured or otherwise to be told that the IB did not recommend any set books. This was indeed a paradigm shift for me (except I doubt that I knew what this meant at that time). It was also an awesome responsibility. Most of all, however, it proved to be a liberating experience, because as a history teacher I was quite literally given the world to discover. It felt as though, at last, someone was treating me as a grown-up.

Of course, within my subject specialism, I had a vague notion of what to do. Not so for the ToK; this was indeed a revelation, and how I valued the communication between my peers in various parts of the world as we attempted to grapple with issues of knowledge alongside our students. Naturally, there was no course-book. Each student charted his or her own path through the systems of knowledge and the ways of knowing, herded and nudged in a general direction by the teacher privileged enough to accompany them on their journey, and by some suggested reading. What a learning experience it was, if only to discover the depth of my own ignorance (and here I modestly tip my hat at Socrates). It felt like frontier stuff alright, and no mistake.

Notwithstanding my personal belief that it is time for the ToK course to be thoroughly overhauled and possibly expanded, is the final ToK essay intended as an assessment of the student or of the teacher? If the intention is the former, then surely the teachers know what each student deserves, based upon observation and assessments throughout the course. If the bonus point concept was removed in favour of a simple pass or fail, then the whole vast structure of moderation could be removed. How many of us have told students not to spend too much time and energy on these essays – because it is simply not worth it for most of our students who are already staggering under the weight of the diploma requirements? Is it not enough that a student has followed a course that is essentially reflective, and that this commitment has been acknowledged by his or her teacher? And does a submitted and moderated essay really add value to the programme? For that matter, doesn't the award of bonus points threaten to turn a personal introspective journey into just another academic course after all?

Further, I have long felt that physical activity in some form should be a central part of any curriculum timetable and at every level in a school. Similarly, creative opportunities should be, and often are, devised by schools, through school-wide events and celebrations, debates and conferences, exhibitions and visits or through service opportunities. A school should be trusted to meet its obligations on behalf of each and every student, irrespective of whether or not they are diploma candidates.

Although I am a great believer in the philosophy of CAS (the creativity, action, service component of the diploma), it has always taxed my patience as an administrator. If a school cannot be trusted, then what right has it to be authorised by the IB? The bureaucratic process necessary to unpick the individual tangled threads of CAS and record them for judgement and the general record is, quite frankly, a burden. But worse, it has the capacity to diminish the nature of the whole experience. As an example, I am reminded of putting an end to a project that involved 'gardening' for a teacher (which conveniently seemed to embrace all three aspects of the CAS programme); typing a teacher's dissertation was another creative interpretation that I proscribed. We all have our war stories and the scars of ingratitude to prove it. While setting a prescribed number of hours may well seem to be the fairest and most expedient way to ensure compliance, what a bureaucratic and time-consuming nightmare monitoring all this can become for schools as well as for the IB.

To the purist, taking some responsibility away from the student may seem a retrograde step, or may even open up the diploma to abuse, but I would argue that the best schools (sorry, the more efficient schools) already do this. They have constructed frameworks to ensure that each student complies with all obligations without undue stress being placed upon either the student or, indeed, the school administration, thereby releasing more time for more important stuff (please note the intended irony). Compare this scenario with those students who have to get on with it themselves, devise their own programmes, and face the equivalent of the Spanish Inquisition to defend every hard-earned minute. And at the end of all the bureaucracy and cost (in both temporal and financial terms), who out there, within the world of higher education, is scrutinizing the final CAS records of the individual students?

Really?

Finally, the EE. Although it would seem to be a burden in many ways, it is one of the most rewarding exercises for the student, and certainly for those destined for higher education. It is now quite common to 'get it out of the way' following the end of the first year or by early on in the second year. Again, because of its limited impact upon the final points tally, a common recommendation for overburdened students is not to waste too much time and energy on it. A pity, and not an intended consequence of the diploma structure – merely a pragmatic response to overload. So many wonderful research papers crumble into disillusion and despair, crushed up against the deadline by the weight of other subject demands.

The dilemmas

How times change. Small, cabalistic gatherings of enthusiastic administrators and teachers from international schools once plotted world domination and the dawning of an educational Golden Age. The reality, however, is a lot more prosaic, and it seems the pioneering efforts have culminated in an exercise in global logistics. Inevitably, the 'brand' had to be protected, and the course books were produced, as the diploma seemed to slide effortlessly into national systems and into independent school marketing strategies. Of course, there is a problem (oops, I mean challenge) for us when highly selective, highly competitive schools embrace the Diploma Programme; many of these schools know a thing or two about getting outstanding results, and universities are fast becoming spoilt for choice, unlike many of our less fortunate, well-travelled diploma holders. Can the diploma evolve and remain innovative once caught in the vice-like grip of so many and varied vested interests, all reeling from the heady fumes of success? Perhaps size does matter after all.

The full diploma provides a healthy differential scale of success, and conditional offers to applicants by UK universities, at least, seem to be creeping ever higher with an increasing emphasis on the specific points gained for higher level subjects (and many schools around the world are responding by achieving average diploma scores that I could only dream of in my early experiences of teaching IB courses). Although the number of successful diploma students is increasing each year, this is not necessarily matched by the number of university places being made available for them. Some years ago I assured a group of parents that the full diploma was within the grasp of almost all students, and that it was the attributes of perseverance and organisation that would result in a minimum of 24 points and subsequent academic success. I also believed that it was the acquisition of the full diploma, with all that this entailed, that was the ultimate litmus test of achievement and potential, for life as well as for academia.

Today, I suspect that my advice would be different: the diploma model for breadth and balance is fast becoming an academic millstone for many worthy, but not necessarily high-flying, students who, for all the right reasons, may be forced to compromise their specific talents and interests in pursuit of breadth, resulting in the more modest full diploma scores that are fast losing currency in the increasingly competitive world of higher education. Is it enough that they have become more internationally-minded? Indeed, has this ever been tested as an assumption?

Also, if the IB is pragmatic enough to recognise that a limited range of subjects from the hexagon is educationally acceptable, or at least a practising reality, to the extent that the philosophical core is being re-packaged for such learners, then it is surely time to reassess and possibly unpack the hexagon itself – a sacred cow if ever there was one. Is the ultimate goal inclusivity or exclusivity? Is the diploma at heart about values or about higher education? Does the hexagon provide for a genuine breadth of experience, or creativity, in a way that is meaningful for students in the 21st century?

It is important to remember that the diploma has always reflected compromise. The optional nature of group 6 subjects (the arts) is an example, even though it is through the arts that cultural synthesis and celebration often achieve their highest expression in our schools, and through channels of communication that are far more accessible and universal. Yet it seems that the arts have always been sacrificed upon the altar of academic expediency, notwithstanding the

CAS component (which is subject to such a wide interpretation). Philosophically, there can be no rationale for this; if it is acceptable to construct a diploma out of five areas of the hexagon, then why not four? Could balance and breadth be achieved in other ways?

Back to the future

The IB diploma became a success, I believe, because it was a pragmatic response to the educational needs of a world emerging from the collapse of empires and two world wars, yet still riven along ideological fault lines. The philosophy seemed to resonate with teachers who hoped for more from their students than just academic success; it was, and hopefully still is, an unabashed attempt to unite people and promote understanding through education and service to others. It seemed to me all those years ago, as I embraced it, a curriculum for global citizenship and peace first and foremost, which nevertheless most certainly had to be based upon intellectual growth; a rounded, moral education that would lead almost seamlessly to higher educational opportunities as a consequence of its rigour, balance and central, humanistic philosophy.

If I am not too enmeshed in my own idealism (and I continue to be reassured by the central importance of the IB learner profile) and, indeed, intercultural understanding in pursuit of peace is a central tenet of the diploma, then the greatest threat may well be that somewhere along the journey, intellectual rigour has become increasingly viewed as its core purpose or, to put it another way, that the purpose of the diploma is to create and promote an academic elite, with an international veneer, to secure access to the best universities. This fear may be unfounded, and I have been encouraged by the way in which educational cultures around the world are embracing those same core values that were placed at the heart of the diploma at its inception. As a result, however, and possibly to the diploma's eternal credit, these core values are no longer so unique to its programme, and the growing importance of social and emotional development, multiculturalism and humanistic values is becoming evident in many educational systems and schools around the world.

It was surely never the intention of the IB diploma to place any school in a curriculum strait-jacket, and through my own experiences as a Head I have been conscious of the need for the culture of a school to shine through the externally imposed academic framework; to emphasise the unique characteristics of location; to acknowledge the value-added of the character of each individual school; to celebrate our differences. Not always easy within the diploma assessment regime, or within an organisation increasingly reliant upon quality control for its very existence. 'Expansion' and 'quality control' are uneasy bedfellows at the best of times, and may result in little room, or time, being left over for schools to express their own individuality of approach.

The above issues are not the result of failure. Quite the opposite: they reflect the outstanding success of the diploma. But the sheer logistical scale and cost of the current enterprise, and the manner in which the central ideas have been widely embraced, suggest that it may be an opportune moment to consider not just new courses for the diploma, but perhaps a new structure to maintain momentum and respond to the needs of the 21st century (and not least to the approach of the other two IB programmes). Using technology to improve delivery and assessment is, of course, a given, but it would be unwise to consider the upgrade of what is essentially a tool as being anything more profound.

Sharing the burden

While the IB worked its way up through the gears and down through the curriculum, information technology – like the spoilt brat it is – demanded our immediate and constant attention, often to the detriment of other important considerations. In particular, developments in the field of neuroscience and evolutionary biology over the past two decades have provided extraordinary insights into the neural basis for the human condition: learning and enculturation; empathy and emotion; brain plasticity and aging. Surely all students should be exposed to this developing field, in much the same way as they have in the past been encouraged to grapple with knowledge issues and approaches to learning. Where better to place such universal considerations than at the core? And although I am also in favour of more focused study on global history and current affairs for all, I am conscious that the obscenely swelling belly of the core can only take so much. Something has to give.

The IB diploma placed emphasis upon breadth, cross-cultural understanding and service at a time when these were not necessarily features of mainstream education, or even of international education. It is worth emphasising that it is, perhaps, in large part due to the diploma's success and subsequent influence on educational thinking that, in broad terms, this is no longer the case. And arguably, there is no longer a need for the IB to shoulder this responsibility alone; school authorisations could focus on provision for the core and internal monitoring structures, after which the authorised school could take full responsibility for assessment in this area. Surely all that is required is a recognition or otherwise that a student has fulfilled his or her core curriculum obligation. We must trust the professionals in our schools, and in so doing ease the bureaucratic burden on the central organisation.

Similarly, the assessment burden, and costs, of the central organisation could be reduced by an internal assessment regime for some or all of the standard level subjects. This would leave only the higher level courses to be externally assessed to which, personally, I would add external assessment of the EE on a seven point scale. Universities could then review the external and internal assessment elements together – surely, more than enough upon which to base their admissions decisions.

While recognising that this may be too radical a proposal, I am left wondering whether the education of our students would be compromised by such a structure. Would schools be liberated and empowered by such a move, and rise to the creative challenge of constructing and assessing elements of the diploma? Somehow, I sense much shaking of heads and the sharp intake of breath, if not outright gnashing of teeth.

Am I, therefore, doomed to remain haunted by that voice from my past: "Which bits can I leave out, and still get a good grade?" Good question, Freddy. I wish I knew the answer.

References

IB (2002): *A basis for practice: the Diploma Programme.* Geneva: International Baccalaureate.

IB (2011a): *IB Learner Profile booklet.* Online (last accessed 26 August 2011): www.ibo.org/programmes/profile/documents/Learnerprofileguide.pdf

IB (2011b): *Diploma Programme developments.* Online (last accessed 26 August 2011): www.ibo.org/diploma/development/

Chapter 4

Moving on from the 1960s: a new model of diploma for our global citizens

James MacDonald

Introduction

Imagine a graduation ceremony. You are watching young people accepting their diplomas then walking off the stage and into the world. With this image in mind, how would you describe the 'ideal' graduate?

Every year, at ceremonies around the world, IB educators watch their students graduate. Those teachers and administrators in attendance normally have a fairly accurate idea of each student's academic achievement level. In fact, many administrators can probably recite their school's DP scores going back a number of years and possibly to at least one decimal place! But we seem to have less of a grasp on non-academic outcomes, including big questions like whether a young person is likely to be part of the solutions to the world's problems. It seems strange (at least to me) that we do not know more about such things, especially considering the mission of the IB.

This chapter is about a proposal for modifying the IB diploma. The underlying premise for change is that the DP in its current form is an excellent academic credential, but does not fully recognize or acknowledge the type of learning outside of the classroom that is so essential to achievement of the lofty aspirations of the IB. In fact, at my school, we are not waiting for the IB to change the DP. We are launching a new model of diploma: the Global Citizen Diploma (GCD). This new diploma, which uses the DP as the academic base, is presented in this chapter; the case is made for how it could be 'scaled' at the IB level and why now is an opportune time for change to take place. If nothing else, it is hoped such ideas will generate more discussion about how we can practically implement a system that will more fully reflect the ideals of a modern international education.

Background and context

International education has a long history. As a concept and in practice it is not new, dating back arguably at least to the 1860s (Sylvester, 2002) and, in the modern form, to 1924 when the first schools to call themselves 'international schools' opened their doors in Geneva and in Yokohama (Hayden, 1998: 3). 'International education' today cannot ignore the influence of this history and any discussion of the future will inevitably build upon what has evolved over generations of students, teachers, and researchers. While 'international education' lacks an agreed definition, Walker provides what many would consider a reasonable summary: 'an education for international-mindedness; an education designed to break down the barriers of race, religion and class; an education that extolled the benefits of cultural diversity; above all else, an education for peace.' (Walker, 2011: 1) The IB mission statement (2011) echoes similar themes:

> The International Baccalaureate aims to develop inquiring, knowledgeable and caring young people who help to create a better and more peaceful world through intercultural understanding and respect. To this end the organization works with schools, governments and international organizations to develop challenging programmes of international education and rigorous assessment. These programmes encourage students across the world to become active, compassionate and lifelong learners who understand that other people, with their differences, can also be right.

However, making statements about something is one thing. Converting words into practice presents different challenges. As Tarc (2009: 2) observes, the challenge of converging its 'global dreams' with the practical demands of delivering a consistently high quality educational service has led to an on-going 'structural tension' for the IB. This is not the only challenge facing international education either. It seems everywhere there are calls for education to undergo a revolution of sorts. There is a growing consensus that we should be approaching teaching and learning differently than educational systems have in the past and, in the process, rethinking the outcomes we are producing via our schools. Depending upon one's perspective, this is either a very exciting time to be an educator or a very daunting one. But whichever perspective one adopts, we are facing large challenges.

Measuring success and balancing priorities

In thinking about taking the DP forward, it is hard not to come around eventually to the question of what makes a school organization 'successful'. This is a big question and complicated because any answer given will likely be contested by at least someone. As an educational leader myself, I often envy our counterparts in the business world who can gauge their organization's success via a bottom line figure. For a school organization though, I would argue that success cannot be measured through a single bottom line because, for starters, there is no universal agreement on what are *the* desired outcomes of education. However, as a way of grappling with some of this complexity we face as school leaders, I have found a Triple Bottom Line framework to be useful. This is as much of a mindset as anything and is outlined in Table 1.

A framework like this can help to clarify areas of focus and priorities for a school. In some systems, for example, a school and teachers are judged solely by

Bottom Line	Description
Financial	Financial results reflecting the 'business' side of a school. Schools operate in an economic context, and even the leaders of 'not-for-profit' schools rely on finances for resources. Examples: cash flow statement, profit and loss or income statements, and balance sheet.
Academic	The formal academic curriculum, which has outcomes that are directly assessed, evaluated, and reported. Example: A DP score out of 45.
Intangible Core	All other forms of learning outside of the academic bottom line. It encompasses things such as co-/extracurricular activities, pastoral care programmes, and the social/emotional curriculum, the 'hidden' curriculum, or 'affective domain'. Example: CAS activities.

Table 1: A triple bottom line framework for schools (adapted from MacDonald, 2009)

an academic bottom line figure (often via high stakes examinations). In such a case, the educational focus and priorities become clear to all. A Triple Bottom Line model, however, separates academics from other types of educational focuses and then puts academic and non-academic activities on equal standing by assigning each a bottom line. Doing this is a deliberate attempt to highlight the importance of 'intangible core' activities, while using the language of the business world in an attempt better to communicate with those who have the power to influence education (such as school owners or some school governors or politicians) but whose thinking tends to centre around the bottom line.

Bringing the conversation back to the IB, and looking at things through a Triple Bottom Line lens, consider words such as 'active', 'compassionate' and 'caring' in the IB mission statement. These are probably best developed outside of a formal classroom setting. In the DP, however, assessment and criteria for awarding diplomas allow the academic bottom line to dominate.

What about CAS?

At this point, some will be quick to point out that CAS is compulsory, non-academic, and focuses very much upon the 'intangible core'. While this is true, it should also be put into perspective. Until recently, CAS was measured in time and students were required to perform, for example, 50 hours of service over the course of a two-year programme. While the IB has moved away from this metric, there is no reason to believe that this time commitment for students has been changed substantively. Many would agree that service has the potential significantly to shape 'active', 'compassionate' and 'caring' young people. However, 50 hours divided by the length of time students are in the programme equals just minutes a day.

Added to this observation, Roberts argues that service is not 'structurally related to the rest of the curriculum' (2011: 87) and that attempts to offer formal credit have been resisted. He suggests, too, that some students may interpret this to mean CAS requirements are marginal. Roberts also points out that 'anecdotal evidence suggests that perhaps relatively few teachers are engaged in regular service in their own personal lives', which no doubt has implications for schools attempting to embrace the spirit of CAS in their schools (2011: 87). Also, despite what is known about the importance of physical fitness and creativity for today's high school graduates, 'action' and 'creativity' are similarly weighted. Thus, we need to be realistic about what CAS can do and what it cannot do. With only minutes of the day, it is hard to imagine how even the best CAS programme will consistently lead to long term impact for students, especially considering how CAS is presently structured within the DP. As it stands, the DP is basically an academic qualification – but it could be much more.

Persistent challenges

There is an old management axiom that 'what gets measured gets done'. In other words, if people know their performance is going to be measured they will be more motivated to complete a task. Many educators can probably attest to this notion too, having seen students 'chasing grades'. While measuring performance seems to have a motivational effect, there are also challenges. One challenge is summarized in Campbell's Law; the idea that the more a quantitative social indicator is employed in social decision-making, the more pressure there will be to corrupt the social process that the figure is intended to measure and monitor (Campbell, 1976). In other words, if you use a number to help make decisions in a social context, you should assume that over time (and despite the best of intentions) this metric will become corrupted to a certain point. So, for example, if police are being evaluated by crime rates then this may create a new incentive to, among other things, make fewer criminal charges in order to show 'improved performance'. In education, the pressure to meet the goals of the 'academic bottom line' can lead to accusations of cheating by teachers and administrators. (One recent and high profile example of such accusations comes from the Atlanta area, where 38 principals and 178 teachers were accused of colluding to change student examination responses in order to meet the goals set out from the No Child Left Behind legislation (*Economist*, 2011).) I suspect Campbell's Law could be one reason why CAS requirements are no longer quantified as hours.

Related to Campbell's Law is the difficulty of attributing cause and effect relationships within a complex social context. In education, for example, it is

Moving on from the 1960s: a new model of diploma for our global citizens

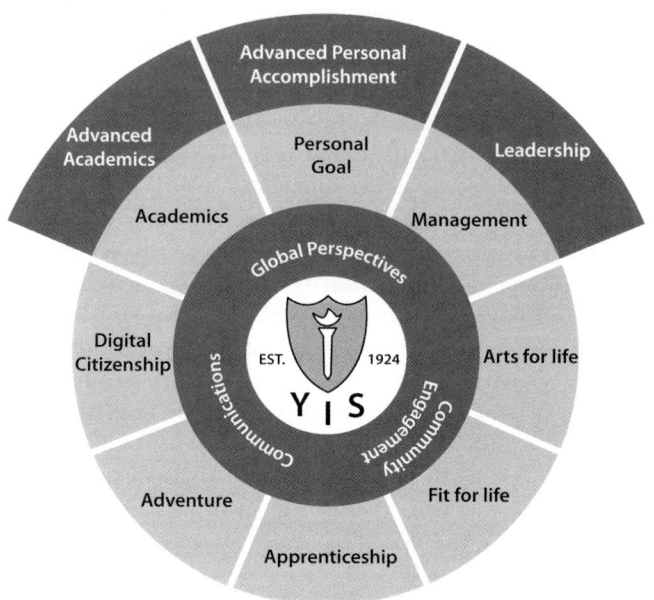

Figure 1: The Global Citizen Diploma (for Grades 9–12)

Global Citizen Diploma

Figure 2: How to earn a Global Citizen Diploma (50% of YIS graduates)

problematic to say with full confidence that certain interventions will lead to specific results because, when changes do occur, especially over the long term, it is difficult to say for certain what influence caused the change (was it the school curriculum, individual teachers, parents, peer group, and so on).

Looking at another challenge, and especially within the context of moving the IB diploma forward, we must also consider credentialism, which occurs when one group of students begins catching up to the credentials held by another – and then the latter group seeks additional credentials to maintain the gap (Brown & Lauder, 2006). We know that inequality gaps are growing in many places in the world (Walker, 2011: 14) and that the IB is laudably trying to increase access to its programmes (Guy, 2011). Any changes to the DP that might disadvantage certain groups require pause for reflection.

Finally, DP students are busy young people. Pressure on our high school students is as high as ever. One recent graduate of my own school, Yokohama International School (YIS), when asked what advice he would give to younger students, replied: "Tell them they can't complain about stress until they are in the DP." Our students are busy, stretched and their plates are full, and this must be acknowledged in any plans to change the DP. How then can the DP move forward while mitigating these types of persistent challenges?

A different model: the Global Citizen Diploma

At YIS we are attempting to introduce our own model, the Global Citizen Diploma (GCD), which will run for the first time in school year 2011-12. The GCD, at its heart, is a recognition programme. We believe our students do many great things that are not fully recognized by the DP. This is not to say that we are rejecting the DP. On the contrary: the DP forms the academic base for the GCD. We think of it as an extension of the DP, acknowledging learning and accomplishment occurring outside of the classroom that the DP structure does not recognize.

As can be seen from Figure 1, the GCD has three main categories. The core requirements are in the centre and are for all students. They consist of global perspectives, communications, and community engagement. The eight extended elements are: personal goal, management, arts for life, fit for life, apprenticeship, adventure, digital citizenship, and academics. There are also three advanced elements: advanced academics, advanced personal accomplishment, and leadership. More details, including criteria for each category, are available online (www.yis.ac.jp/gcd).

To earn the diploma (see Figure 2), students must achieve all of the core requirements, five of the extended elements plus academics. (In terms of academic achievement, a student would need to be roughly in the top half of the class and be enrolled in the full IB diploma.) Thus we anticipate roughly half our graduates will be able to earn the full diploma. To ensure the GCD carries weight with university admissions, we feel setting the academic bar

Global Citizen Certificate

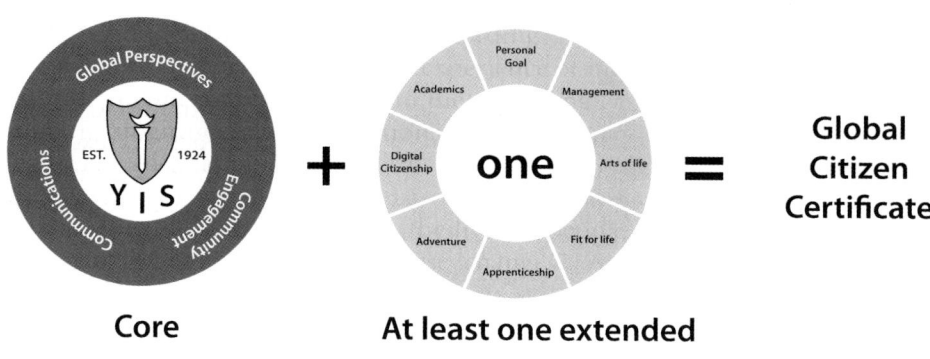

Figure 3: How to earn a Global Citizen Certificate (90% of YIS graduates)

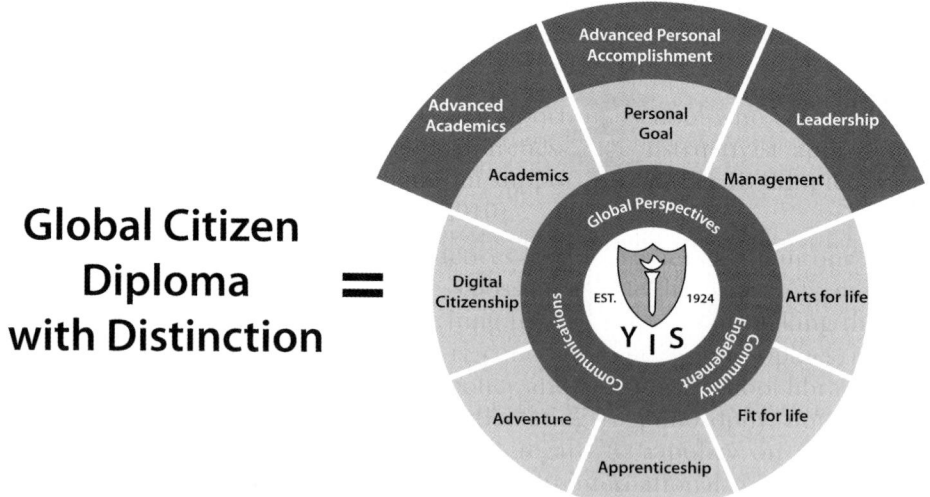

Figure 4: How to earn a Global Citizen Diploma with Distinction (10% of YIS graduates)

relatively high is important.

To make the benefits of the GCD accessible to a wider range of students, we have also introduced the Global Citizen Certificate (see Figure 3). To earn this, a student would need to complete all the core requirements, plus at least one extended element. We believe almost all of our students will be able to achieve this requirement from the outset, as we will not require the same level of academic achievement as for the diploma.

We also anticipate that some of our students will be able to attain the GCD with distinction (see Figure 4). To acquire this, a student must achieve excellent academic results (around the top 10 per cent of the class), have a significant personal accomplishment (as determined by a rubric) and have demonstrated leadership in a meaningful way (note we distinguish between management and leadership in our criteria).

As one can see, while academics centred on the DP remain a foundation, there is considerable focus on activities outside the classroom. We also believe this is in step with what some of the leading educational thinkers are calling for in terms of educational change. For example, in outlining 'five minds for the future', two of the five minds Gardner proposes are outside of the cognitive domain (2011: 10). The 'strategically influential' (Hargreaves, 2011: 334) *Partnership for 21st Century Skills Framework* (2011) has five major categories: one is 'core subjects' (which are essentially academic) and the other four all incorporate elements that fall within the 'intangible core'. November (2011: 278-279) states that there are three key things students today need to learn: 'how to make meaning with overwhelming amounts of information; how to work with people around the world (empathy); and how to be self-directed, interdependent, and a superb lifelong learner.' For all three, it is difficult to imagine how these outcomes could occur without a considerable focus outside the traditional realm of academics. Furthermore, and as Thomas and Brown nicely summarize: 'the kind of learning that will define the twenty-first century is not taking place in a classroom – at least not in today's classroom. Rather, it is happening all around us, everywhere, and it is powerful.' (2011:17). So, I would argue, when we think of schooling our thoughts should not automatically turn to a classroom setting. Instead, we need to think bigger and broader.

Development of the Global Citizen Diploma

The process of developing the GCD was led by a small team at YIS. Along the way there were many iterations. As part of the process, we held multiple feedback sessions with the staff (both formal and informal), conducted parent and alumni surveys, held sessions with students, spoke to university admissions officers and external consultants (both formally and informally), and received feedback from the Board. In short, there was considerable community input. We are, nonetheless, conscious that in many respects designing the new diploma was the easy part; implementation will be quite challenging.

Implementing and managing the Global Citizen Diploma

Central to making the GCD successful in practice are student portfolios (created digitally on blogs). Here students will demonstrate their learning and accomplishments and they will also be allocated time to develop their portfolios throughout the year in extended homeroom sessions. As Saltman (2011) argues, 'an insistent drumbeat of research findings' is for more of the work of learning to shift 'from teachers to the ones doing the learning', and we think student portfolios being in the centre of the programme will help us to step in this direction. Incidentally, these online portfolios will assist with college applications and will also meet part of the diploma's digital citizenship criteria. On the teacher side, one staff member will provide top-level oversight of all blogs/portfolios, working with homeroom teachers who will work more closely with individual students as they update and develop their work.

Looking at the challenges that lie ahead, it seems fair to assume that developing a new diploma could be called an adaptive challenge: 'it requires creating the knowledge and the tools to solve the problem in the act of working on it.' (Wagner *et al*, 2006: 63). We know the diploma will evolve and improve over time as we learn through our experience and adapt as necessary. We are also aware of potential pitfalls. We are conscious that the GCD could be seen as an additional requirement for our students, rather than as a means of naturally recognizing the many achievements already occurring as a result of our high school programme. In the first few years in particular, while we are aligning all of our programmes with the diploma criteria, this will be a key challenge. We also know that some students may try to 'game' or manipulate the requirements, knowing that something like a GCD will help positively to differentiate them in their college applications. While we have no foolproof solution for Campbell's Law to offer, and know we cannot be certain that prescribed student activities will lead to all the outcomes we hope for, we believe the GCD is better aligned to fulfil our school mission than are present systems. We also expect that by offering a diploma that aims to acknowledge some of the things students like ours are doing, our students may very well be given an edge over others in university admission. In that sense we are promoting credentialism. However, we are very open to sharing the ideas rather than keeping them to ourselves. We also are committed to being at the forefront of what a modern international education should be and therefore, on balance, think it is important that we take this next step despite the challenges.

Articulated shared vision

The GCD fits into our school's overall desire to shift fully our programmes to reflect what we think a 21st century international education should look like in practice. Through the structure and specific criteria of the GCD, we are saying 'this is our ideal graduate'. With over 40 nationalities of students, teachers hailing from 14 different countries and with diverse experiences, having a common vision for an ideal graduate should make our professional dialogue more focused and, by extension, our school organization more effective and unified. Along these lines, one could argue that something like the GCD could act as a self-organizing mechanism as activities, decisions, and priorities will need to refer back to our agreed diploma criteria. The new diploma becomes then a shared vision – or what Fullan might describe as a 'collective moral purpose' (2005: 68) – for our entire community; more concrete than a mission statement and more vibrant than most strategic plans.

So while we think it is time for a change where we are, could it also be time for change on a broader scale?

Why the time for change has come

The DP has been serving international education very well for over 40 years. In fact, the six-subject structure was created in 1965 with CAS (originally known as CASS: creative, aesthetic or social service activities) being added at the same time, and ToK introduced in 1967 (Tarc, 2009: 11). Much has changed in the world since the 1960s and, as mentioned previously, our generation of educators is being called upon to create a revolution in education.

Tarc contends that international educators must re-animate the founding dreams of international education 'under the changed and changing conditions of the present' (2009: 135). I think the GCD offers one model showing how such 're-animation' can occur in practice, but as Abbott and Ryan pointed out a decade ago, 'winning of intellectual support' for educational change is easier to do than garnering 'full emotional acceptance' (2001: 185) for that change.

Nevertheless, assuming one agrees with our philosophical rationale for change and sees practical merits in the model, the question then becomes could something similar be 'scaled' for the IB? The next section explains why the timing for change is excellent and possibilities are exciting.

Reason 1: Technology

While the internet has been around for decades, today Web 2.0 technologies mark a major step forward. Today, anyone with internet access can be both a consumer and creator of content; peer-to-peer learning can occur more easily and more naturally as well (Thomas and Brown, 2011: 50), and 'anyone can now learn anything from anyone at anytime' (Bonk, 2009: 7). The implications for educators, and for a global programme like the IB, are significant. For example, one technology already shaping education is blogs (Thomas and Brown, 2011: 71-70). Blogs are easy to use, often free, and offer a highly versatile publishing platform (users can upload and share text, videos, files for download, links to other sites and more). Blogs are also complemented by other free 'cloud computing' productivity tools such as Googledocs, with the advantage that files can be accessed from anywhere with internet access as the files are not stored on local hard drives.

So what does this mean for the DP? Students can, from anywhere at any time, demonstrate achievement, reflect upon learning, collaborate with other students and have their work moderated. While doing so, students will also learn about their own digital presence (something that was not necessary in the 1960s!), because, whether they like it or not, their digital footprint today is not unlike a tattoo that will stay with them for the rest of their lives. Moreover, maintaining a portfolio will alleviate some of the pressure on DP students, as an online portfolio can be part of the college application process. In short, the technology is providing exciting opportunities for learning, shifting more control over learning to students while helping to shape wiser and more responsible 'digital citizens.'

Reason 2: Young people want a better world

There is a growing recognition that people are increasingly expecting organizations and those around them to be acting in socially and environmentally responsible ways. Take the observations of two business gurus: Porter contends that creating societal benefit is a very powerful way of making economic profit and that more companies are realizing this opportunity (2011); marketing expert Kotler in the book *Marketing 3.0* argues that today businesses must address people's deepest needs for social, economic, and environmental justice (Kotler *et al*, 2010: 3-5) if they want to sell products and services. If two of the world's leading business thinkers are saying these things – and historically the business world has been seen as one of the least socially and environmentally minded sectors – I would contend something is afoot.

I would also suggest that if we are seeing this trend in society in general then we should expect it will be amplified in the idealism of our youth. Today, as much as ever, it seems that our high school graduates are looking for opportunities to make a positive difference in the world. It follows then that this generation of students may well be interested in expressing themselves and succeeding in ways that cannot be recognized through academic achievement alone. We should listen to the students.

Reason 3: Ideals of the IB and the practicalities of growth

If the IB continues to grow at its present pace, there will remain significant challenges related to retaining the ideals of an international education while maintaining quality. A model like the GCD highlights many of the ideals of an international education. Moving the DP framework more towards acknowledging activities outside of the academic realm would serve to reaffirm the IB's commitment to its ideals and critical time in the organization's development.

Reason 4: Influence on universities

Most people familiar with the DP know that, over the past decade, strides have been made in the area of university recognition. In the past, I think it was fair to say that universities could dictate their entrance requirements to high schools; now there seems to be more opportunity for dialogue between the two sides. Added to this, few universities these days are solely relying on academic scores for admission decisions as they may have done years ago, but rather look much more holistically at applicants. Students need to convey such information on their application and convince admissions personnel of their experience. So why not formally acknowledge the great things students are doing outside of the classroom and allow such information to be readily factored into the decision-making of university admissions offices in a more reliable fashion?

No doubt universities will continue to influence the IB with their requirements, but this is no longer a one-way street and the IB is now in a position where it can influence universities. It should embrace this position and it should be working with universities in redesigning the DP requirements. I sense they are listening.

Conclusion

The IB diploma is a good programme, designed in the 1960s, and has stood the test of time. But the world is not standing still and neither are our schools. We, as the IB community, need to rethink elements of the DP and now is an opportune time for change. In writing this chapter, I have attempted to demonstrate that change is possible in a practical sense. By arguing that the structures and assessment mechanisms of the DP do not reflect to the degree possible the IB mission, I aim to lay out an idealistic argument for practical change. Outlining some of the reasons why change could happen now is an attempt to demonstrate the opportunities that now exist.

But, more than anything, my argument boils down to this: ask yourself which diploma structure – the IBDP or something more holistic such as the GCD – better reflects the 'ideal graduate'? Neither this question, nor your answer, can be ignored.

Acknowledgements

The vision, passion and intellectual energy of my colleagues on the 'Global Citizen Diploma design team' made creating the diploma a very rewarding experience. I would like to thank each of these individuals: Dennis Stanworth, Adam Seldis and Eddie Levisman. I would also like to thank Neil Richards – also contributing a chapter (chapter 3) in this book – as he was the inspiration for many of the initial ideas about creating a new diploma at YIS.

References

Abbott, J and Ryan, T (2001): *The Unfinished Revolution.* Stafford: Network Educational Press.

Bonk, C (2009): *The World is Open: How Web Technology is Revolutionizing Education.* San Francisco: Jossey-Bass.

Brown, P and Lauder, H (2006): Globalization, Knowledge and the Myth of the Magnet Economy, in H Lauder, P Brown, J A Dillabough and A H Halsey (eds), *Education, Globalization and Social Change.* Oxford: Oxford University Press, pp317-340.

Campbell, D (1976): *Assessing the Impact of Planned Social Change.* The Public Affairs Center, Dartmouth College, Hanover, New Hampshire. Online: www.eric.ed.gov/PDFS/ED303512.pdf (last accessed 26 August 2011).

Economist (2011): Low marks all round, in *The Economist*, July 16-22, 2011.

Fullan, M (2005): *Leadership & Sustainability: System Thinkers in Action.* Thousand Oaks California: Corwin Press.

Gardner, H (2011): Five Minds for the Future, in J Bellanca and R Brandt (eds), *21st Century Skills: Rethinking How Students Learn.* Bloomington IN: Solution Tree Press, pp9-33.

Guy, J (2011): Challenges to Access, in G Walker (ed), *The Changing Face of International Education: Challenges for the IB.* Cardiff: International Baccalaureate, pp139-158.

Hargreaves, A (2011): Leadership, Change, and Beyond the 21st Century Skills Agenda, in J Bellanca and R Brandt (eds), *21st Century Skills: Rethinking How Students Learn.* Bloomington IN: Solution Tree Press, pp327-48.

Hayden, M (1998): International education in practice, in M Hayden and J Thompson (eds), *International Education: Principles and Practice.* London: Kogan Page.

IB (2011): *Mission and Strategy.* Online: www.ibo.org/mission/ (last accessed 26 August 2011).

Kotler, P, Kartajaya, H and Setiawan, J (2010): *Marketing 3.0: From Product to Customer to the Human Spirit.* Hoboken, NJ: John Wiley & Sons.

MacDonald, J (2009): Balancing Priorities and Measuring Success: a triple bottom line framework for international school leaders, in *Journal of Research in International Education*, 8, 1, pp81-98.

November, A (2011): Technology Rich, Information Poor, in J Bellanca and R Brandt (eds), *21st Century Skills: Rethinking How Students Learn.* Bloomington, IN: Solution Tree Press, pp274-83.

Partnership for 21st Century Skills (2011): *Framework for 21st Century Learning.* Online: http://p21.org/index.php?option=com_content&task=view&id=254&Itemid=120 (last accessed 26 August 2011).

Porter, M (2011): *How to Fix Capitalism.* Interview, Online (last accessed 26 August 2011): http://blogs.hbr.org/ideacast/2011/01/how-to-fix-capitalism.html

Roberts, B (2011): Engaging with the Community, in G Walker (ed), *The Changing Face of International Education: Challenges for the IB.* Cardiff: International Baccalaureate.

Saltman, D (2011): Student-Directed Learning Comes of Age: Teachers Adopt Classroom Strategies to Help Students Monitor Their Own Learning, in *Harvard Education Letter*, 27:4, pp4-6.

Sylvester, B (2002): The 'first' international school, in M Hayden, J Thompson and G Walker (eds), *International Education in Practice.* London: Routledge, pp3-17.

Tarc, P (2009): *Global Dreams, Enduring Tensions: International Baccalaureate in a Changing World.* New York: Peter Lang.

Thomas, D and Brown, J S (2011): *A New Culture of Learning: Cultivating the Imagination for a World of Constant Change.* USA: CreateSpace.

Wagner, T, Kegan, R, Lahey, L and Lemons, R (2006): *Change Leadership: A Practical Guide to Transforming Our Schools.* San Francisco: Jossey-Bass Education.

Walker, G (2011): Introduction: Past, present and future, in G Walker (ed), *The Changing Face of International Education: Challenges for the IB.* Cardiff: International Baccalaureate, pp1-17.

Chapter 5

The IB Diploma Programme as pedagogic discourse

James Cambridge

Introduction

This chapter will discuss the structure and implementation of the International Baccalaureate (IB) Diploma Programme (DP) and draw comparisons both between the IBDP and other upper secondary programmes of study, and between the IBDP and other IB programmes. The framework for the description and analysis of the respective programmes is provided by Basil Bernstein's (1975, 2000) theories of pedagogic discourse. The chapter concludes with a discussion of possible avenues for school-based academic and professional enquiry into curriculum development and the implementation of the IBDP.

Bernstein on pedagogic discourse

The pedagogic device

The pedagogic device comprises the rules for the distribution, recontextualisation and evaluation (*ie* assessment) of knowledge. According to Bernstein (2000) these rules comprise:

- *Distributive* rules that govern the distribution of different forms of knowledge to different social groups.
- *Recontextualising* rules that construct the 'what' and 'how' of official pedagogic discourse.
- *Evaluative* rules that provide the criteria and standards for the transmission and acquisition of knowledge.

Distributive rules distribute access to the 'thinkable' (*ie* official knowledge) and the 'unthinkable' (*ie* the possibility of new knowledge). In so doing they distribute different forms of consciousness to different groups in society. Consequently, distributive rules produce division of labour in society and (re)produce economic and social stratification. Selective education systems that implement sorting policies, which may be based on psychometric or other forms of measurement of 'aptitude' or 'ability', distribute differential access to knowledge by students. Fitz *et al* (2006: 87) argue, with reference to the British context, that higher education institutions have pressured schools 'to identify and give children credentials with different types and levels of qualifications. Employers and universities have made it clear that this is the key function of schools'.

Knowledge, as it is created in universities and elsewhere, must be selected, sequenced and paced in order to be made available to learners in schools. This process is referred to as the 'pedagogic recontextualisation' or 'pedagogisation' of knowledge (Singh, 2002). Curriculum and assessment organisations such as the International Baccalaureate, Cambridge International Examinations and the US-based College Board may be identified as sites of pedagogic recontextualisation. Political reform of education in many parts of the world has resulted in a shift in control over pedagogic recontextualisation, away from decentralised bodies independent of direct governmental control, such as examination boards, towards increasing centralisation and government control (Ball, 1990; Fitz et al, 2006; Ross, 2000). Centralised control of the curriculum in this way is identified with the so-called 'Official Recontextualisation Field' (ORF), which comprises Ministries of Education and other government departments that exert power over education policy (Singh, 2002). However, the power of the ORF extends beyond the control of the curriculum alone. It may be argued that legislation has privileged the national curriculum in England, for example, not only as a body of 'official' knowledge but also as a means of assessing students' learning and judging the performance of teachers and schools (Fitz et al, 2006).

Educational assessment exerts a backwash effect on pedagogic practice. That is to say, how learning of the curriculum is assessed has a strong influence on how it is taught. Two contrasting models of pedagogic practice may be identified with a focus on the assessment of *performance* and *competence* respectively. The performance model 'places the emphasis upon a specific output of the acquirer [*ie* the learner], upon a particular text the acquirer is expected to construct and upon the specialised skills necessary to the production of this specific output, text or product' (Bernstein, 2000: 44). Fitz *et al* (2006: 6) describe the performance model as 'the dominant, established model ... with the focus upon acquirers' past and future accomplishments, with strong apparent progression and pacing, evaluation focused on what was missing from their texts in terms of explicit and specific criteria of which they were made aware'. By contrast, in a competence model of pedagogic practice, the learners 'apparently have a great measure of control over selection, sequence and pace... The emphasis is upon the realisation of competences that acquirers already possess, or are thought to possess' (Bernstein, 2000: 45). Competence models may be identified with 'liberal/progressive', learner-centred approaches to education (Fitz *et al*, 2006: 7). However, such approaches may be criticised on the grounds that they are expensive to produce and maintain because of the time required for the development of resources, communicating with students and parents, and personalising the learning of individuals.

Classification and framing

Underlying the theory of the pedagogic device are Bernstein's concepts of *classification* and *framing*. The construction of the curriculum is based on

The IB Diploma Programme as pedagogic discourse

relations between different forms of knowledge. In some contexts, there are strong boundaries insulating the different subjects such that what goes on in the science laboratory, for example, is separate from and unrelated to what goes on in the modern foreign languages classroom. In the high school or upper secondary school, there is frequently strong classification between the academic subjects. In other contexts, such as in the primary school, classification between curriculum contents, and the boundaries insulating the different subjects, can be weak. For example, cross-curricular teaching and learning can bring together diverse strands such as literacy and numeracy in the same lesson.

The internal organisation of subjects is also variable. In some subjects, knowledge is hierarchically ordered such that learning must be approached in a particular sequence. In other subjects, learning may not be dependent upon prior knowledge or experience so that content can be approached in a variety of different sequences. Selection, sequencing, and pacing of curriculum contents are indicators of framing.

Bernstein (1975, 2000) proposes two ideal codes that describe relationships between and within contents of the curriculum. The 'collection code' demonstrates strong classification and strong framing, whereas the 'integrated code' demonstrates weak classification and weak framing. The strong framing of collection codes means that pedagogic discourses and practices may vary between subjects, and that individual teachers may operate with considerable autonomy and have divergent ways of addressing their particular subjects in terms of selection of content, order, pacing, and assessment. Bernstein (1975: 101) argues that the integrated code, with weaker classification and weaker framing, 'will not permit the variations in pedagogy and evaluation that are possible within collection codes'. He suggests that:

> There will be a pronounced movement towards a common pedagogy and a tendency towards a common system of evaluation. In other words, integrated codes will, at the level of the teachers, probably create homogeneity of teaching practice. (Bernstein, 1975: 101)

Moreover, 'integrated codes may require a high level of ideological consensus, and this may affect the recruitment of staff' (Bernstein, 1975: 107). That is to say, teachers in schools that implement an integrated curriculum may be expected to require and to gain access to continuing professional development courses that coordinate their practice in order to be most effective.

Furthermore, collection and integrated codes are inscribed with contrasting discourses pertaining to the social location and ownership of knowledge. Bernstein (1975: 97) proposes that:

> Knowledge under collection is private property with its own power structure and market situation. This affects the whole ambience surrounding the developing and marketing of new knowledge. Children and pupils are early

socialised into this concept of knowledge as private property. They are encouraged to work as isolated individuals with their arms around their work.

In contrast to this perspective, Bernstein (1975) argues that attempts to weaken classification, as found in the integrated code, 'can be regarded as attempts to break or weaken existing monopolies' (1975: 97). Hence, teaching and learning may be seen as an individualised experience under a collection code, whereas it may be seen as a socialised common experience under an integrated code.

The IB Diploma Programme as pedagogic discourse

Distributive rules

As outlined above, Bernstein (2000) argues that distributive rules govern the ways in which knowledge is made accessible to different groups in society. A common way of implementing differential access to knowledge in school is to impose some form of educational selection. For example, a school might identify the IBDP as a programme of study that is most appropriate for 'gifted and talented' students. As such, only those deemed to be in this category would be considered capable or worthy of having access to the IBDP. 'Gifted and talented' programmes may be organised as a 'school within a school' (Matthews and Kitchen, 2007). In other words, certain students may attend a particular school but be segregated from their fellows as a consequence of curriculum arrangements. Here is a powerful example of what Siskin (1994: 37) refers to as the relationship between 'the formal organization of the school and the disciplinary organization of knowledge'. The way in which a school is organised reproduces and embodies discourse about the structure of knowledge, in terms of the composition of academic subject departments. It also reproduces and embodies discourse about division of labour and social stratification by regulating access to knowledge, academic subjects, and programmes of study. This may seem to address separate issues about selection and access, on the one hand, and what subjects schools have decided to offer, on the other, but in practice these two can be intimately linked. This is because the distributive rules control differential access to knowledge. Students following the IBDP in different schools may not be pursuing the same programme of study because:

> One school might be non-selective, offering an open access whole-school programme, whereas another might be selective, offering a restricted access school-within-a-school programme. The values and assumptions underlying the criteria for entry on to the programmes of study are different in either case. (IB, 2008: 22).

Cambridge (2010: 211) explains this distinction in Bernsteinian terms by proposing that 'the non-selective, open access approach is inscribed with a discourse of weak classification and weak framing, whereas the restricted access, school-within-a-school represents a discourse of strong classification and strong framing'.

Examples can be found in the literature arguing that the curriculum may be used to widen access to and participation in education by weakening classification. Hence, in the US context, Kugler and Albright (2005) describe the IBDP as a means of serving 'underserved' (*eg* Afro-American and Hispanic) communities with equity. They discuss how the IBDP was introduced into a public high school with the intention of increasing inclusion by encouraging greater enrolment from 'minority cultures' in high school classes. This was achieved by changing policy 'from the "gifted and talented" model that admitted students mainly on the basis of their performance in standardized tests to an "honors" approach that focused on students' motivation and performance in class' (Kugler and Albright, 2005: 43). The adoption of this approach meant rejecting the implementation of 'a diploma-only program as a school-within-a-school' (Kugler and Albright, 2005: 43). However, a conclusion that may be drawn from this example is that a quality such as 'inclusiveness' is not implicit in a programme of study such as the IBDP. Such a quality is an outcome of the policy environment in which the programme is implemented and not an attribute of the programme itself. Under different circumstances and in different contexts, different policy outcomes could be achieved using a similar programme of study. In other words, the school a student attends and the policies it implements are (at least) as important as the programme of study followed by that student.

Recontextualising rules

Does the pedagogic discourse inscribed in the IBDP constitute a collection code or an integrated code? There appears to be some debate about the way in which the IBDP may be characterised. Thompson (1998) suggests that grouped programmes of study such as the IBDP present opportunities for 'interstitial learning', being the 'learning that takes place *between* the subjects of the curriculum, and that arises from the various styles of inter- and transdisciplinary processes that are part of the planned and unplanned experience for the students and teachers' (p 286, italics in original). This may be seen as a proposal that grouped programmes of study such as the IBDP are inscribed with weak classification. Cambridge (2011: 134) observes that it is unclear whether or not it is valid to interpret Thompson's references to transdisciplinary processes and boundaries between subjects in terms of classification and framing because Thompson makes no explicit reference to Bernstein's theories in his writing. On the other hand, Doherty (2010: 7-8), citing the work of Remillard (1978), proposes that the IBDP has been characterised as 'a curriculum with strong classification along traditional Western disciplinary lines, and strong framing with reduced opportunity for student choice or teacher control within the externally examined regime'. Doherty (2010) argues that while the theory of knowledge (ToK) course appears to offer the prospect of integration across the IBDP, 'it also serves to expose, contrast and reify the differences between [subjects], in terms of how their knowledge is legitimated' (page 8). She also draws attention to how limitations placed on the choice of topic for the extended essay maintain the strength of classification in the IBDP:

> The Extended Essay ... must be undertaken within the guidelines set for the selected disciplinary fields and interdisciplinary projects, such as in biotechnology, are expressly discouraged, thus strong disciplinary classification is largely maintained. More recently a minor 'Group 4' project combining enquiries across a number of experimental sciences has been required, but at this stage, has little impact on assessment and thus has had marginal impact on the strength of disciplinary boundaries. (Doherty, 2010: 8)

However, it has also been proposed that the 'internationally-minded values' that underpin the IBDP may contribute to the mitigation of classification. Walford (2002) discusses how religious values in education might produce an overarching discourse that weakens classification in the curricula of Evangelical Christian and Muslim schools in England and The Netherlands:

> There still may be a collection code of subjects, but there is an attempt to integrate these subjects at a deeper level by relating them back to belief in a Biblical view of God, creation and the role of human beings in that creation. To the extent that teachers are successful in making each of the subjects and topics examples of God's creation, humanity's fall and redemption, they produce an integrated code with an 'overarching weak classification' between contents. It is a way of linking all subjects through the superimposition of one master-viewpoint on all. (Walford, 2002: 416)

Cambridge (2011: 134) speculates that 'international values' might constitute a similar 'master viewpoint' that weakens classification in IB programmes. This is an attractive proposition but it may be criticised because it is not clear that 'religious values' and 'international values' are analogous. Individuals might be able to claim certainty of the religious values in which they believe because they are located in specific religious texts, but there are no corresponding bodies of scripture that express 'international values'. Hence it may be argued that international values are contested in a way that religious values are not. On the other hand, as Roberts (2009) attempts to demonstrate, there is potential for the whole curriculum to be permeated with 'internationally-minded values' in order to produce an 'education for global citizenship'. This may be interpreted as an argument in support of Walford's perspective.

Notwithstanding these theoretical debates, it seems evident that the IBDP is inscribed with a collection code showing strong classification, if only because the candidate is strongly constrained in terms of choice of subjects from the hexagon of grouped subjects, and must complete the compulsory common core activities, comprising the ToK course, creativity action service (CAS) and the extended essay (EE), in order to be eligible for award of the IB diploma. Candidates who do not fulfil these requirements are not eligible for award of the diploma but may be awarded a certificate 'noting the courses they took and the marks they earned' (IB, 2011a). It may be argued that, in contrast to the IB diploma, the award of IB certificates represents a weakening of classification because candidates are less constrained in their subject choice. However, this argument may only apply if a student elects from the outset of a programme of study to take only individual certificates. Choice is still constrained if the student is awarded certificates after having failed to meet the conditions for the award of the full diploma.

Evaluative rules

Evaluative rules provide the criteria and standards for the assessment of learning. Two modes of assessment are identified: performance and competence. The IBDP creates a context for a wide variety of modes of assessment within a performance model:

> The nature of the examination questions varies considerably from paper to paper and from subject to subject. Objective tests comprising a set of multiple choice questions are used in some subjects, but short answer questions, structured questions, extended response questions, essay questions, data analysis questions, text analysis questions and case study questions are all used where appropriate. (IB, 2002: 16)

Corbett (2007: 27) identifies the IBDP as an example of 'outcomes-based education' (OBE) because it 'starts with a clear picture of what is important for students to be able to do, then organises the curriculum, instruction and assessment to make sure learning happens'. From this point of view, it may be argued that assessment in the IBDP corresponds with a performance model.

> Within the IB, the learner profile, subject aims, objectives, content, some teaching time, and summative criteria-based assessments are all mandated by the IB ... It's a system in which teachers seem to have little control, and students even less control, of their educational landscape. Compliance to outcomes is mainly enforced through international standardised examinations that account for up to eighty per cent of assessed material, and through moderation of the remaining internally-assessed components. Add to this the extensive content that must be covered in certain subjects, and the curriculum might be considered highly prescriptive and restrictive. (Corbett, 2007: 28-9)

However, there appears to be some scope for at least a small proportion of evaluation according to a competence model that acknowledges the agency of the learner. Making reference to the IBDP *Biology Subject Guide* (IB, 2001), Corbett (2007: 29) notes that 'some types of learning cannot be effectively evaluated':

> To indicate that parts of the aims will be assessed is to imply that parts of the aims will not be assessed, which is to say that teachers and students are working with a critical curriculum which cannot be effectively evaluated, let alone be

measured, by anyone other than the learner. Thus, the IB curriculum and assessment structure not only recognises that students should be self-reflective critical learners, but also allows some room for this to happen in a way 'uncontrolled', or not wholly controlled, by assessment. (Corbett, 2007: 29)

Comparisons with other upper high school programmes

Bernstein (1975: 91) proposes a typology of educational knowledge codes that display varying degrees of collection, and hence strength of classification. He proposes that at one end of the range, with the greatest collection, are specialised 'pure' combinations of GCE Advanced Level (A level) courses, such as pure mathematics, applied mathematics and physics. These constitute 'a small number of subjects, which are normally related or cognate to each other' (Ross, 2000: 100). 'Impure' combinations of specialised subjects, 'drawn from different universes of knowledge, *eg* Religion, Economics, Physics' (Bernstein, 1975: 91) are inscribed with weaker collection codes. A still weaker variety of the collection code is found in the 'non-specialised, *subject*-based models' of the curriculum found in certain European countries. It may be argued that the IBDP resembles this model most closely. Stenhouse (1975) proposes that English and many European curricula share strong classification in common but vary in their strength of framing, with European curricula showing 'exceptionally strong framing' in terms of the 'central direction of the selection, organization and pacing of knowledge' (1975: 48). However, numerous reforms to curriculum have been implemented since the time of Stenhouse's writing. A fourth 'non-specialised, *course*-based' variety is the US form of the collection code. This has even weaker classification because 'a far greater range of subjects can be taken ... and are capable of combination' (Bernstein, 1975: 92). The formulation of a valid distinction between concepts such as course and subject is problematic, but Ross (2000: 100) proposes that courses are structured as 'knowledge units' rather than whole subjects. It may be argued that the award of 'certificates' for combinations of subjects that are not eligible for award of the IBDP resembles this variety most closely.

Comparisons with other IB programmes

Bernstein's typology of knowledge codes also embraces curriculum models that are inscribed with an integrated code and that demonstrate the weakest classification. A distinction is drawn between teacher-based and teachers-based modes. The former involves learners spending an extended block of time studying a range of subjects with a specific teacher. However, it is acknowledged that this teacher 'may operate a collection code and keep the various subjects distinct and insulated, or he [*sic*] can blur the boundaries between the different codes' (Bernstein, 1975: 93). In the latter teachers-based mode, 'integration involves relationships with other teachers. In this way, we can have integration in terms of the number of teachers involved' (Bernstein, 1975: 93).

Furthermore, two varieties of 'teachers-based' integration can be identified 'according to whether the integration refers to a group of teachers within a common subject, or the extent to which integration involves teachers of different subjects' (Bernstein, 1975: 93). Integration by definition demonstrates weak classification but there may be variation in strength of framing, *eg* whether the lessons are teacher-centred or learner-centred.

IB programmes of study are inscribed with contrasting degrees of collection and integration. Compared with the IBDP, the IB Middle Years (MYP) and Primary Years (PYP) Programmes are inscribed with weaker classification and, hence, show greater integration. This approach is exemplified by the transdisciplinary themes that underpin the PYP because

> ... educating students in a set of isolated subject areas, while necessary, is not sufficient. Of equal importance is the need to acquire skills in context, and to explore content that is relevant to students, and transcends the boundaries of the traditional subjects. (IB, 2007: 11)

As documents relating to the PYP such as *Making the PYP Happen* (IB, 2007) make explicit, a whole-school approach to curriculum planning is required, and it is necessary for teachers to work collaboratively. This corresponds to Bernstein's (1975: 107) observation that 'integrated codes will only work when there is a high level of ideological consensus among the staff'. This is because integrated codes 'call for greater homogeneity in pedagogy and evaluation, and therefore reduce differences between teachers in the form of transmission and assessment of knowledge' (Bernstein, 1975: 107). Consequently, it may be proposed that there are profound differences in the nature and content of professional development workshops for PYP and IBDP teachers because the demands for 'ideological consensus' are different. This would make a productive topic for research. Cross-phase liaison between different stages of education, and continuity between different programmes of study, would also be useful topics for systematic study. For example how might the form and content of pedagogic discourse be compared and contrasted between the PYP and the MYP, or between the MYP (or another junior high school programme of study such as the Cambridge IGCSE) and the IBDP?

The introduction of the IB career-related certificate (IBCC) in 2012 will mark a new development in the pedagogic discourse of the IBDP (IB, 2011b). This certificate 'bridges the gap between academic and career-related programmes, allowing highly motivated career-oriented students to also have the opportunity to take advantage of an IB education' (IB, 2011b). It is intended for students 'who may not wish to take the full IB Diploma Programme but instead want to relate their academic studies to their career-related aspirations' (IB, 2011b). Hence, it may be argued that the pedagogic discourse inscribed in the IBCC is less strongly classified than that of the IBDP. It will be interesting to see how the introduction of elements of vocational education into a hitherto exclusively academic approach to education will be implemented, particularly in those contexts in which academic studies have historically been ascribed with higher status than vocational studies.

Conclusion

From the arguments outlined above, it is evident that the IBDP may be implemented in different ways in different contexts. Bernstein's theories about pedagogic discourse offer a language for the description and analysis of these differences. Furthermore, Bernstein's theoretical perspective, particularly in connection with classification and framing, may be viewed as a heuristic device that assists in the formation of research questions about curriculum. Rather than draw any definitive conclusions about the structure or implementation of the IBDP, this chapter would be of greatest use to the reader if it were to identify some potential avenues for professional or academic enquiry that could be pursued by school-based practitioners.

In schools that implement two or more IB programmes of study, for example the IBDP and the MYP, it would be of value to make a critical comparative review of the discourses inscribed in each of the programmes. To what extent does the IBDP exhibit stronger classification when compared with the other programme(s)? How can this strong classification be characterised? What observations can be made with validity and reliability that demonstrate these differences? How might the transition of students between programmes of study be organised so that the changes in the pedagogic discourse do not disrupt their learning? How might a smooth continuity between programmes of study or cross-phase liaison be achieved?

Similarly, in schools where a variety of programmes of study are offered to cohorts of students of similar age, how might the discourses inscribed in the different programmes be characterised? Bernstein (1975: 91) proposes a typology of educational knowledge codes that display varying degrees of classification and framing. How might the different programmes offered by the school be characterised? Do they conform to the pattern described in Bernstein's typology? How might it be recognised if they did fit the typology? What observations would need to be made?

Does a school implement the IBDP as a non-selective, open access programme or as a selective 'school-within-a-school' programme? Cambridge (2010) proposes that these contrasting approaches are inscribed by discourses with contrasting degrees of classification and framing. In the latter case, what criteria are used to regulate access to the programme? How is the programme viewed by those students and teaching staff who participate in it? How is the programme viewed from 'the outside', by students and teachers who do not participate in it? What boundaries exist between the IBDP and the rest of the school? What forms do these boundaries take? How strong are these boundaries? How can such boundaries be characterised?

Some schools implement the IBDP as an open access or whole school programme. However, not all students complete the whole diploma; some, instead, opt for the award of 'certificates'. What criteria are involved in the decision to opt for 'certificates' rather than the whole IB diploma? In what aspects of the IBDP do all students participate? From what aspects of the IBDP do 'certificate' students opt out? Might the discourse inscribed in the 'certificate' programme be characterised as having stronger or weaker classification when compared with the whole diploma? What observations need to be made in order to answer this question with validity and reliability? What boundaries exist between the students pursuing the whole IBDP and those opting for 'certificates'? What forms do these boundaries take? How strong are these boundaries? How can such boundaries be characterised?

How will the introduction of the IBCC impact on the function and organisation of the school? What will be the relationship between learners following academic studies in the IBDP and those following vocational studies in the IBCC? Will there be integration between these groups, or will the introduction of the IBCC increase differentiation between factions of the students and teaching staff?

To reiterate Caffyn's (2010: 324) response to an earlier book in the present series, the International Baccalaureate 'needs independent research and both focused and pragmatic texts that critically engage and explore the essence and component parts of each programme'. It is hoped that research questions such as those outlined in this chapter can contribute to the development of a practitioner-led research culture associated with critical studies of the implementation of the IBDP.

References

Ball, S J (1990): *Politics and policy making in education: Explorations in policy sociology.* London: Routledge.

Bernstein, B (1975): *Class, Codes and Control, Vol. 3: Towards a theory of educational transmission.* London: Routledge and Kegan Paul.

Bernstein, B (2000): *Pedagogy, symbolic control and identity: Theory, research, critique* (revised edition). Lanham, MD: Rowman and Littlefield.

Caffyn, R (2010): Book review: Davidson, S, and Carber, S, (2009), Taking the PYP Forward, in *Journal of Research in International Education*, 9 (3), pp324-26.

Cambridge, J (2010): The International Baccalaureate Diploma Programme and the construction of pedagogic identity: a preliminary study, in *Journal of Research in International Education*, 9 (3), pp199-213.

Cambridge, J (2011): International curriculum, in R Bates (ed), *Schooling Internationally: Globalisation, internationalisation and the future of international schools*. Abingdon: Routledge, pp121-47.

Corbett, M (2007): Building blocks for a critical curriculum: Outcomes-based education and the International Baccalaureate, in *Professional Educator*, 6 (2), pp26-31.

Doherty, C (2010): *Re-centring the curricular market: Pedagogic identities in IB Diploma programs in Australia.* Paper presented at the International Basil Bernstein Symposium 2010, Griffith University, Brisbane, Australia, 30 June-3 July 2010. Online (last accessed 7 March 2011): www.griffith.edu.au/_data/assets/pdf_file/0008/221759/Doherty-RT.pdf

Fitz, J, Davies, B and Evans, J (2006): *Educational Policy and Social Reproduction.* London and New York: Routledge.

IB (2001): *DP Biology Subject Guide.* Cardiff: International Baccalaureate.

IB (2002): *The Diploma Programme: A Basis for Practice.* Geneva: International Baccalaureate.

IB (2007): *Making the PYP Happen: A Curriculum Framework for International Primary Education.* Cardiff: International Baccalaureate.

IB (2008): *A review of research relating to the IB Diploma Programme.* Cardiff: International Baccalaureate. Online (last accessed 7 March 2011): www.ibo.org/programmes/research/resources/dpresearchreview.cfm

IB (2011a): Frequently asked questions (FAQ). Online (last accessed 7 March 2011): www.ibo.org/faq

IB (2011b): *IB Career-related Certificate now available.* Online (last accessed 7 March 2011): www.ibo.org/announcements/ibcc.cfm

Kugler, E G and Albright, E M (2005): Increasing diversity in challenging classes, in *Educational Leadership*, 62 (5), pp42-45.

Matthews, D and Kitchen, J (2007): School-Within-a-School Gifted Programs: Perceptions of Students and Teachers in Public Secondary Schools, in *Gifted Child Quarterly*, 51 (3), pp256-71.

Remillard, R (1978): *Knowledge and social control in a multinational context: An analysis of the development, content and potential of the International Baccalaureate.* Unpublished PhD thesis, State University of New York at Buffalo, NY.

Roberts, B (2009): *Education for Global Citizenship: A practical guide for schools.* Cardiff: International Baccalaureate.

Ross, A (2000): *Curriculum: construction and critique.* London: Routledge.

Singh, P (2002): Pedagogising knowledge: Bernstein's theory of the pedagogic device, in *British Journal of Sociology of Education*, 23 (4), pp571-82.

Siskin, L S (1994): *Realms of Knowledge: Academic Departments in Secondary Schools.* London: Falmer Press.

Stenhouse, L (1975): *An introduction to curriculum research and development.* Oxford: Heinemann

Thompson, J J (1998): Towards a model for international education, in M C Hayden and J J Thompson (eds), *International Education: Principles and Practice.* London: Kogan Page, pp276-90.

Walford, G (2002): Classification and framing of the curriculum in Evangelical Christian and Muslim schools in England and the Netherlands, in *Educational Studies*, 28 (4), pp404-19.

Chapter 6

The IB diploma in a national education system: a case study of curriculum convergence in Turkey

Jale Onur

National systems that have undertaken responsibility for mass education are slow in responding to the fast-changing global needs of our times and are usually burdened with excessive bureaucracy, while popular politics can often interfere with education policies. The UNESCO report on 21st century education (Delors, 1996: 85) points out that traditional methods are not sufficient to prepare future generations for a globally interdependent world. Independent and international schools, which are not hampered by the bureaucracy and politics of national education systems, have been quicker than state systems in responding to the educational needs of our rapidly changing global conditions.

Gardner (2004) reflects on the impact of globalisation on the school curriculum, arguing that it is high time to bring multi-perspective thinking into our classrooms and to teach young people formally about global systems, such as worldwide markets. The Turkish National Education Programme (TNEP) is among the national educational systems that is lagging behind global developments, while the contributions of courses to be found in the International Baccalaureate (IB) Diploma Programme (DP), such as business and management, economics, and the theory of knowledge (ToK), help students learn to look at issues from different perspectives and with a critical mind. According to my observations, in a situation where teachers teach both IBDP students and students who are following the TNEP, once teachers adapt their teaching skills to IB pedagogy, they apply the same skills in teaching non-IB groups too.

Our context

The Koç School in Istanbul was founded in 1988 as a bilingual, K-12, non-profit private Turkish school by the philanthropic organisation Vehbi Koç Foundation. It accepts most of its students through competitive central examinations. There is a total enrollment of 2000 Turkish students and 300 teaching faculty, one quarter of whom are expatriates. Unlike in many international schools, the student population is very stable. Pedagogically this is an advantage, and all graduates are strong candidates for universities both at home and abroad.

The school is defined as 'a Turkish school, where some subjects are taught in a foreign language'. Such schools under the Turkish Ministry of Education offer the Turkish language and literature, plus the so called 'culture courses', *ie* social sciences, arts and physical education, in Turkish; the rest can be offered in a different language, which is English in our case. So mathematics, sciences and IBDP electives such as economics, business and management, information technology in a global society (ITGS), environmental systems and arts (for IB) are all taught in English. This is the make up of the bilingual programme. Also a third language (French, German or Spanish) is offered in addition to the required courses mentioned above. The decision to add an international component was taken and the IBDP was introduced to the Koç School (as the first IB school in Turkey) in 1994, after obtaining the approval of the Ministry of National Education. The students study between 12 and 14 different subjects in a 40 period week, as well as engaging in extracurricular activities. Approximately 30 percent of the students, who are all university-bound, graduate from the Koç School with double diplomas: the TNEP and the IBDP. (Access to Turkish universities requires completion of the TNEP, and cannot be secured on the basis of the IBDP alone.) Some apply to universities both at home and abroad, which is undoubtedly demanding but presents additional options and provides time to make important decisions about their future. Both groups (approximately 30 percent who take both TNEP and IBDP, and the remaining 70 percent who take the TNEP alone) are equally successful in university admissions and they are usually placed in one of their first five university choices either in Turkey or internationally.

Reasons for parental choice

Whether for idealistic, political or economic reasons, parents desire a good future for their children, wish them to be able to cross borders and to survive, feeling at ease and at peace globally as well as within national borders. They want education to provide their children with skills that equip them with competencies for a transnational, cosmopolitan life. If cosmopolitanism is 'feeling at home in the world' as Brennan suggests (1997), there are many cosmopolitans among our alumni. About 40 percent of them go abroad for tertiary education every year, while others travel abroad for postgraduate education after they achieve their BA degree in Turkey. Many find a job and stay on to get some work experience abroad, while some choose to work all around the globe. They are not afraid of changing jobs and gaining new experiences, which is testament to the success of the IBDP offered at school.

Pragmatic concerns of parents for the future of their children do not necessarily preclude the idealistic outcomes of bringing up internationally-minded people. It is a source of both pride and relief for them that both the pragmatic and ideological education of their children is addressed by the school curriculum. IB claims that their programmes contribute to the student's developing international understanding, which supports our school mission. 'Quite what the balance should be between the emphasis on pragmatism and ideology is clearly a matter for the school to decide, not only in relation to the programmes it chooses to offer but also in relation to how it implements them' says Hayden (2006: 139). The effects of our choices for our students' school experience as a whole may be seen years later. Recently I undertook a mini-survey, which revealed that quite a few of our alumni are either working or have worked for non-governmental organisations, which may be interpreted as an effect of a school education that encourages responsible citizenship.

Why converge?

Students in the non-IB group firstly started taking part in the IB creativity, action, service (CAS) activities voluntarily. They then asked to be allowed to take some IB courses: arts, music, economics, and business and management were especially desired. Finally, they objected to being referred to as 'non-something' (as in 'non-IB'), which they rightfully claimed to have a negative connotation. The school administration came up with the label 'regular', but that did not satisfy them. All the signals were pointing toward either merging the two programmes or enduring the negative, divisive effects they were having on the school culture.

Convergence in staffing

Observing the energy emanating from the co-existence of the two programmes and the spontaneous cross-breeding of methodology, the school administration first decided to encourage all teachers to teach in both IBDP and TNEP sections if the schedule permitted. IB workshop leaders were invited to the school to train all department members about the IB programme and pedagogy, and some teachers were sent to workshops organised by the IB. It was observed that the teachers carried over to the TNEP classes the IBDP skills and methods they had learned at IB workshops. Deliberate attention was paid to eliminating the perception that different methodologies were used in the two programmes, and that one was better than the other.

Convergence in content

To achieve convergence in content, the academic departments were asked to compare the two programmes. Overlaps were far greater than expected, and departments were asked to generate a convergent programme from both the TNEP and IBDP. In some areas complete convergence was achieved in a short time but in others, where content showed more discrepancy, there was greater resistance because they felt the time pressure while attempting to cover both. As the Ministry becomes more familiar with the IB syllabi, their amendments to the TNEP increasingly resemble IBDP – making converging easier. For example, the content of the new TNEP contemporary history syllabus is very similar to the history in the IB school-based syllabus Turkish social sciences (TSS). Similarly, there are many other features of the IB programme that affected change in the TNEP. Holland (1975: 262) explains that organisms in an

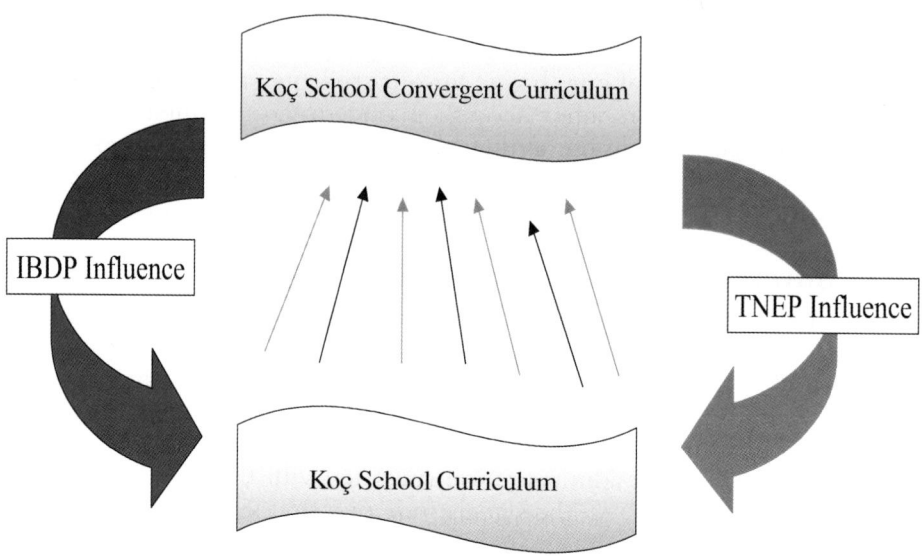

Figure 1: Koç School Convergent Curriculum (adapted from Morrison, 2002: 10)

eco-system do not just evolve, they co-evolve, and this is a powerful force for emergence and self-organisation. In a similar way, from the co-existence of the TNEP and the IBDP emerged the convergent curriculum of the Koç School. It is a synthesis of the national and international. Figure 1, adapted from Morrison (2002: 10), represents the convergent Koç School curriculum.

The confluence of the two programmes, with different properties, gives rise to a new holistic programme that encompasses the properties of both the local (national) and the global (international). The overlapping content, shared resources, professional development opportunities, selectivity in student enrolment and good teachers aided their co-existence and convergence, which in time influenced the school culture, and the unique Koç School programme emerged.

Walker (2004) says that there is no point in simply adding disciplines to a curriculum. In the TNEP it is the case that disciplines have been added to the curriculum, as the existence of some courses has been secured by the Constitution. For example, a 'traffic' course was mandated by Parliament as a result of public lobbying for the prevention of traffic accidents, which could have been a unit in another subject. Walker (2004) continues: 'There has been some deliberate attempt to balance breadth against depth [in IBDP], if necessary to sacrifice some quantity in the name of quality.' As he put it: 'the programme has had the courage to leave some gaps.' The word 'courage' pinpoints some political realities. Some practices have been so deeply rooted in our culture that bringing them up for discussion requires courage. The traditional framework of the old French system adopted in the early 20th century, with its compartmentalised, subject-based approach, seems to be locked in. Eleminating a course that has been taught for almost a century brings with it the fear of leaving important gaps in the education of our youth. There are also other political decisions that require courage to enact in relation to pedagogical changes, such as in relation to possible ensuing teacher unemployment. Timing and economic resource allocation questions need long term planning, and consistent and courageous leadership.

The Koç School programme

The Koç programme, resulting from the confluence of TNEP and IBDP, is represented in Figure 2. The well-known IBDP hexagon, created originally by Thompson (1988, in Fox, 1998) and now widely used to represent the IBDP structure (IB, 2011) with six IB courses shown at the tips of the hexagon, is surrounded by a circle representing the breadth of the numerous smaller courses of the TNEP on both sides of each corner related to an IB course. The two approaches combined (IBDP + TNEP) provide a more holistic educational programme.

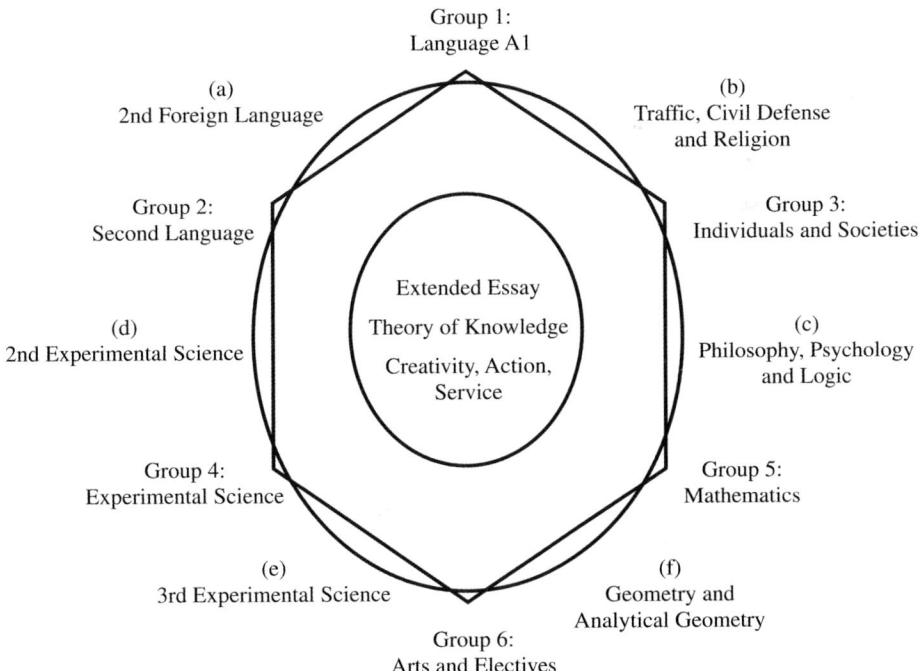

Figure 2: The Koç convergent curriculum

In addition to its academic programme, the IBDP targets the development of the whole person. At the heart of the hexagon there are three main components: the theory of knowledge (ToK), extended essay (EE) and creativity, action, service (CAS). CAS addresses aesthetic, athletic and humanistic aspects of the curriculum, leading to creative, balanced and caring individuals. It is often described as experiential education. ToK bridges the compartmentalisation of the separate courses, training the learner to look at issues from multiple perspectives, developing reflective people. EE puts the academic skills necessary for tertiary education into practice, developing the inquirer and the critical thinker in the IB learner profile with a two-year piece of research that teaches thesis writing with attention to academic honesty. These three components at the heart of the IBDP hexagon are of paramount importance, for they help students to experience a holistic education and prepare them for tertiary education and life with different approaches.

At the Koç School, although there have been a number of problems due to the co-existence of the two programmes such as overload, resistance to change from some teachers, or problems stemming from either the Ministry or from the IB (such as announcing a change of policy without allowing sufficient time to make the necessary adaptations), the existence together of an international programme and national programme caused a synergetic transformation making the school more dynamic and open to change. Since the first IB programme started in Turkey at the Koç School in 1994, many others – including a public school – have become IB World Schools, which is a significant indication of the growing acceptance of the programme in Turkey.

The IBDP's worldwide acceptance

Thompson (1998: 279) describes the IBDP as one example of an international curriculum that was developed by the bringing together of 'best practices' from a range of 'successful' curricula 'to determine a curriculum that may be operated across a number of systems or countries'. If it were the curriculum of one country only, many national systems could have rejected the IBDP's implementation for fear of cultural imperialism. For example, at present in Turkey there is public debate on changing the university acceptance system from one based on a central examination to one with alternatives such as the IB diploma, SAT and TOEFL scores. There are those who object to these as 'imported systems', and find it insulting for a national system to be thinking of using them. However, the assessment policy of the IBDP with its criterion-based examinations, evaluated both internally and externally under the same conditions for students of the same age group around the world, has an important effect on its acceptance as a worldwide standard of education. Many world famous universities recognise it for direct entry, and accept credits earned in IBDP subjects as credits at college worldwide. The Higher Education Council in Turkey is also considering some special quotas for direct entry of IB graduates into universities.

Centralisation

Standardisation of assessment makes assessment more consistent, but it also brings with it more centralisation. This leads to less flexibility for individual differences, possibly hampering innovation and creativity. Similarly, a major criticism of the TNEP has always been its central control, which cannot accommodate unique differences among schools. The same is true of the IBDP, because of its fast growth seeming to be in danger of losing its flexibility in answering unique requests from schools. For example, the IB wants to withdraw the non-regular diploma option they had granted earlier for Turkish students who need to take three sciences because of the way the curriculum is designed and the combined science section at university examinations in Turkey. The IB's reasoning for the withdrawal of this option is that the number of students using it has exceeded the allowable figures for it to be treated as an exception.

Although it enhances the credibility of the IBDP worldwide, recognition by universities also imposes restrictions on the IBDP's flexibility *vis-à-vis* new developments and educational needs that emerge with changing times and conditions. One positive aspect is the stability it gives to the programme in the fast-changing world of teenagers. Its predictability also facilitates long-term planning for the professional development of IBDP teachers, which is one of the strongest aspects of the IB, along with teacher materials. In interviews I undertook as part of my research on the convergent IBDP/TNEP curriculum, a mathematics teacher at the Koç School described the IB lesson plans as foolproof. For novice teachers, this is a big advantage while guaranteeing equal success for teachers around the world.

Teachers

The OECD Programme for International Student Assessment (PISA) test champions, Finland, explain the secret of their success as good teachers. A Master's degree is required to be a teacher. Then teachers are trusted to do a good job and given autonomy. There are no common examinations to ascertain standards, yet they have proved their standards by consistently high results on the international PISA tests (Gürses, 2011). Walker (2004: 199), a previous Director General of the IB, says that 'without good teachers, nothing will happen and not even the most imaginative curriculum will survive'. The new IB teacher award scheme recognises that the performance of teachers in the delivery of the curriculum is a key factor. Their commitment is possible only if they understand and accept the basic principles and philosophy underlying curricular decisions.

Of the 300 teachers at the Koç School, approximately three quarters are Turkish, and more than half are bilingual Turkish and English; the remaining one quarter are international, coming from approximately 15 different countries. In recruitment there is a deliberate attempt to have teachers from around the world so that students learn to understand, work with, and get along with people of different nationalities and cultures. Teachers from different backgrounds are expected to cooperate with both the other international staff and the Turkish staff, to understand the system, the curriculum, the Turkish students and school culture, and to teach in a system attempting to converge the national and the international. Living and cooperating together, they learn about each others' cultures, exchange different applications in their subject areas, and their implementations enrich the school curriculum.

Of course, a support system provides orientation, mentor teachers and a lot of professional development to help the teachers cope. Though there are difficulties in bringing together people of different backgrounds, the emerging collective wisdom and innovative ideas are invaluable. Accumulation of such contributions over the years is very important, and department heads are responsible for keeping data banks for the future.

Along with collaboration among teachers, there is constant support from the administration for improving teaching methodologies and programmes through the professional development opportunities provided. The popularity and respect enjoyed by IB programmes worldwide is largely a result of serious training prepared in collaboration with practising teachers. There is a continuous flow of feedback to and from teachers. Open communication and transparency facilitate improvements to the programme and quick problem-solving. Teachers are invited to assist with curriculum revisions, which increases teacher committment to the programme and differentiates IBDP from the more top-down national curriculum.

In addition to IB training in their subject fields, faculty and staff at the Koç School are also provided with professional training opportunities to develop the whole person, which are not related directly to the curriculum. For example, this year we have had coaching, communication and leadership trainings for the middle management, critical thinking for the secondary faculty and neurolinguistic programming for the elementary faculty.

Issues to be considered by the IB in taking forward the development of the DP with national systems in different countries

Since IB programmes are not implemented solely in international schools as was envisaged in the late sixties, the problems encountered in many national schools offering the IB, and the ways in which schools are resolving their issues, may shed light for the IB in offering advice to yet other schools with similar problems. I undertook a piece of research that observed the effect of the confluence of the two programmes, the national and the international, on the teaching styles of the teachers who were teaching the IB groups as well as the non-IB groups (Onur, 2008). I did not observe any difference in the teaching styles of teachers according to whether they were in the IBDP or TNEP sections.

IBDP workshops (which were attended by our non-IB, as well as IB, teachers) help all teachers to use the same language and ensure global standardisation. This may have helped to ensure consistency of teaching methods, as evident from my observations and interviews.

Overload, lack of time and bias

Overload, time and bias emerged in my study as the three main factors that affect the way in which the curriculum is applied. These factors are quite interrelated and one affects the other. From the analysis of my observations, the self-reflection forms that teachers were asked to complete, and the interviews with teachers, it is clear that differences related to the two programmes are partly due to bias, time pressure and overload. Total convergence of the programmes and its official declaration by the administration may resolve some of these issues to a great extent.

Bias

The teachers I observed said that they were doing the same things and using the same style in all lessons. Although they converged the IBDP and TNEP, the students falsely assumed that different applications were made in the different classes. Teachers' perceptions were supported by my observations, which leads to the interpretation that the students are biased. Students are not, however, the only ones who are biased. Some of the teachers spoke about differences in the nature of the students in the TNEP and IBDP groups, although all students were from the same background. Teachers were of the opinion that students were influenced by whether they wanted to attend university at home or abroad, in other words whether or not they were going to take the highly competititive Turkish university examination and had to attend the weekend cram courses. In fact, teachers seemed somewhat prejudiced towards the students according to which programme they were taking, and this appeared to affect their expectations and treatment of the students. Although the technical aspects of the teachers' teaching (for example, their plans and the methods they used) did not show much difference, their personal styles (*ie* how they behaved in class) differed reflecting their bias towards students of a particular programme.

It appears that some Koç School teachers – perhaps as a result of habit, professional comfort zone, and culture – may believe that one of the programmes is superior to the other, or that the students following the programme they favour are superior to the others. This affects their attitudes towards the students and their performance and quality of teaching, leading to a chicken-and-egg scenario. Teachers may have varying affinities to the different programmes or the students because they understand and feel more comfortable with one programme than with the other. The Turkish teachers were themselves educated with the TNEP, while some international teachers may be coming from countries where parts of the IBDP curriculum are taken.

Bias may not seem as important as some other factors, but the 'make or break' effect of teachers' attitude must be borne in mind. For example, as observed in this study, a mathematics teacher might think that TNEP students are overloaded because they attend weekend courses, and may therefore be more tolerant towards them. A language teacher, on the other hand, might think that IBDP students are more interested in language and may therefore be more enthusiastic and enabling with that group, lending books to students without books, while s/he does not show this tolerance with the TNEP group. If the teachers become aware of their biases towards the different programmes and the students taking them, they can change their attitudes. 'Awareness training' during orientation, and professional development programmes at school, can be useful because all teachers, and particularly the more seasoned ones who are more set in their ways, can benefit from understanding the effects of the biases they hold.

Time

One of the recurrent themes mentioned by teachers as a main reason for insufficiencies in teaching and learning activities was the time factor. The basic claim of *Bloom's Taxonomy* (Anderson and Sosniak, 1994) of 'mastery learning' is that 90 to 95 percent of students can learn basic principles and skills if they are given enough time. Although lack of time is probably a universal complaint of both teachers and students, it is a fact that students with such high ambitions of making it to competitive universities are trying to 'fit too many watermelons under one arm' as a Turkish proverb goes. The same may be true for the schools, which try to be all things to all people, trying to cater to individual student differences, accommodating the local, national and international, and answering parent requests of all kinds. At the Koç School there are student systems, such as teachers who reside on campus giving remedial sessions after school (especially to boarders), CAS activities organised for peer tutoring and a mentorship programme that also involves alumni.

Time lost for assessment is the subject of constant debate among teachers at the Koç School. According to TNEP regulations, courses that meet for a minumum of three periods per week must have a minimum of three examinations per term (otherwise two examinations suffice); one of these must be common, taken by all students at that level and corrected with the same criteria by teachers. With a minimum of 12 different subjects weekly, time spent on assessment is a matter of heated debate among teachers, and alternative assessments (such as class presentations and portfolio assessment) are seen as something that can help with this problem.

Saving time as a result of convergence

Portfolios, take-home papers and projects have been new models of alternative assessment introduced to the school culture by the IBDP. These help to save teaching time by decreasing testing time, but they are not yet accepted by the culture at large because teachers worry too much about academic honesty issues (hence the debates). The Turkish Social Sciences (TSS) school-based syllabus is another good example of how converging the curriculum creatively has helped save time in the weekly programme. By creating an interdisciplinary school-based syllabus from the separate TSS courses, we reduced the number of courses students had to take. Three separate required courses (history, geography and sociology) were reduced to one, saving also on assessment time. IB does not easily approve a school-based syllabus, because schools then have control over the programme, and one programme sets a precedent for others. Both the creation and the control of developments that are out of the norm may be difficult. However, the advantages to student and teacher learning and development outweigh all the disadvantages; therefore, it is worth undertaking and supporting such creative, out-of-the-box initiatives. Learning from the social sciences experience, we tried to merge mathematics and geometry by assigning them to the same teacher, who is supposed to handle the two related syllabi in a holistic manner.

The contribution made by international teachers to local teachers at the school usually includes introducing student-centred activities that enhance constructivist teaching. This also seems to address the question of whether the synthesis of the local and global enhances the practice and teaching styles of teachers. It does enhance their pedagogical skills, knowledge, and style, but does so even more if they are committed to the idea that it is possible, and put time into developing the convergent curriculum, which ends up saving time in the whole school programme.

Overload and time

Naturally, trying to merge two programmes in a single school leads to overload complaints. It may be seen as a problem unique to the Koç School because of the convergent curriculum. However, researchers such as Stoll *et al* (2003), Hargreaves and Fink (2000), and Block *et al* (1999) show that in fact it is quite common even in schools with only one programme to follow. Stoll (2003: 186) has itemised reasons for teachers needing time to do a good job professionally: planning, learning new techniques and processing what is learned from professional training to integrate into their teaching, observing peers' work and researching their own work, reviewing data, reflecting, examining and clarifying ideas, and working collectively and creatively with the school community to provide the richest possible learning experiences for their students. This can have implications for professional training in time management, planning, and organisation for efficient and effective planning for both teachers and students. Many administrators would agree that while staff complain about insufficient or lost time, general observations at school indicate that a lot of time is spent unwisely. It is a natural tendency to plan more meticulously when there is limited time allocation to courses than when there is plenty of it. Professional development in new teaching strategies and collaborative learning techniques can lead to improvement in teachers' use of time.

Stoll *et al* (2003: 41) also note that: 'Time has become a precious resource. Educators everywhere are grappling with decisions about how to schedule it, how to use it, how to preserve it and so on.' At the Koç School, which is located on the outskirts of Istanbul where traffic is a major problem, late arrival home by both teachers and students is a constant reason to ask for early dismissal, fewer class hours, less time spent on after-school activities, and so on. Great pressure is put on the administration, who try to create a balanced schedule that can satisfy all curricular and extracurricular needs while dealing with the issues discussed above.

Saving time by technology

One of the major influences of the IBDP on the TNEP and the school programme has been the prioritisation of the use of technology. Teachers attending IB workshops learned about newer approaches using technology and were instrumental in introducing them into their departments. This saved time compared to the more traditional methods, and that time could be used for inquiry. On the other hand, TNEP's extra content and the rote memory skills associated with it, which sometimes leads to a different way of time saving such as multiplication tables, is another technique. The ability to use all of these in an eclectic manner as necessary makes the Koç programme more holistic, encompassing both quality and quantity.

IB serving as a spur to change the national systems

Because students studying for very competitive places in Turkish universities have had no tangible rewards in university admissions terms for completing the IB diploma, some students, feeling overburdened with the extra requirements of the DP, have dropped it, as it is an add-on programme leading to a second diploma. The IBDP schools in Turkey have been working with universities to achieve some tangible benefits that would serve as incentives for completing the IBDP. Universities have no freedom to determine their own acceptance regulations and have to adhere to the rules set by the Higher Education Council (YÖK). However, there are public discussions aimed at starting new baccalaureate examinations at the end of secondary education in Turkey. The head of the Higher Education Council is talking about the IB diploma being recognised for direct entry into universities in the near future, as is the case for IBDP graduates from abroad. These are examples of the IB serving as a spur to change national systems. Caine and Caine (1991: 153) suggest that individual schools can determine their own models, but what matters is that most of the members of the community take ownership of the decisions and genuinely implement them.

Together with other IB schools, the Koç School has been making a special effort to introduce the IBDP to other stakeholders. Presentations have been made to senior officers of the Turkish universities. Recognising the superior qualities of IB graduates, private universities started trying to attract more IBDP graduates, with some benefit. Koç School counsellors and administration advise the students and their families of such developments and inform them about transfer and double major opportunities, scholarships available and possible future benefits such as special quotas at university entrance. As a result of such tangible incentives the number of students who take the IBDP is increasing, which justifies our efforts in merging the TNEP and IBDP.

While success with one programme is already challenging and highly competitive, we target success while fulfilling the requirements of two programmes. The standards and expectations are very high, and we have to operate in a state of flux because nothing is completely stable; student groups change, teachers change, syllabi change and even university examination times and conditions change. Conditions are not conducive to long-term planning. While going through this process, students learn a lot of organisational and survival skills, as well as acquiring the knowledge necessary for higher education and life.

Overlooking the need to equip our students with the skills required to solve intercultural conflicts would be a huge shortcoming for those with responsibility for educating future generations. In our case, the TNEP is providing our Turkish students with the cultural foundation necessary for the formation of their national identity, while the IBDP provides them with the intercultural mindedness necessary for them to form international ties and to understand 'others' more effectively than the national curriculum could do.

Einstein said that so long as the two different patterns of gene activation were not too different, they would tend to converge (Waldrop, 1992: 110). Using Einstein's terms as a metaphor, the gene combinations of the IBDP and the TNEP, their goals and content, must not have been too different for them to co-exist at the Koç School. The bigger difference was in approaches to teaching: in the IBDP more student-centred, using more comparative and interdisciplinary approaches and constructivist methods, compared with more teacher-centred and rote learning-oriented in TNEP, mainly because of content overload and difference in assessment systems. Their confluence improved the teaching and learning experience for both the students and teachers, as well as having a positive impact on the school culture as a whole. The rapid increase in the number of IB schools in Turkey is an indication that this has been observed and taken on by other schools. The national education system is adapting some of its features, and the higher education institutions are encouraging this rapid increase by trying to attract more IBDP students to their universities, which means spreading the IB ideology. If IB can take on the pedagogical leadership role globally, collaborating with national systems more courageously, international-mindedness can spread faster and the ideological goal of peace building through increasing global communication and understanding might stand a chance of success. After all, schools like ours – in the national systems – have already done the piloting for co-existence successfully.

References

Anderson, L W and Sosniak, L A (1997): *Bloom's Taxonomy: A Forty year Retrospective.* Chicago: University of Chicago Press.

Block, J, Everson, S T and Guskey, T R (eds) (1999): *Comprehensive school reform: a program perspective.* Dubuque, IA: Kendall/Hunt, pp179-191.

Brennan, T (1997): *At Home in the World: cosmopolitanism now.* Cambridge: Harvard University Press.

Caine, R N and Caine, G (1991): *Making Connections, Teaching and the Human Brain.* California: Addison-Wesley Publishing Company.

Delors, J (1996): *Learning: the treasure within. International Commission on Education for the 21st Century.* Paris: UNESCO.

Fox, E (1998): The Emergence of the International Baccalaureate as an Impetus for Curriculum Reform, in M C Hayden and J J Thompson (eds), *International Education: Principles and Practice.* London: Kogan Page.

Gardner, H (2004): *Changing minds: the art and science of changing our own and other people's minds.* Boston: Harvard Business School Press.

Gürses, B (2011): *Egitimde Fin Mucizesi Dosyası* (Finnish Miracle in Education File), in *Artı Egitim,* May 2011, pp38-43.

Hargreaves, A and Fink, D (2003): Sustaining leadership, in B Davies and J West-Burnham (eds), *Handbook of Educational Leadership and Management.* London: Pearson Education, pp435-450.

Hayden, M (2006): *Introduction to international education.* London: Sage Publications.

Holland, J H (1975): *Adaptation in Natural and Artificial Systems.* Ann Arbor: University of Michigan Press.

IB (2011): Online: www.ibo.org/diploma/curriculum/ (last accessed 30 August 2011).

Morrison, K (2002): *School leadership and complexity theory.* London: Routledge Falmer.

Onur, J (2008): *A study of the effects on teaching methods and teaching styles of converging national and international curricula at the Koç School, Istanbul.* University of Bath: unpublished EdD thesis.

Stoll, L, Fink, D and Earl, L (2003): *It's about learning (and it's about time).* London: Routledge/Falmer.

Thompson, J (1998): Towards a model for international education, in M C Hayden and J J Thompson (eds), *International education: principles and practice.* London: Kogan Page, pp276-290.

Waldrop, M (1992): *Complexity: the emerging science at the edge of order and chaos.* New York: Simon and Schuster.

Walker, G (2004): *To Educate the Nations 2: Reflections on an international education.* Saxmundham: John Catt Educational.

Chapter 7

Extending access to the Diploma Programme: IB courses online

Keith Allen

The International Baccalaureate (IB) organization has regularly regaled us with growth statistics. In the 1980s and 1990s it looked – to this observer – as if there was competition between regions in signing up schools. Certainly, the growth statistics were significant. But, as the IB's paper *From Growth to Access* (IB, 2006a) pointed out, the average per annum growth rate in programmes of nearly 18 percent disguises two features. Firstly, the growth is heavily skewed towards a handful of countries – the USA, Canada, the UK and Australia. Secondly, the quantification of 'programmes' disguises the number of *students* benefiting from IB programmes. At present, the only publicly available statistics are of the number of students *completing* programmes such as the DP. These *Statistical Bulletins* (*eg* IB, 2006b; IB, 2010b) reveal a growth in the number of students taking the full Diploma Programme of 12 percent per annum over the last decade. This is impressive growth.

Growth creates a number of challenges. In a March 2009 presentation to IB schools in the UK, the Director General listed six key steps to deal with the growth of the IB. Amongst these was to 'invest in technology infrastructure to support growth'. In the same presentation, Jeffrey Beard also raised the fundamental access issue – how to give a wider range of students the opportunity to follow IB programmes (Beard, 2009). The same issues were presented with slightly different emphases in the *Annual Review 2009*. An introductory letter from the IB Chair and Director General reported that 'digital collaborations formed a large part of our work in 2009', adding 'fast moving technology will enable us to continue to provide high quality services to schools in professional development and assessment'. The letter continues by referring to the introduction of online DP courses that 'will expand the curriculum options for existing IB World Schools as well as enable us to reach students in remote locations'. (IB, 2010a)

That the IB is investing in technology in support of its agenda is not surprising. Impressive as the growth of the IB is, it is as nothing in comparison with changes in technology. Whilst many of our students are 'digital natives' (Prensky, 2009) and seem to be unfazed by each new development, those of us with more years under our belts have often been awed by the changes over the last 40 years. I remember joining a prestigious university in the UK in 1967 and learning that it did not possess a computer; in order to learn programming, I had to log in via a dedicated cable to a computer in a neighbouring city. Before I started teaching in IB schools in the 1980s, I was using a portable computer. But it only had 32K of RAM. I am typing this chapter on a laptop with a modest 2GB. This growth rate matches the prediction of Gordon Moore in 1965 – now known as Moore's Law – that computer power would double every two years (BBC, 2005). Growth in the speed and power of computers is, of course, only one aspect of the phenomenal developments within information and communication technology (ICT). The evolution of the World Wide Web brings many more opportunities and challenges. Already, we have moved from Web 1.0 with shared access to information, to Web 2.0 with enhanced options for interaction, changing content, sharing and subscribing. Web 3.0 is knocking on our doors with the promise of the semantic web (focusing on the interpretation of data), the personalisation of information and intelligent searches.

Within IB schools and colleges around the world, these technological developments have had – and continue to have – major benefits for, *inter alia*, teaching, learning, assessment, management and marketing. But the new technology also raises continuing challenges for the IB community in dealing with potentially increased opportunities for plagiarism, as well as web-based access by students to, for instance, past papers and markschemes that teachers might have preferred to retain for mock examinations. IB-led online developments have occurred in many areas. Initial steps such as the 1999 launch of the Online Curriculum Centre (OCC) and the evolution of the IB website have had significant impacts and, in 2007, the IB began its Digital Space Initiative to create an online, web-based virtual community (Bunnell, 2011). This chapter will focus particularly on online courses, with a brief reference to online workshops.

The notion of online DP courses

One of the drivers for online IB courses has been the access agenda. In July 2006 the IB Council of Foundation organised a retreat to discuss the strategic goal of access. Amongst the plans were to 'develop an online version of [the] IB Diploma Programme that can both support delivery in existing IB World Schools but also reach out to completely new communities of students that cannot physically attend an IB World School' (IB, 2006a). The first experiment with online DP courses came in 2005, with the establishment of a virtual classroom comprising 11 students from four schools to study economics standard level (SL) in one year. The course was offered via the Virtual High School (VHS) in Boston, MA (Bunnell, 2008). This pilot scheme was evaluated by Susan Lowes of Columbia University. Student retention was high and the students achieved grades above the world averages. They also reported that they enjoyed the opportunity to interact with students in different countries – especially when discussing the impact of economic policies around the world.

This pilot was taken further in 2008 when enrolment opened for more online courses offered by VHS in both economics and information technology in a global society (ITGS). VHS is a major player in online courses. Unlike some other providers of online training, their courses create virtual classrooms where students work together with pre-prepared materials overseen by an online teacher. As Susan Lowes (2005) states: 'VHS's pedagogical approach emphasizes student-centred teaching; collaborative problem-based learning; small-group work; and authentic performance-based assessment.' A much more expansive scheme was started the following year following the creation of Pamoja Education (PJE). PJE was established to develop and deliver the DP online. In September 2009, students joined classes for business and management SL, economics SL, economics higher level (HL) and ITGS HL. Eleven subjects were on offer for September 2011 and more are in the planning process, in line with the aspiration expressed in the IB's *Annual Review 2009* to 'develop and deliver a minimum of 27 high-quality online courses by 2015 with the aim of increasing this to 70 or more courses by 2020' (IB, 2010a).

The growth of online courses

Online courses are, of course, available widely outside the world of the DP. Stephenson (2001) reported that too many were based on the traditional paradigms of 'teacher control and tightly specified tasks and outcomes' instead of the technology driving pedagogy towards 'a more learner managed approach'. Countering the view that online courses might be little more than 'electronic page-turning' of a course manual, Stephenson suggests course designers should consider the new features that might be incorporated. For example:

- online libraries of resources and the use of simulations
- collaboration within diverse study groups
- the tracking of student activities and feedback assessment loops
- multi levels of engagement and choice of learning styles to facilitate differentiation

He added that 'the overriding feature of online learning is that it has the potential to allow [these] features to be controlled by the learner', and argued that 'there needs to be significant changes in the roles of the teacher and the development of the skills to carry out those roles' (Stephenson, 2001). Stephenson adds that technology – even in 2001 – allowed resources to be 'dis-aggregated' into bite-sized learning objects, for these objects to be 'meta-tagged' to facilitate retrieval to suit the learner's needs, and for 'intelligent agents' to present material in a format appropriate to the learner's requirements. He predicted that online teaching would evolve into learner-managed learning. He ends by stating that 'the challenge facing teachers is not *whether* to give their online students responsibility for their own learning, but *how much* responsibility are they going to *deny* or *facilitate*, and *how* they are going to do it' (Stephenson, 2001). [Italics in original.]

Echoing the notion that the new technologies might encourage revised pedagogies, writers such as Sontag (2009) have suggested that, in the light of students' usage of Web 2.0, we need a new paradigm for learning theory in this post-information age. This is clearly a two-way street. While technological opportunities encourage a re-thinking of pedagogy, our goals must influence the tools we use (Manning and Johnson, 2011). Selecting and developing online technologies must be closely related to our educational goals – and this must be done with care. In a thorough evaluation of e-learning, Pachler and Daly warn that 'too often digital technologies are "sold" on a false premise of inflated benefits, mostly around efficacy and effectiveness, without due consideration of the disruption they invariably cause to established pedagogical and administrative practices' (Pachler and Daly, 2011). They continue by listing the important drivers for e-learning, including:

- the abundance of e-resources and the need for learners to become sense-makers
- the expectation that learners can study where they want and – increasingly – when they want
- the growth of cloud-based technologies and decentralised IT support
- increased realisation in the value of collaborative student work

By looking at this macro-level – rather than trying to base online courses on specific tools – it should be possible to develop effective learning experiences through the new technologies.

In summary, online technologies provide educators with hugely expanded opportunities, but these also act as challenges to our approaches to teaching and learning. Some aficionados of the new technologies warn that we are doing learners a disservice if we do not develop enhanced competences in this field. For example, Prensky (2009) suggests that familiarity with modern ICT is essential for every profession. Others are more sceptical – arguing, for example, that reliance on technologies reduces our innate skills. A further driver for schools to engage with online learning is provided by changes within tertiary education. There has been significant growth of online courses in this sector. The Sloan Consortium surveys have shown that such courses are part of the mainstream in US colleges (Allen & Seaman, 2010). In the autumn of 2009, nearly one-third of higher education students in the United States were taking at least one online course. In the UK, a paper entitled *Collaborate to compete* looked at how 'UK higher education (HE) might maintain and extend its position as a world leader in online learning' (Online Learning Task Force, 2011). Some universities are reported as favouring students who can demonstrate that they have successfully completed an online course prior to admission. Even if that is not a common approach, might we not be doing our students a disservice if we fail to prepare them for e-learning within the university sector?

The development of the DP online

The role of the IB in the design and development of DP online courses has been significant and, possibly, surprising. As Judith Fabian, IB Academic Director, has recorded, the founders of the DP did not get deeply involved in pedagogy. But she goes on to suggest that the organisation should pay greater heed to encouraging appropriate pedagogy as it moves into the 21st century (Fabian, 2011: 22). Signs of interest in how teachers work is evident in documents such as *DP: From principles into practice* (IB, 2009). For the DP online, there has been very close interest within the Cardiff-based IB Curriculum and Assessment Centre in relation to the structure and processes of DP online. This ranges from discussions as to which courses to offer, through the selection of subject matter experts (SMEs) for decisions on course content and teachers for course delivery, to the online tools to be used and the systems for monitoring course delivery and student progress. This involvement is unprecedented in the IB world where, for schools, the IB is clearly involved in authorisation, reviews, syllabuses and assessment – but not in *how* schools deliver the IBDP. Yet this is a feature of the DP online.

DP online courses are, currently, developed in collaboration with course designers at VHS and Florida Virtual School (FVS), but PJE has plans to bring design and delivery in-house. Whilst both VHS and FVS have significant experience of online courses, the nature of DP online courses goes beyond their normal range. Two of the main differences are that DP courses operate over two years – rather than over the single semester for many US-based courses – and the specific demands of IB assessment. Other, lesser, differences include the complexities of operating over broad time-zones. But the general concepts of VHS's pilot schemes are still retained. These include:

- Class 'sections' comprising up to 25 students from all over the world with one teacher – with structured processes for integrating them into coherent study groups.
- Students log into a site giving many resources – from the syllabus and an online textbook to assessment rubrics and guides on using Web 2.0 tools.
- Each week students are given tasks to perform – and the resources to support them. Some are to be undertaken individually, many are collaborative.
- The teacher monitors the work, answers queries and intervenes where appropriate – either directly to an individual student or more widely to the 'section'.
- Within each student's school there is a site-based coordinator (SBC) to liaise with the student and, as needed, the teacher.
- PJE monitors students' (and teachers') activity, grades achieved, and so on.

Course design and development is a highly collaborative process. As Oblinger and Hawkins (2006) have noted, the development of effective online courses is far from trivial and best practice requires teamwork incorporating a variety of skills. Wang *et al* (2009) report that 'a course development support team generally includes a project manager, a faculty course developer, an instructional designer, a graphics and animation specialist, a video production specialist, and a media services specialist'. For the DP online, course development incorporates for instance SMEs, instructional designers, web developers and system administrators. As the courses are under continuous review (Hughes, 2011) in order to utilise new tools and resources, the costs associated with these experts extend beyond start-up. Assessment of the impact of these innovations will continue for many years to come – but some initial analyses are considered in the following sections.

The access issue

One of the drivers behind DP online courses was the desire to improve access. Longer-term plans suggest that, in the future, online courses may also be accessed by students who are *not* enrolled in IBDP schools, which may be appealing for groups such as home-schooled students. But, for the present, only students in authorised DP schools may enrol. How might allowing students to enrol for DP online assist in moving forward the IB's access agenda? Within the first cohort it was obvious that, for many students, online courses allowed them access to subjects that were not taught at their school. The online courses can – and do – provide solutions, especially in schools with small DP cohorts. Picciano and Seaman (2010) report that schools in the United States are interested in online courses in order to overcome scheduling difficulties and to open up opportunities for students to study new subjects, as well as for credit recovery – whereby a student takes a course to compensate for others that were failed, or where the student underachieved.

Two other client groups have become obvious for the DP online. One is students with many external commitments. Typically, these are athletes whose training and performance schedules conflict with the timings of regular school. Online courses permit students to access materials and work on tasks at times – and in places – that they find convenient. Hence, academic achievement can be blended with excellence in, for instance, sport or music. FIS Academy is one example of a school that is targeting athletes with the offer of the DP online (FIS, 2011). The second client group is that of transfer students. Within the international sector, schools have been all too aware that globally-nomadic families switch schools with high frequency. When this occurs in the middle of the IBDP, a student may find that the new school does not offer all the same subjects. If some of the previously-studied subjects are offered online, a degree of continuity can be ensured. Recently, a variant on this has occurred with DP online courses being used to support students relocating due to events in Libya,

Egypt and Japan (Lawless, 2011). The DP online may promote access in other areas. One idea is to widen student selection of options. Fabian (2011) suggested that the development of independent learners could be facilitated through allowing students in a DP class to select different options within a subject. Online courses could facilitate these – with a student able to study option X in an online 'section' rather than option Y in a face-to-face class, if that better met the student's needs and interests.

These examples are far from making major changes in access. The most likely impacts seem to be in better catering for choice of DP subjects for students already in IB schools, supporting students whose education is disrupted by migration, and marginally increasing the number of students taking IB diploma subjects in small DP schools. Could the impact be greater than this? George Walker (2011) has suggested that 'new technology offers powerful ways of reducing costs and opening up huge new audiences for the IB as, for example, in the newly developed Diploma Programme online'. Sadly, the DP online is not particularly cheap – not least because it is breaking into new ways of operating. In comparison with the costs of hiring another teacher, US$1900 for an online DP subject may represent a saving for a school. But how many schools would hire another teacher in response to one student's request for a subject? If the DP online were to attract – or retain – a student who might otherwise study elsewhere, then US$1900 may compare favourably with the funding that a school might attract as a result of that student.

Within national systems there may be other complexities. As Picciano and Seaman (2010) report, 'state and local education policies that follow strict attendance-based funding formulae do not easily accommodate students taking online ... courses'. Regardless of the financial impact, the DP online does not sound like a system for 'opening up huge new audiences'. As identified in *From Growth to Access: developing an IBO access strategy* (IB, 2006a), 'despite our best intentions, our growth is not distributed evenly ... indeed, there is good evidence to show that our growth is mainly benefiting the economically advantaged'. Tristan Bunnell has argued that 'by growing into new markets through innovation, the IB risks creating a product that is too expensive and complicated for many current constituents who might seek a simpler and more pragmatic alternative' (Bunnell, 2011). Might this also apply to the DP online? PJE is counteracting the issue of expense to a certain extent by offering scholarships to ten schools (Pamoja Education, 2011). This is to be welcomed, but is it enough?

Price is one constraint on access, but it is not the only one. The technology required for online study is not as widely available as those of us in the affluent north may imagine. While 74 percent of the North American population has internet access, only 19 percent of Asia and seven percent of Africa is similarly connected (Walker, 2011). Even within IBDP schools, there are many students without fast, stable, reliable internet access in their homes – and sometimes without access in their schools. As has been noted before (Allen, 2002), the 'net' provides great opportunities for those on the net, but there are big gaps in the mesh of the net and those living in the gaps are increasingly disadvantaged. There really is a digital divide – and it is growing. Bunnell (2008) has also warned that 'online provision of the IBDP could in the long run facilitate a stronger view that it is an exclusive curriculum, offered by a largely hidden elite body of schools for the benefit of other elite schools with access to, for example, sophisticated technology'. It is true that online DP courses are only an option and that schools can still deliver the IBDP effectively in purely face-to-face mode but, if students joining the online courses are perceived as having an advantage, the IB could stand accused of supporting even more fully the economically advantaged. As Judith Guy (2011) has pointed out, the challenges to access go beyond socio-economic and technological factors to incorporate linguistic and pedagogical barriers. The DP online is currently only available for courses in English and for the May examinations session (in other words, not in French and Spanish, the other DP working languages, or for the November examination session). Automatically this restricts access – at least in the early years of development – for francophone, hispanophone and many southern hemisphere IB schools.

DP online courses are most appropriate for students who are motivated, organised and technologically astute. They are designed by a course team, and the teacher has only limited options for adjusting them to individual student needs. This is a challenge. The online course may be deemed appropriate for the 'norm', but what about catering for linguistic, cultural or other diversity? Will different learning styles be adequately catered for? It is a double-edged sword that gives new opportunities to some but not to others. All these notions are based on the early stages in the introduction of DP online courses. With careful planning, the courses may become more economical, more flexible and more accessible. As such they could have a significant impact on the access agenda.

The global dimension

A second key feature of DP online courses is that they create genuinely global communities of learners. IB courses originated in 'international schools' – many catering for a hugely diverse range of nationalities. But passports are not the best measure of diversity, and these schools have been described as exhibiting a substantial monoculturalism as to values, mitigated by tolerance of exotic detail (Zaw, 1996). National schools will often be similar. So the creation of a truly global group of students within the DP online could be a major step forward. It provides potential for them to learn from their counterparts living in diverse cultures. It is also a much better way of adding a global dimension than is the trend towards expensive projects abroad (Roberts, 2011). How fully this can be achieved depends on two main factors. Firstly, the course structure must encourage students to report on – and, just as importantly, to listen to and reflect on – circumstances facing their locale. Within business and management, for example, it is easy to see how students could be tasked with investigating and reporting on how employment practices operate in their environment. It is also self-evident that courses such as global politics are particularly appropriate for DP online – where interaction among a truly transnational cohort of students can lead to fascinating insights. But can the course design team find comparable activities for subjects such as mathematics HL?

Secondly, how well do the students use the opportunities? This is crucial. Many teenagers are compulsive communicators. They readily engage in online communities. But how much of this engagement leads to the sort of reflective analysis that supports global understanding? Fabian (2011) argues that we should find ways for students to hear the world views of others (p 25). As many teachers will confirm, listening and hearing are not the same. Online courses have the potential to support genuine global understanding as the 'section' becomes a cohesive learning unit and as the teacher acts as an effective facilitator. Practice suggests, however, that it is far from easy to engage students in an online course. Whilst growing numbers of them are extremely comfortable online – as Prensky (2009) calls them, 'digital natives'– developing group coherence and genuine collaboration is a challenge. For most students, learning as a social activity is easier in a face-to-face class than online. As Pachler and Daly (2011) point out, 'social bonding is the preliminary to successful learning online' (p 75). More recent developments in the DP online have taken this idea on board.

In her review of VHS courses, Lowes (2005) reports that 'in the online environment, a whole host of issues – including teacher-student and student-student communication, the extent and nature of reflection, student accountability, and assessment – are very different from the face-to-face classroom'. She also noted that 'some teachers … find that face-to-face interaction is an essential component of their teaching and quickly leave the online classroom' (Lowes, 2008). But in a later reflective footnote Lowes suggests that teachers may have been thinking of communication in too narrow a sense. If a student is contributing to a discussion forum this is 'communication', just as it is in the more direct exchange of comments. In monitoring individual student contributions, it is worth noting that online classes provide a clear record. This e-trail allows the teacher to monitor closely how each person has contributed to group work and collaborative projects. Such knowledge is rarer in the face-to-face environment, especially when students are working on tasks outside the classroom. In essence, online communication is different from that in a face-to-face classroom. Teachers for the DP online need to be aware of these differences and be able to monitor and encourage communication effectively.

A related challenge is motivation. Picciano and Seaman (2010) report 'the need for motivation and maturity levels, study habits and organizational skills, and adequate academic preparedness for online students to succeed'. Lowes (2005) gives a similar impression: 'To be successful in online courses, students need to be self-motivated, well-organized, and independent learners, but at the same time, taking online courses can help students to develop these characteristics.' Evidence from the initial years of DP online courses shows that student activity online was highly variable. Some students were clearly engaging with the course for many, many hours each week. They logged in several times per day, accessed lots of resources, contributed extensively to collaborative and communicative tasks and reliably posted assignments. Others were far from this extreme.

Susan Lowes reports that online teachers stated that 'distance emphasizes the students' need for constant reassurance' (Lowes, 2008). How many students in face-to-face classes share that same need? Another teacher reported: 'I like the technique of weekly assignments and then students having the responsibility to budget/manage their time accordingly. When possible I do this in my face-to-face classes.' Surely, this is a good example of Fabian's urge that we 'democratize the classroom' (Fabian, 2011). DP online courses have the potential to make a dramatic impact in creating global communities of learners. Careful design can facilitate this. But successful achievement also requires sensitive and effective monitoring and management of the global 'section' by the online teacher.

Issues relating to skills and time

DP online courses advertise that students develop '21st century skills' in the process. Putting to one side the point that we cannot know the skills that are needed for the next 90 years – 'Educators in 1910 would have had a hard time predicting 20th century skills' (McKenzie, 2011) – there seems little doubt that students successfully completing a DP online course will have acquired a range of skills that match closely those anticipated as being of use in the future. This includes e-skills as well as communication and organisational skills. Learning these skills takes time and hence successful completion of a DP online course is more time-consuming than a face-to-face class. Not only does the student have to gain mastery of new technologies, but s/he also needs to arrange time to fit in with students around the world. Almost inevitably, asynchronous collaboration requires very frequent log-ins and this adds to the time needed.

The time issue also relates to other aspects. In addition to opening access to students with time-restricting commitments such as the athletes mentioned earlier, advocates of asynchronous online learning argue that it supports reflection. In a face-to-face situation, immediate responses tend to dominate. In the DP online, students will be responding and reacting at different times throughout the week. This allows all to contribute *and* for contributions to be better researched and considered. A negative implication of the temporal organisation of DP online courses has been hinted at by other authors. They warn that the flexibility afforded by asynchronous, mobile learning platforms may undermine the importance of the task. If you are able to do work in a coffee shop that previously could only be done in a school or office, or if you can work when you like instead of during predetermined hours, the perceived importance of the work may be reduced. As Kanuka and Rourke (2008) point out, e-learning gives improved access by removing 'temporal, geographical and situational barriers'. But, they also point out that this can result in the work becoming subordinated to other responsibilities.

DP online courses provide highly beneficial opportunities to promote the habits of independent learning, to facilitate collaboration and to acquire contemporary skills. But, each of these opportunities hides a danger. In order to make the most of the opportunity, students need to be motivated, organised, effective communicators and have the time to acquire the necessary skills. There is a *digital dividend* that comes from effective use of e-learning.

Online professional development

IB schools rely on well-trained teachers. The IB has, for many years, supported workshops for teachers. Since 2007, this has included the offer of online professional development (PD). In 2010, approximately 2500 delegates participated in online PD (Drennen, 2011). The attractions of online PD are threefold – cost, timing and nature. As school administrators know, the cost of a conventional face-to-face workshop includes workshop fee, travel and accommodation costs, costs within the school caused by the absent colleague and opportunity costs lost. Estimates vary, but in the UK the estimate was £1500 per participant before cost-price organisations such as the IB Schools and Colleges Association of the United Kingdom (IBSCA) were authorised to run workshops. The price of an online workshop is approximately £390. Clearly, this represents a saving for schools. Face-to-face workshops are typically run over two or three consecutive days. Online workshops operate over a much longer timescale – typically six weeks. This can be less disruptive for the participant's classes – although many may prefer a shorter, sharper experience. The longer timing, however, allows a very different experience – affecting the nature of the training.

Just as online DP courses are not just e-versions of face-to-face classes, the adoption of an online medium for professional development affords important opportunities for re-thinking training. One report (Godwin and Kaplan, 2008) identifies strategies for making online workshops 'experiential'. In addition to creating a virtual environment that supports a range of experiential activities, the longer timeline allows participants to take their learnings and apply them in offline, job-specific projects. For an IB workshop, for example, there could be discussions with colleagues, research into practices in another part of the school, surveys of students, and opportunities to try out a new classroom approach. Training can take on a new dimension. Godwin and Kaplan also argue that there is a need to present material in multiple formats to support more fully those with different ways of learning, and they give participants a choice of online tools. 'With the right kind of assignment, we found that interpersonal connections and learning, rather than technology, became the focus of activities' (Godwin and Kaplan, 2008). Technology then fades into the background as participants engage in the activities. They end by arguing that their ee-workshop (electronic and experiential) model is particularly valuable for 'globally dispersed audiences' and by warning that 'the greatest challenge ... is the time commitment from both participants and facilitators'. As with other asynchronous programmes, participants may be logging in at very different times. The facilitator/teacher/leader must be available almost daily, which can be a major commitment. This matches the experience for DP online courses.

In exploring some of the issues surrounding online courses (and workshops), it seems clear that carefully constructed online provision can provide valuable alternatives to face-to-face classes and training. Participants in online learning environments are likely to acquire additional skills and benefit from the increased time for reflection and global communities generated. But neither should be seen as an easy option. Early evidence suggests that online workshops are seen as an interesting – and cheaper – option for professional development for IB teachers. But the case for DP online courses acting as an avenue to greater IBDP access still has to be made.

References

Allen, I E and Seaman, J (2010): *Class Differences: Online Education in the United States, 2010.* The Sloan Consortium. Online (last accessed 27 August 2011): http://sloanconsortium.org/publications/survey/class_differences.pdf

Allen, K (2002): Atolls, Seas of Culture and Global Nets, in M C Hayden, J J Thompson and G R Walker (eds), *International Education in Practice*, London: Kogan Page.

BBC (2005): *Moore's Law on chips marks 40th.* Online (last accessed 21 July 2011): http://news.bbc.co.uk/1/hi/technology/4446285.stm

Beard, J (2009): *Preparing today's IB for tomorrow's future.* Presentation to IBSCA Spring Conference, 6 March 2009, Croydon, UK.

Bunnell, T (2008): The International Baccalaureate and its Diploma Programme online: the challenges and opportunities, in *Journal of Research in International Education*, 7(3), pp327-344.

Bunnell, T (2011): The Growth of the International Baccalaureate Diploma Program: Concerns About the Consistency and Reliability of the Assessments, in *The Education Forum*, 75 (2), pp174-187.

Drennen, H (2011): Professional development, in G Walker (ed), *The Changing Face of International Education: Challenges for the IB*. Cardiff: International Baccalaureate.

Fabian, J (2011): Principled teaching and learning, in G Walker (ed), *The Changing Face of International Education: Challenges for the IB*. Cardiff: International Baccalaureate.

FIS Academy (2011): Online: www.fis-academy.org (last accessed 16 May 2011).

Godwin, L and Kaplan, S (2008): Designing ee-Learning Environments: Lessons from an Online Workshop, in *Innovate: Journal of Online Education,* 4(4). Online: http://innovateonline.info (last accessed 27 August 2011).

Guy, J (2011): Challenges to access, in G Walker (ed), *The Changing Face of International Education: Challenges for the IB.* Cardiff: International Baccalaureate.

Hughes, D (2011): personal communication, 10 June 2011, Oxford, UK.

IB (2006a): *From Growth to Access: Developing an IBO access strategy.* Cardiff: International Baccalaureate.

IB (2006b): *Diploma Programme Statistical Bulletin: May 2006 Examination session.* Cardiff: International Baccalaureate.

IB (2009): *The Diploma Programme: From principles into practice.* Cardiff: International Baccalaureate.

IB (2010a): *Annual Review 2009.* Geneva: International Baccalaureate.

IB (2010b): *The IB Diploma Programme Statistical Bulletin: May 2010 examination session.* Cardiff: International Baccalaureate.

Kanuka, H and Rourke, L (2008): Exploring the Non-Neutrality of e-Learning Technologies, in *Technology, Pedagogy and Education,* 17(1), pp5-16.

Lawless, E (2011): personal communication, 10 June 2011, Oxford, UK.

Lowes, S (2005): *Online Teaching and Classroom Change: The impact of Virtual High School on its teachers and their schools.* Unpublished manuscript. Online (last accessed 27 August 2011): www.ilt.columbia.edu/publications/lowes_final.pdf

Lowes, S (2008): Online Teaching and Classroom Change: The Trans-Classroom Teacher in the Age of the Internet, in *Innovate: Journal of Online Education,* 4(3) Online: http://innovateonline.info (last accessed 27 August 2011).

Manning, S and Johnson, K E (2011): *The Technology Toolbelt for Teaching.* San Francisco: Jossey-Bass.

McKenzie, M (2011): Conclusions: Reflections and refractions, in G Walker (ed), *The Changing Face of International Education: Challenges for the IB.* Cardiff: International Baccalaureate.

Oblinger, D G and Hawkins, B L (2006): The Myth about Online Course Development, in *EDUCAUSE Review,* 41 (1), pp14-15.

Online Learning Task Force (2011): *Collaborate to compete: Seizing the opportunity of online learning for UK higher education.* Report to HEFCE, January 2011.

Pachler, N and Daly, C (2011): *Key Issues in e-Learning.* London: Continuum.

Pamoja Education (2011): Online (last accessed 10 June 2011): www.pamojaeducation.com/schools/scholarship/id/36,scholarship-information

Picciano, A G and Seaman, J (2010): *Class Connections: High School Reform and the Role of Online Learning.* Babson Survey Research Group. Online (last accessed 27 August 2011): www.babson.edu/ESHIP/research-publications/upload/Class_connections.pdf

Prensky, M (2009): H. Sapiens Digital: From Digital Immigrants and Digital Natives to Digital Wisdom, in *Innovate: Journal of Online Education,* 5 (3). Online: http://innovateonline.info (last accessed 27 August 2011).

Roberts, B (2011): Engaging with the community, in G Walker (ed), *The Changing Face of International Education: Challenges for the IB*. Cardiff: International Baccalaureate.

Sontag, M (2009): A Learning Theory for 21st Century Students, in *Innovate: Journal of Online Education,* 5 (4). Online: http://innovateonline.info (last accessed 27 August 2011).

Stephenson, J (2001): *Learner Managed Learning: an emerging pedagogy for online learning?* Conference paper delivered to BECTA, November 2001.

Walker, G (2011): Introduction: Past, present and future, in G Walker (ed), *The Changing Face of International Education: Challenges for the IB*. Cardiff: International Baccalaureate.

Wang, H, Gould, L V and King, D (2009): Positioning Faculty Support as a Strategy in Assuring Quality Online Education, in *Innovate: Journal of Online Education,* 5 (6). Online: http://innovateonline.info (last accessed 27 August 2011).

Zaw, S K (1996): Locke and multiculturalism: toleration, relativism and reason, in R K Fullwider (ed), *Public Education in a Multicultural Society*. Cambridge: Cambridge University Press.

Chapter 8

Schools' contributions to curriculum innovation in the IB diploma: a case study of the world studies extended essay

David Wilkinson, Cyrus Vakil and Veronica Wilkinson

Introduction

It is now over 40 years since the International Baccalaureate (IB) Diploma Programme (DP) was launched in a handful of pilot schools. Since that time, it has always drawn on and encouraged the teachers within its member schools as a source of curriculum innovation. From the earliest days the United World Colleges (UWC), a group of now over a dozen largely scholarship entry, residential colleges situated worldwide have been active in developing school-based syllabuses as part of the DP. In a small number of cases, the IB has authorised an IB World School to offer a school-based syllabus that, ultimately, was adopted as an official diploma subject. One such example is the marine science syllabus developed by the United World College of the Atlantic, South Wales, which eventually led to the environmental systems and societies subject. This chapter follows the process through which another such school-based initiative, the world studies course developed by the Mahindra United World College of India to be offered in addition to IB diploma requirements, became adopted as the world studies extended essay available to all IB diploma schools.

In the beginning

The IB is quite specific in its mission statement: through its graduates it seeks to create a 'better and more peaceful world through intercultural understanding and respect' (IB, 2011a). The UWC movement, in whose member schools the IB diploma forms the backbone of the curriculum, shares these most laudable aims (UWC, 2011). However, as the DP also requires students to become critical thinkers, it is not surprising that students ask whether, in this respect, it is fully fit for purpose. During 2000, at the Mahindra United World College of India's weekly and informal global affairs sessions (offered as a supplement to DP requirements), the students asked very specific questions:

- Firstly, do all IB subject combinations guarantee a real understanding of the key global issues of our time?
- Secondly, does community service in the CAS programme ensure an adequate understanding of the local manifestations of these global issues?

The co-authors of this chapter, together with Guenther Lanier then head of humanities (all then teachers at the Mahindra College), quickly came to the conclusion that the IB ideals needed more rigorous implementation. This group was not a politically homogeneous one: one Marxist and one globalist were united in their distrust of nationalism but little else. A third believed passionately in bringing together different language speakers as a prerequisite to any cross-cultural understanding. The fourth believed that the cultural and linguistic diversity of international schools and the elite IB was false; it catered to the same globally mobile elite.

The group met as a working party in late 2000 to discuss a proposed extension to the IB diploma curriculum in the light of these questions. They suggested a formally structured course in world studies to replace Mahindra's more informal global affairs programme. Such a course, they believed, should enable students to gain a sufficient understanding of the issues that underlie many of the world's most pressing problems and hence to become, more closely, the young adults described in the IB mission statement. Excited by the potential of such a course for strengthening the IB hexagon they approached the IB. This chapter tells the story of this utopian venture and its encounter with the IB Curriculum and Assessment Centre (IBCA) in Cardiff, South Wales. It provides a case study in curriculum development and of how both inertia and assessment needs influence the process.

The early years

How could the core issues that underpin an understanding of current global problems be brought into focus without adding to the workload of diploma students? Three possibilities were put forward. First was that of converting the service component of CAS into a mainstream subject that would require competency in the local language, as well as awareness of local culture and history and of the local economic context. Second was the possibility of the service component becoming a research project that could be offered as an extended essay (EE) or that could replace the EE. Thirdly, that a syllabus based on the existing weekly global affairs discussions could be developed and introduced as a mainstream subject or as a source of an EE was discussed.

The world studies proposal thus grew partly out of our in-house global affairs programme. Our criticisms of this programme, the majority of which were raised by students, were based on the fact that much of the discussion in the 90 minute sessions did not rest on an underlying understanding of the issues and as such was very much an exchange of uninformed opinions. Many students felt that we talked too much and did too little. From the outset, however, discussion of a formal world studies course raised major concerns among students about the additional workload that this would place upon them. As we regarded such a course as the key to students building their own knowledge base about the major issues underpinning matters of real global concern, it was essential to look at ways in which it could be introduced without creating a major work overload for students. A number of options were considered and, as they had serious implications for the hexagon structure of the Diploma Programme, the project team set out their recommended changes in an email to George Walker, who was at that time IB Director General. The proposals were set out in what was regarded as order of importance:

- The need for a compulsory world studies course, which could provide students with an effective knowledge base and the intellectual tools with which to examine the current international order.
- Replacing CAS as a requirement by the service component, and making creativity and action part of an extracurricular programme. Furthermore, there would be the need to ensure that a student would reflect on the purpose of his or her service by requiring a report as an assessed part of the course.
- The introduction of cross-disciplinary courses that would create room for the world studies course without sacrificing diploma breadth.

In response, George Walker wrote: 'Do you see emerging from this a new UWC version of the IB Diploma Programme (presumably open to others who wish to join in) or do you envisage a wholesale reform of the programme?' (Walker, 2001). Essential to his response was the issue of a possible change to the IB diploma hexagon implied by our proposals: in particular, the balance provided by the six subject groups. In this context, he further asked: 'Are you pinning your faith on the new trans-disciplinary subjects to restore the balance which you *do* believe to be an essential feature of the diploma?'

In responding to this last question we wrote:

> The only way to put world studies at the centre is to reduce the load elsewhere. In order to do so, we believe that trans-disciplinary subjects are crucial to ensure that the balance of subject areas is maintained. We do not wish to reduce the ways of knowing that students will encounter. (2001)

All of this was very much in line with the reasons behind the development of the world studies course. College-wide discussions had led to a consensus view; action without thought is at least as undesirable as thought without action. Hence the support grew to build a course that would oblige students to confront the issues upon which many of the world's present problems rest. Apparent through discussions concerning the nature of such a course was the belief that the breadth of understanding needed to make sense of the global issues should be complemented by an in-depth study of their impact at a local level. This is precisely what could be achieved by having the EE written on world studies. The required approach to the essay would be a narrowly focused topic, to which would be applied the skills of analysis, the collection of raw data from fieldwork undertaken on a local manifestation of a global issue and its interpretation, and hence the formulation of a hypothesis. Since most real life problems cannot be studied from the perspective of one academic discipline (or else they would have been solved ages ago!), it was natural that this EE would have to be multidisciplinary. The idea of an EE in world studies was hence, from the outset, a means of furthering the aims of the world studies course.

With these considerations in mind, a draft proposal was prepared for the UWC Heads' meeting in July 2001. The arguments for a world sudies course were set out in the introduction to the proposal:

> Past and present experience shows that IB schools achieve a high academic standard, manage to prepare their students well for the excellent universities that the majority of them will go to in different parts of the world, and generally offer exciting and invaluable personal experience to their students. However, the 'internationalism' often lacks depth. Sitting in the same classrooms and participating in community service with fellow students from different countries leads in most cases to cross-border friendships that may last a lifetime, but understanding and awareness of world affairs in many cases remains under-developed. Largely unchallenged, students and graduates often stick to traditional patterns of thinking and acting. Despite their IB experience, they may maintain prejudices ... such students and graduates thus stay far below their potential of making a difference and achieving change. (Mahindra IB/UWC Project Group, 2001)

The proposal set out the way in which the world studies course would fit into the IB hexagon. World studies would become a central element of the IBDP, complementing the theory of knowledge (ToK) course and subsuming the EE. Together with CAS, these would constitute the international, intellectual and affective core of the IB Diploma Programme. Following discussion of the proposal by UWC Heads, it was agreed that critical comments should be solicited from within the UWC community as a whole and from a number of other IB schools. The responses raised issues of a practical nature such as overload and of a more philosophical nature, including objections to the concept itself.

One international school teacher felt that the most commonly heard complaint at all levels is about overload. To add another taught course, however valuable, is neither practical nor desirable. Such a course may well be viable in the rather unique context of a UWC, but not in the overwhelming majority of non-residential schools that have to juggle other requirements along with those of the IB. Some raised concerns regarding the perceived need for a world studies course, and yet others objected to the point of world studies; one teacher from another UWC, for instance, objected to David Wilkinson's original assertion that the IB does not provide students with appropriate thinking skills. Strong objections were raised to the idea of the EE being written on world studies rather than on one of the IB subjects. One UWC teacher stated that he was vehemently opposed to any EE requirement that would take it away from the subject area that the student is most passionate about, adding that the proposal suggests that locally-based work carried out by a student should be central to the essay. This teacher noted that this struck him as an uncomfortably narrow requirement being placed on what should be a free choice.

Behind the liberal rhetoric there was perhaps a natural conservatism: 'Why fix something that ain't broke?' The Mahindra contention that both the hexagon and the world *were* 'broke' was not accepted even by the UWC Heads' meeting. Had the meeting happened a few months later in 2001, after 11 September rather than before, the tone may well have been different.

David Sutcliffe, then Head of the UWC Adriatic College, wrote:

> Give students a choice between two alternatives:
>
> • Write an Extended Essay on World Issues instead of one of the traditional six IB subjects.
>
> • Write a standard Extended Essay but add a (say) 1,000 word section that relates the theme of the Essay to World Affairs.
>
> The adoption of this twin track approach not only opens up a splendid opportunity for those students (and teachers) who want to emphasise the world issues approach; it also safeguards the 'academics' who wish to preserve a free choice of research subject, but with the challenges, surely reasonable for all UWC students, of relating their academic concerns to world problems. Just suppose Oppenheimer and others had been required to write a social 'world issues' audit alongside their research studies which led to the atomic bomb. We would be setting a valuable precedent which would have immense significance in international schools worldwide. (Sutcliffe, 2002)

The suggested subject matter of the course itself raised a further issue with another UWC: that it smacked of political correctness and socio-political indoctrination. One member of the Mahindra core group, Cyrus Vakil, feared that the course had an anti-globalisation world social forum stance uncritically embedded in it. He asserted that the course should invite students to explore the connection between globalisation, capitalism and poverty and not be taken as *a priori*. 'Unless there was this openness, world studies would have the ironic effect of undermining globalism.' (Vakil, 2002)

The criticisms received resulted in a clarification of our objectives. We remained convinced that a taught world studies course was essential if students were to gain an understanding of the crucial issues that underpin the major problems that face our world. The course would enable the students to choose a service on the basis of local knowledge, and this would provide the hands-on experience that would serve as the basis for their EE research. In dealing with the complexity of real issues, the course would need to draw on several disciplines as appropriate to each of the topics covered. In turn, this would necessitate an interdisciplinary approach to the EE. It was at this point that Ian Hill, Deputy Director General of the IB, asked: 'Have you considered approaching the world studies concept via the Extended Essay? Is there not a strong case for insisting that the Extended Essay be devoted to a topic of global or humanitarian concern?' (2001). Hill's suggestion acknowledged that global concerns should be added into the core, but mitigated any radical implications for the IB hexagon or even for a world studies course. Hill's proposal would win the day.

The relationship of the course to ToK now came into focus. It was clear that the critical thinking skills forming a crucial element of the ToK course would make a vital contribution to our objectives if applied in the context of the real-world situations to which the proposal was directed. Was there a way that, by applying such thinking skills to these ends, aspects of the ToK course could be subsumed within the world studies course? We believed that this could be done. However, any suggestion that the ToK course be amended met with fierce opposition, not least from the students themselves. George Walker expressed this admirably when he responded to our thoughts on this matter: 'Suggesting a modification of ToK is a bit like the removal of the gospels from the New Testament.' (Walker, 2002)

The stage was now set for us to write a formal proposal for discussion with representatives of IBCA; Guenther Lanier was chosen to represent the Mahindra core group and to put forward the proposals at a Cardiff meeting in April 2002. The purpose of the meeting, as set out by IBCA representatives, was to establish a working group to examine the overlap between Lanier's proposals and the existing components of the Diploma Programme. The group was also asked to consider what revision might be acceptable of the central components of the programme, both ToK and EE, to accommodate world studies. The meeting considered a two-pronged approach: firstly, world studies as a pilot project by the Mahindra UWC of India with EE in world studies to be made possible for non-pilot schools, and secondly, wherever appropriate, ensuring an international context of the existing curriculum in all subjects, the EE and the CAS programme.

In fact, the first of these proposals was the one that found favour with the IBCA that:

> Mahindra UWC of India be invited to submit candidates for an Extended Essay in world studies, based on guidance notes and assessment criteria to be prepared by the College and approved by the Diploma Review Committee. These guidance notes and assessment criteria would follow those of other subjects in the Extended Essay guide. This is a slightly unusual approach in that the guidance notes would be based not on an approved IB syllabus but on an in-house syllabus taught at Mahindra. In the first instance only candidates from Mahindra could submit an Extended Essay in world studies and in this way the College would act as a testing ground for this kind of assessment. (IB, 2003)

A single-school pilot with no clear timeframe for going mainstream, and no clear mandate? What was it piloting and for whom? Was it really, as Walker had said in March 2002, going to bring back the 'I' into the IB hexagon? The world studies suggestion had arisen from the conviction at Mahindra that both the IBDP hexagon and a deeply divided world needed thoughtful fixing. The IB would not, then or now, agree to this. After 9/11, however, it became difficult to deny that deep divisions exist. When the October 2002 Bali bombing claimed the lives of 202 people, including two IB teachers who had arrived a few days earlier for the IB conference scheduled to be held there, it became even more difficult to deny that the world was beset with deep problems of mutual misunderstanding and mistrust, with terrifying local implications. At the re-scheduled conference, held in Singapore in March 2003, George Walker made his most anguished speech: 'Terrorism, tolerance and the human spirit – the challenges for international education.' In it he insisted that the IB 'must surely have a view on the conditions that produce extremism' and that it was his intent 'to create a sense of discomfort' among conference participants. At this conference, while Walker announced that the IB was changing gears from curricular innovation to consolidation, he also announced the Mahindra world studies pilot as a key IB initiative to address the in-depth study of global issues (Walker, 2003).

Walker himself was now down a road that would lead to his 2006 book *Educating the Global Citizen* in which his troubled questions of 2003 would find an answer. Faced with the passions and the complexities of globalisation, international education should, he felt, facilitate a three-stage evolution: from international to global awareness and finally to global citizenship. He would acknowledge Howard Gardner's ideas on globalisation and education in that book, and in 2007 Gardner's Project Zero, at Harvard, would be given the mandate to take world studies mainstream.

From Mahindra to mainstream: refinement or dilution?

The Mahindra project was accommodated by IBCA but the basic purpose proposed for world studies, to re-invigorate the IBDP hexagon and provide a beacon for the IB, was not accepted. It was analogous to a school-based subject and seemed destined to remain that way. As such, further development now took on a top-down approach.

Things were to change, and the impetus came from an unexpected direction. The reason was a growing realisation at IBCA, in mid-decade, that the IBDP was 'behind the curve' in interdisciplinary work: it was behind other competing curricula, behind the interdisciplinary wave sweeping North American universities since the 1990s and, most significantly, behind the IB Middle Years Programme (MYP). The MYP was rapidly coming into its own in those years, and the objective of integrating the MYP and the DP into a coherent full-school curriculum sharing an educational philosophy came to the fore. Unlike the DP, the newer MYP had embraced interdisciplinarity wholeheartedly: both in its final personal project and elsewhere. The DP had not. All its interdisciplinary efforts had come from individual schools: the human rights school-based syllabus from Nordic UWC, peace and conflict studies from UWC of the Atlantic, Chinese studies developed at Li Po Chun UWC, for example – and none were slated to go mainstream. It was in this context that officials at IBCA saw the world studies EE as a useful exemplar of interdisciplinarity within the Diploma Programme. These years also saw IBCA putting two interdisciplinary subject pilots on the fast track: environmental systems, and then text and performance. Both, in a modified form and with new titles, are now mainstream subjects. The idea of an interdisciplinary world studies course was not revived. It remained an EE.

The Diploma Programme, however, lacked a theoretical framework for interdisciplinarity. Hence it found funding to bring Harvard Project Zero (HPZ) on board in order to provide the framework for the world studies EE. Simultaneously, a few more schools joined Mahindra as pilot schools. In two stages, HPZ's Veronica Boix-Mansilla and her team would visit these schools in late 2009 and early 2010, along with IBCA officials. Students and faculty involved with the world studies EE would be interviewed and questionnaires administered. As a result, the world studies EE guide and grading schema was produced by HPZ and IBCA in July 2010. It was not a consultative process. When the pilot schools met in Cardiff in October 2010, IBCA officials made it clear that the EE guide and assessment criteria had been internally finalised, and already sent for publication and translation into French and Spanish (the other IBDP working languages). The pilot schools gathered were to review and proof-read the teacher support material. At this time, concerns about intellectual property were so high that documents for discussion were not circulated to pilot schools before the conference and were taken for shredding at the end. While these security precautions may be necessary for examination papers they impede preparation (before) and reflection (after): two essentials for curriculum development.

It was evident also in reading the world studies EE guide that much more than the abandonment of the world studies course had happened. The guidelines of the pilot, Mahindra guide (MG), had been transformed in the IB draft of 2010, IB guide (IBG), in the following six ways:

1) *From global 'concern' to global 'issue'*: whereas the MG required an in-depth local study of 'an issue of global concern' (Mahindra IB/UWC Project Group, 2005), in the IBG this becomes 'an issue of contemporary global significance' (IB, 2010). The essay no longer needs to be centred on a global problem. Hence in the IBG an example of a research question is 'How and why have two Japanese graffiti artists used American hip hop art for the purposes of self-expression and community organisation in their country?' A celebration of intercultural hybridity is now possible rather than a matter of wider global concern.

2) *The displacement of the local*: the MG required students to make an 'effective linkage ... between the global question or concern and the local case study or studies' (Mahindra IB/UWC Project Group, 2005). The insistence on one or two in-depth case studies was not just inspired by a 'think globally, research locally' ideology; it was a means to ensure the rigour expected of an EE in the in-depth investigation. The Mahindra group was haunted by the fear that essays in world studies would become little more than internet-based surveys or syntheses of issues such as malnutrition, global warming or child labour in various countries. In fact, the word 'local' does not appear at all in the assessment criteria of the IBG, even though the global-local perspective is exemplified in each of the four examples. In the absence of a clear embodiment of the 'local' in the actual assessment criteria, one fears its demise.

3) *From fieldwork to reflection*: earlier sections of this chapter make clear that the world studies EE was an experiment in experiential learning: requiring, even forcing, students to connect what they learned in the classroom to what they encountered in the real world, in CAS and in their EE fieldwork. Data gathering, interviewing, designing and administering questionnaires, and workshops in statistics and qualitative/quantitative social science research techniques were always offered to world studies students. As a result, the best essays at Mahindra emerged from CAS experience at the college or in project weeks or summers across India. Whilst fieldwork was never an absolute requirement (in the same sense that a laboratory experiment is not an absolute requirement for a science essay) it was strongly encouraged, and 'fieldwork initiative' was explicitly rewarded in the holistic judgement criterion. The same criterion in the IBG makes no mention of fieldwork. Instead it rewards the acquisition of 'global consciousness', as demonstrated by 'personal reflections embedded in the essay' or extracts from the researcher's reflection space (IB, 2010). While this is modelled on the IBDP *Visual Arts Workbook*, which is a space for research and reflection required of IB visual arts students, it is interesting to note that IB CAS assessment is taking a similar turn: from actions and hours to student self-reflection.

4) *No expectation of solutions or implications*: the MG required students to 'examine the implications of the research findings' within an 'academic or political discourse', whilst the IBG does not. The former made it clear that: 'The best essays will display analytical rigour in the use of evidence and in the identification of causes *and creativity and realism in their proposed solutions*.' A study of a global issue or hybridity is now sufficient.

5) *Objectivity and balance*: in the MG, objectivity and balance required candidates to pay 'detailed attention' to 'differing viewpoints and perspectives'. Essays that engaged in 'advocacy' scored zero on this criterion. This insistence ensures that students who are interested in being

'agents of change' are required to 'look at the other side' to ensure rigorous scholarship. This focus on differing perspectives is at the heart of the Cambridge Pre-U global perspectives course, which was developed around the same time as the world studies EE pilot. However, the IBG does not explicitly demand this sense of objectivity and balance. It simply requires two subject perspectives: 'Students are expected to employ theories, methods and findings from two or more subjects. While journalistic and media sources are permitted, the essay should also include perspectives based on selected subjects.' (IB, 2010)

6) *Integrated approach*: every criterion in the IBG speaks of the need to integrate and demonstrate the integration of two subjects, with one calling for, in a manner reminiscent of ToK, 'explicit awareness of the strengths and limitations of the individual subject concepts or ideas', as well as for the candidate to reflect on 'the success and limitations of their own integrative approach to the issue'. What is now clear is that the candidate is not allowed to forget that the main objective of the essay is not the exploration of a global-local problem-context. Instead it provides the IB with a way forward in interdisciplinary studies. Our initial project was *incidentally* interdisciplinary, because real-life problems rarely lend themselves to adequate study within the confines of a single discipline. In its final form, the initiative has become *systemically* interdisciplinary.

The way forward?

Since the IBG did not evolve through a transparent or inclusive process including Mahindra or the other pilot schools, one can only guess at the motivations for these six shifts, beyond the prioritising of a particular interdisciplinary model. Collectively the six key points discussed above reveal a paradigm shift. Whether it takes the IB forward or backward is for the reader to judge. A few of these shifts were unavoidable as the process moved from curriculum planners to assessment specialists. However, the big joker in the pack, responsible first for the renewed interest in world studies at IBCA but then also for its re-definition, was IBCA's sudden interest, mid-decade, in interdisciplinarity. This was not Mahindra's motivation for pioneering it, nor was it Walker's intent in accommodating it. Walker envisaged world studies EE candidates, first at Mahindra and then elsewhere when the pilot spread, being supported by a world studies EE course. This is made clear in his initial mandate: 'that the guidance notes would be based not on an approved IB syllabus but on an in-house syllabus taught at Mahindra.' (IB, 2003).

Neither Walker nor Mahindra ever saw world studies as an amalgam of two subjects. Mahindra's conception of a rigorous and successful world studies EE was based on fieldwork, designed objectively to analyse a global problem, and based on sound social science quantitative and qualitative investigation methodologies or hands-on collection of environmental data. Whether this in-depth inquiry took students into one and a half subjects or four, or into a non-IB subject discipline such as education or law, was largely irrelevant. The first shot across the bow was not long in coming from IBCA. One IB official argued in 2005 that two examiners should grade world studies EEs: one from each of the disciplines represented. We argued strongly against this and fortunately an examiner was found for the first essays. If the world studies EE is written by thousands of candidates annually, the shortage of such examiners may, one fears, tempt IBCA towards a two-examiner 'solution'. Yet the 'two-subject' definition of rigorous interdisciplinarity does nothing to make us feel hopeful.

The way forward, we felt, was a pilot interdisciplinary HL course drawn from diploma groups three, four and six that also integrates the service element of CAS. This will not only support students and supervisors in their EEs; it will take things full circle since it was as a course, not as an EE, that world studies was born. The Cambridge Pre-U global perspectives and independent research requirements, which are mandatory for the award of the Pre-U diploma, illustrate not only the value other international awarding bodies place on global awareness, but also the viability of such courses and their attractiveness to universities. Yet IBCA, in a communication with one of the authors of this chapter, rejected the need for, or viability of, such a world studies course (IB, 2003).

Imagine, by way of analogy, an environmental systems EE without a course in the subject. Imagine a definition of rigour in environmental systems that requires students to demonstrate a rootedness in chemistry and biology – or politics and history for a human rights EE. One is likely to read contrived explorations that draw extensively on different curricula to score well, but do not really reach the heart of environmental or human rights issues. This would inevitably result in a genuine 'follow the leads to their conclusion' experiment in experiential learning taking a backseat. Until such time as a world studies course is piloted, CAS could be acknowledged as one of the two 'acceptable' IB subjects. It has a clear guide and philosophy and it is central to the IB; so, why not? Yet in its present form, in our experience service is often a shoddy, feel-good exercise, in which students frequently have no intellectual conception of why they are doing what they are doing. Hence, at the very least, they may well be doing more harm than good: 'nothing in the world is more dangerous than sincere ignorance.' (King, 2007: 492). At the outset, our contention was that this is the case; to sail through the two years of the diploma without having been brought face-to-face with issues that underlie many of the major real world issues is an effortless exercise within the present structure of the hexagon, and this is a grave weakness in an education that claims to be international.

And finally

What issues are highlighted by the interactive curriculum development model described here? It is clearly a great strength that the IB is able to draw upon – and actively encourage – the involvement of its member schools as a source of continuing educational innovation. This case study of world studies, however, suggests that what follows is not a truly consultative process, and that the rich experience of the pioneering school may be scarcely drawn upon when it goes mainstream. The reason for developing a course in world studies was not to support an EE that could be written on it. It was to ensure that IB diploma students were brought face to face with the issues that underline many of the present major real-world problems. In graduating, students would therefore more closely match the IB learner profile (IB, 2011b) and the IB mission statement. The continued absence of a world studies course handicaps both students and schools attempting the standalone world studies EE. More importantly, it belies its *raison d'être*.

References

Hill, I (2001): Quoted in personal correspondence to D Wilkinson from G Walker, 13 March 2011.

IB (2003): Personal correspondence with C Vakil, 1 November 2003.

IB (2010): *World Studies Extended Essay Guide*. Cardiff: International Baccalaureate.

IB (2011a): *IB Mission Statement*. Online: www.ibo.org/mission/ (last accessed 7 June 2011).

IB (2011b): *IB Learner Profile*. Online (last accessed 8 June 2011): www.ibo.org/programmes/profile/documents/Learnerprofileguide.pdf

King, M L Jr (2007): *Advocate of the Social Gospel: September 1948-March 1963*. Berkeley, CA: University of California Press.

Mahindra IB/UWC Project Group (2001): Discussion paper prepared for the UWC Heads' meeting of July 2001.

Mahindra IB/UWC Project Group (2005): Guidelines for the World Studies Extended Essay pilot.

Sutcliffe, D (2002): Extract from a paper written for the Academic Committee of Pearson UWC of Canada, July 2002.

United World Colleges (2011): Online: www.uwc.org (last accessed 31 August 2011).

Vakil, C (2002): Cautions to Global Affairs presenters – notice to the Mahindra UWC of India community, 13 February 2002.

Walker, G (2001): Personal correspondence with D Wilkinson, 12 March 2001.

Walker, G (2002): Memo to D Wilkinson and J Thompson re possible pilot starting in January 2003, 24 January 2002.

Walker, G (2003): Terrorism, tolerance and the human spirit – the challenges for international education. Speech at IBAP conference, Singapore, 2003, in *To Educate the Nations 2*. Saxmundham: Peridot Press Ltd, 2004.

Walker, G R (2006): *Educating the Global Citizen*. Saxmundham: John Catt Educational.

Wilkinson, D (2001): Personal correspondence with G Walker, 12/13 March 2001.

Chapter 9

Supporting the school and the IB diploma community through the school library

Anthony Tilke

Introduction

One major conduit of information available in a school is its library. The term 'library' readily translates into a number of languages, not least in the Latin or romance and italic languages, but also in languages that employ other alphabets, such as Arabic (*maktaba* – phonetic translation), Japanese (*toshookan* – Romanji realization) and many others. This in itself feeds into one of the big ideas of the International Baccalaureate (IB): internationalmindedness. Interestingly, though, the idea of translating the word 'library' does not quite work with related terms used instead of the word 'library', such as resource centre or some other current terms, and may be an issue for students and parents whose mother tongue is not English. So, in an international context, the term library may have more universal meaning, and therefore remains the term used here.

Libraries in some cultures and countries are currently going through stretching times, partly to do with the way information (rather than technology *per se*) works in the 21st century, and political and financial issues. The challenging times faced by libraries are also being experienced in the educational world, though many educators have a regard for libraries in general, and school libraries in particular. They consider a library as a 'good thing', though it may be that the term remains ill- or softly-defined, given that it relates more to individuals' impressions and experiences of both libraries and librarians; this feeds into how school libraries are perceived and used. For instance, it would be interesting to ask members of a school faculty to define both 'library' and 'librarian', as one practitioner-researcher did, with varying results in general and, in particular, with regard to the IB Diploma Programme (Tilke, 2009), not least because some of the results were in tension with each other. For instance, one teacher considered a library should purely support individual, silent study, whilst another thought it was useful for group work, with resources and with ongoing student discussion and debate.

School libraries in IB documentation

In the context of the Diploma Programme (DP), one expects to receive guidance from IB documentation. Guidance is certainly provided for the programme in general, for specific groups and subject options, as well as for core requirements such as the extended essay (EE). However, as one DP librarian noted (Clark, 2006), the library is not a subject in the DP, so where does guidance come from? There are of course some references to libraries in IB documentation. For schools new to the IBDP, the *Guide to Programme Evaluation* is the most obvious starting point. The exact requirements vary between IB regional offices, but generally there are two questions that relate to the library, in terms of the self-study element of the evaluation. One question, as may be expected, is concerned with input measures that a school will put in place over a five-year period to support the development of the DP in that school; this question specifically mentions the school library. The other question concerns use of the school library. Here, the information relating to the library emanates from the school itself, and may be a useful encouragement for subject departments and others to reflect on how they use the library as part of their pedagogy. However, little specific guidance has been available from IB documentation, as noted in a study of DP resource input factors for a group of schools in Canada (Buchanan *et al*, 2005).

The other seminal IB document in this context is the *Programme standards and practices* (IB, 2010b). In its revised form, standards common to all three programmes (Primary Years Programme, Middle Years Programme and Diploma Programme) are articulated, followed by specific standards for individual programmes, with recommended or highlighted practices for support. The specific reference to the school library occurs in Standard B2.6. This refers to a central role for the library in the programme and, specifically for the DP, that the library should contain sufficient resources to support the implementation of the programme. Another major DP document, *The Diploma Programme: from principles into practice* (IB, 2009), refers to the need for librarians amongst other staff to experience professional development about the DP, though there is no mention of libraries in the document.

In the context of the core requirements, the EE document (IB, 2010a), for instance, includes pithy references to use of the library and librarian, which suggest there is a perceived benefit to students, thus aptly focusing on use of – as opposed to input measures about – library provision in the programme. These IB documents may be read by all concerned with teaching the programme, but it is likely that most teachers seek regular guidance from their subject/group documents, where there is a general lack of reference to the role of the school library and librarians in the DP. This is an important point; it is generally held in library and information science (LIS) literature, and borne out by a study of the role of the school library in the DP (Tilke, 2009), that the role of the teacher in using, supporting and encouraging use of the library and librarian is a crucial factor.

A school library and librarian

As both school library and librarian may be ill-defined concepts in the DP educational landscape, perhaps it is useful to consider what they actually are. Generally, people will have a clear idea of what a library contains and looks like, and some studies of both students and staff refer to book-filled rooms, a quiet atmosphere (perhaps with some technology), which may be colonized by particular groups of students (KRC Research, 2003; Rafste, 2005; Tilke, 2009). With respect to how a school library was *used*, opinions varied. Of the librarian, perceptions ranged from them being supervisors and maintaining a quiet atmosphere, to them being information professionals, providing a tutorial and teaching role in the use of information. In two of these studies, though, relationships with the library were deemed to be purely for students and librarian to develop, and not for teachers.

It is important to note that styles and infrastructure of school libraries vary worldwide, and this is also true of the education and professional background of librarians (Turner, 2007). There is no lack of standards relating to school libraries, though these have mostly been developed by (national) LIS agencies, and reference to libraries/ians has not enjoyed synergy in mainstream curricular documentation (Pratt, 1994; Montiel-Overall, 2005), therefore echoing the DP situation. Furthermore, these documents, and the professional development imperatives for school librarians, promote and work best in the context of a constructivist approach to learning, as librarians are aware of the importance of real inquiry, making connections with, for instance, previous and concurrent learning, critical thinking – though librarians need to be aware of pedagogical practice in their own schools, and the philosophy that underpins such pedagogy (Hepworth and Walton, 2009).

Partly because the curricular role of the library may be hidden (Streatfield and Markless, 1994), school librarians have used research findings and professional practice as advocacy in order to develop the role of the school library and that of the librarian, generally on an individual school basis. In this, they have used their vision and professional development, and sought to convince administrators and faculty colleagues about the importance of these roles. As such, librarians are adept at looking into documents and the way that programmes develop in schools, to seek and create learning situations that may provide added value for students.

School library impact on the Diploma Programme

The school library contributes to the overarching themes of the DP in various ways. This may be through provision and promotion of information and stimulating reading material that explain and elucidate notions of culture and language, as well as other attributes of international-mindedness and our global environment. This has the most obvious connection with DP group 1 subjects (meaning that liaison, cooperation, even collaboration with relevant subject faculty members is vital), though it may not be limited to that; for instance, there may also be links with the EE world studies option, and the theory of knowledge (ToK).

The library can make a contribution to the various dimensions of the IB learner profile; in addition to providing resources that explain these attributes, the library also provides a practical environment for putting them into practice. An example concerns the qualities of being open-minded and balanced, where a student could be encouraged to be open to different ways of learning and other people's points of view, as expressed in printed documentation. As a risk taker, a student could be encouraged to pick up a book s/he glanced at, in order to enquire further (Tilke, 2011). Of course, these are just surface aspects – good as they are – and more analysis of the learner profile attributes can benefit from a contribution by the library, through *use* of the facility by students. A more concrete example relates to the quality of being principled, where a student may practise strategies of academic honesty. Indeed, it can be readily appreciated that students and others can practise academic honesty in the school library, and this is recognized in the *Academic honesty* document (IB, 2011). This document contains the most comprehensive account of the role of the library/ian in the Diploma Programme, and indicates that the librarian can play a key role in the school through teaching research methods and strategies for avoiding plagiarism, so simultaneously contributing to another 'big idea' of IB programmes: inquiry and research.

In terms of the focus of such activity, the most obvious role for the school library may relate to the EE. As several practitioners noted:

> Teachers and IB coordinators can make better use of their own time, and help students plan and deliver more effectively, if they allow librarians to support individual students. This can be by teaching 'just in time' courses on research and citation skills and by producing related knowledge products, which are often web-based (such as guides to citation and bibliography construction)… [providing support] for students facing a daunting academic challenge, while additional support takes in everything up to and including help with the abstract-writing requirement. (Barrett *et al*, 2011)

A librarian may support individual students, for instance in guiding the student through using online subscription databases that typically provide detailed, relevant information for very specific EE titles, and which simply is not available in a practical way in printed form or on the internet. Indeed, research suggests that current students (both at secondary and tertiary levels) need support in interrogating online information, in spite of popular perceptions of students being 'techno-savvy' digital natives (Head and Eisenberg, 2009; Rowlands and Nicholas, 2008). As educators who have undertaken Masters and Doctoral degrees may attest, navigating numerous – perhaps esoteric – databases is something of an art form, and generally does not come naturally.

Indeed, providing advice about relevant sources can be valuable support and help for individual students, especially if approached early in the process (Clark, 1995); this can be developed on a more systematic basis, though close liaison with the DP coordinator (Jones, 2004), and indeed structured into the school's EE process on an ongoing basis, with electronic support as well as support in the physical sense (Viner, 2007).

A librarian may also act as a supervisor for an individual student, as the library could be a focus for an essay; for example, one student was known to have critiqued the selection process and various technical products for a new computer system for the school library, as an EE for information technology in a global society (ITGS). Librarians can provide support for supervisors too, in the form of information about what the library/ian can provide, so that supervisors can better support students during their regular meetings. A librarian can also model good practice in this regard in any knowledge product s/he generates. Previous years' EE for the school could be showcased in the school library, too, as powerful exemplars of the achievements of previous students. Library and librarian support for the research process could therefore be a contribution to one of the valuable experiences that DP students can take and use in tertiary education (Taylor and Porath, 2006).

The library's role is not limited to supporting the EE process. Another area of contribution relates to ToK, which is included in various IB library workshops around the world, where one activity is to provide a fourth ring of the traditional ToK circle diagram, headed 'ToK and the library'. The list of suggestions below was brainstormed (from actual practice, as well as imagined possibilities) by just one table group during a 2009 IB continuum library workshop in Sydney, Australia:

- Displays of relevant resources, *eg* of banned books
- Teach information skills, in terms of identifying primary/secondary sources; promote critical thinking and analysing resources
- Databases of specific information, *eg* for debates, essay and presentation
- Promote new relevant resources/magazines *etc*, to ToK teachers and students
- Collaboration with ToK teachers – attend meetings, approach them, send them information
- Be available to listen to students (*eg* for presentation) – active listening!
- Make a discussion area available in the library
- Directing and helping with selection of resources
- Questioning students, engaging them and keep motivating them

Although by no means exhaustive, this list shows the thinking of librarians on how to make connections between library services and facilities and the curriculum. Other possibilities range from providing a discrete collection of ToK-related titles in the library to the librarian being part of the ToK teaching team.

According to one administrator, the library may have a more 'hidden' role with regard to supporting the work of the various group subjects of the diploma. In practice, this will tend to vary according to specific subjects, pedagogy employed, and the previous library experience of individual teachers – whether as students themselves or earlier in their teaching career (Tilke, 2011). Library support might be quite traditional, for example in providing copies of textbooks and scientific periodicals for support of group 4 subjects (Clark, 2006). Or the library could be a case study for ITGS, in group 3, of the social way in which technology changes the lives of people (in one case the librarian spoke to ITGS students about these changes). Alternatively, students could group visit and ask questions of the library staff, to provide an inquiry-focused learning situation. Indeed, group 3 and group 1 subject teachers may be good users of the library, though their use may be 'hidden' because it is so natural and ongoing. It may only surface as in the case of a group 6 student who appended an explanatory note to her/his displayed art at an international school in Asia, indicating how the library had helped:

> I've searched through the library to find sources that could show me how the body of a monkey could be sketched ... most of my research came from the library, magazines and the internet. During this process, I found an artist called James Reekie, [also] Decamps and Tenners, but I was most influenced by Lassetter's photo collage of Bob Dylan. (Tilke, 2011: 26)

The librarian may be another source of support in a school who can, through education, professional practice and awareness of constructivist approaches and real inquiry, work with colleagues in support of another IB-adopted idea: concurrency of learning (Marshman, 2010).

To return to the IB standards and practices, although these contain one overt reference to the library, it is nevertheless possible to infer library involvement in and support for a school's aim in reaching these standards, and taking the DP forward in that school. Standard A is concerned with philosophies in the school. There should be a philosophy, policy and aims for a school library and, in a DP school, the latter should be articulating IB philosophy, not only in general terms but also, for instance, with regard to a policy on developing library collections. As the standard also refers to international-mindedness, the library could audit its collection and highlight relevant titles and sections, and furthermore provide this information to the DP coordinator and others concerned in monitoring the school's adoption of the programme standards. Standard B is concerned with school organization, including professional and pedagogical development. The school library could, for example, promote its function of providing a professional development collection, making sure it holds copies of titles promoted in IB literature; such collections may be considered a valuable support (Williams and Coles, 2007). As *Academic honesty* is included in standard B, the role of the library and librarian in this process should be documented and included as evidence of the school's work in this regard. Standard C focuses on curriculum, including collaboration between teachers, pedagogy, development of learner profile attributes and development of skills. These are key areas for the librarian and others to document and record as a contribution to the development of elements of standard C.

IBDP school community use of the school library

Of course, school community use of the library may vary considerably from school to school, and include factors such as space and location, but some research (Latuputty, 2005; Rafste, 2005; Tilke, 2009) suggests that there could be some general features that apply more widely:

- Student use of the school library will depend on teacher encouragement to do so. Pedagogical use of the school library includes teachers using the library as a teaching and learning tool, working with the library to manage a learning outcome or process. It may also range from teachers encouraging students to use the library in specific ways for individual stages of the subject course, to a general encouragement to use the library as an efficient means of studying at the beginning of their DP candidature.

- Student use will also depend on what other facilities are available in the school library for them. If students have access to a lounge for their non-contact times, they will use that accordingly, and tend to focus on use of the library for academic activity. An alternative scenario is where the library becomes a *de facto* student lounge (in the absence of any other provision for students) and this colonization determines how the library is used and perceived, sometimes in a limited way (Rafste, 2005). Students need space for relaxation, and they also need somewhere to work. Because non-contact time is relatively new to them, they benefit from an infrastructure that allows them to differentiate between the two.

- Administrators' and teachers' views on the library could determine the status and perceived value of the library within the individual institution. Administrators may evaluate a library as an ongoing action, and in a casual way as one of the many school facilities and services available (Everhart, 2006) – though completing the self-study element of the *Guide to Programme Evaluation* may prompt some re-thinking in this regard. In evaluating, administrators tend to be influenced by their previous experience of libraries. Equally, libraries have changed over the years, and now may be places for active learning, group work, and making new knowledge, rather than purely quiet places for individual (silent) study.

DP student use of the library will benefit from a heritage of information literacy skills built up earlier in their secondary school career, as the demands of the programme are such that there is little time to develop such skills 'from scratch' once students have embarked upon the diploma.

Some limitations on using the school library need to be identified. In a study of the role of the library in the Diploma Programme (Tilke, 2009), it was found that the prevalence of subject textbooks deterred students from using (or needing) the library, as they had a view that textbooks alone contained sufficient information, especially if those textbooks had an indication of IB approval. (The same scenario was observed in another curriculum in a British study by Madden *et al*, 2007.) Time, or rather lack of it, was another limitation, as well as pressure to cover significant subject content, as two US studies found (Kyburg *et al*, 2007; Vanderbrook, 2006). Another limitation can be other sources of information, specifically teachers' personal book collections and subject departmental libraries. This latter point needs qualifying, though, as some libraries are moving relevant sections into subject departments, either partially or completely, or cataloguing (and perhaps purchasing) resources for departments, with details of each item being recorded on the computer cataloguing system for the library. This represents a different approach to providing information to support the Diploma Programme. Other schools will prefer to have a large centralized collection in the main school library facility.

Benefits to the DP school community from using the library

Research (Tilke, 2009) and professional practice (including ongoing contributions to the IB Online Curriculum Centre (OCC) library forum) indicate variation in student benefits from using the school library during their diploma candidature. Factors include:

- Time management. One study found that this was the most common benefit mentioned, and was considered one of the most important skills that students needed to complete the DP, especially in a school where the entire 16-18 year cohort undertook the diploma. Students used the library for academic work; they completed work, researched for coursework and core diploma requirements, and prepared for final diploma examinations. They were able to practise their time management skills in the library.

- Quality of information. Students and teachers associate the library with quality of information, which is focused on the needs of the school, and derived from the professional knowledge of the librarian, in ongoing liaison and communication with DP teachers to identify resource needs.

- Help with the EE. Whilst support for group 1-6 work varies with subjects chosen, the most common benefit students and teachers have referred to was in relation to the EE, in respect of resources, advice about information, and bibliographic and citation strategies and practice.

- Stress. Students under pressure in the DP felt that the library was an oasis of calm in a busy environment, where they could have space to spread out, and space and time for private thoughts. This benefit was strengthened if they could use headphones for their own music, which helped to support their learning styles and preferred environment.

- Experience of using the library in an individual manner provides good practice for life in tertiary education, though this tended to be something appreciated by students only when they actually reached tertiary education.

Conclusion

The role of the school library and librarian in the DP can be seen through a narrow reading of IB documentation, though the role may well be correspondingly limited. However, taking a wider, more holistic perspective of IB literature relating to the school library will open up various areas so that the facility and – crucially – its manager is positioned effectively to support and enhance the learning process, experiences and information needs of DP students. Such a situation is strengthened where the library and librarian role is well understood within the IBDP school community, involving contributions from a range of stakeholders: students, teachers, administrators and the IB itself, as well as librarians. Together, these contributions strengthen what the library and its librarian can bring to the development of the DP in a school.

References

Barrett, Y, Green, G and Tilke, A (2011): Between the pages: whether it's the culminating projects or everyday research, school librarians' expertise can bring learning to life, in *IB World*, 62, p25.

Buchanan, S, Douglas, L, Hachlaf, K, Varner, E and Williams, P (2005): *Evaluating the International Baccalaureate Programme: an IB proposal for the consideration of the North Vancouver School District.* Unpublished Master's thesis, University of British Columbia. Online: http://slc.educ.ubc.ca/Masters/Buchannan.pdf (*nb* Buchanan name wrongly spelt in url) (last accessed 26 July 2011).

Clark, C (1995): The school library: an under-used resource for the IB programme? in *IB World*, 9, pp43-46.

Clark, C (2006): IB, the sixth form and the LRC: an international school perspective, in G Dubber (ed), *Sixth sense: the sixth form and the LRC*. Swindon, UK: School Library Association, pp40-44.

Everhart, N (2006): Principals' evaluation of school libraries: a study of strategic and non-strategic evidence-based approaches, in *School Libraries Worldwide*, 12 (2), pp38-51.

Head, A J and Eisenberg, M B (2009): *Finding context: what today's college students say about conducting research in the digital age.* Project Information Literacy Progress Report, February 4, 2009. Online: www.projectinfolit.org/pdfs/PIL_ProgressReport_2_2009.pdf (last accessed 21 July 2011).

Hepworth, M and Walton, J (2009): *Teaching information literacy for inquiry-based learning.* Oxford: Chandos Publishing.

IB (2009): *The Diploma Programme: from principles to practice.* Geneva: International Baccalaureate.

IB (2010a): *Extended essay guide.* Cardiff: International Baccalaureate.

IB (2010b): *Programme standards and practices.* Geneva: International Baccalaureate.

IB (2011): *Academic honesty.* Cardiff: International Baccalaureate.

Jones, S (2004): The Extended Essay, in M van Loo and K Morley (eds), *Implementing the IB Diploma Programme: a practical manual for principals, IB coordinators, heads of department and teachers.* Cambridge: Cambridge University Press, pp195-210.

KRC Research (2003): *A report of findings from six focus groups with K-12 parents, teachers, and principals, as well as middle and high school students.* Online (last accessed 4 September 2011): www.ala.org/ala/mgrps/divs/aasl/aaslissues/@yourlibcampaign/krc_research_report.pdf

Kyburg, R M, Hertberg-Davis, H and Callaghan, C M (2007): Advanced Placement and International Baccalaureate programs: optimal learning environments for talented minorities? in *Journal of Advanced Academics*, 18 (2), pp172-215.

Latuputty, H (2005): Improving the school library for IB students: a case study at The British International School, Jakarta, in S Lee, P Warning, D Singh, E Howe, L Farmer and S Hughes (eds), *IASL Reports, 2005: Information leadership in a culture of change, selected papers from the 34th Annual Conference of the Association of School Librarianship and the 9th International Forum on Research in School Librarianship, incorporating IB PanAsia Library Media Specialists (IB PALMS), Hong Kong, China, July 8-12, 2005* [CD-ROM]. Hong Kong: International Association of School Librarianship.

Madden, A D, Ford, N J and Miller, D (2007): Information sources used by students at an English secondary school: perceived and actual levels of usefulness, in *Journal of Documentation*, 63 (3), pp340-358.

Marshman, R (2010): *Concurrency of learning in the IB Diploma Programme and Middle Years Programme (IB position paper)* Online (last accessed 4 September 2011): http://blogs.ibo.org/positionpapers/files/2010/09/Concurrency-of-learning_Roger-Marshman2.pdf

Montiel-Overall, P (2005): A theoretical understanding of teacher and librarian collaboration, in *School Libraries Worldwide*, 11 (2), pp24-48.

Pratt, D (1994): *Curriculum planning: a handbook for professionals.* Fort Worth, TX: Harcourt Brace Inc.

Rafste, E T (2005): A place to learn or a place for leisure: pupils' use of the school library in Norway, in *School Libraries Worldwide*, 11 (1), pp1-16.

Rowlands, I and Nicholas, D (2008): *Information behavior of the researcher of the future.* Online: www.ucl.ac.uk/infostudies/research/ciber/downloads/ggexecutive.pdf (last accessed 29 August 2011).

Streatfield, D and Markless, S (1994): *Invisible learning: the contribution of school libraries to teaching and learning.* London: British Library.

Taylor, M L and Porath, M (2009): Reflections on the International Baccalaureate Program: graduates' perspectives, in *Journal of Secondary Gifted Education*, 17 (3), pp21-30.

Tilke, A (2009): *The impact of an international school library on the International Baccalaureate Diploma Programme: a constructivist grounded theory approach.* Unpublished PhD thesis. Charles Sturt University, Australia.

Tilke, A (2011): *The International Baccalaureate Diploma Program and the school library: inquiry-based education.* Santa Barbara, CA: Libraries Unlimited.

Turner, R (2007): The use of independent school libraries in England and Wales, in *School Librarian,* 55 (1), pp11-15.

Vanderbrook, C M (2006): Intellectually gifted females and their perspectives of lived experience in the AP and IB programs, in *Journal of Secondary Gifted Education,* 17 (3), pp133-148.

Viner, M J (2007): *IB diploma – extended essay library program.* Paper presented at the IBAP Teachers' Convention: Information Literacy across the programmes, Singapore. Online (last accessed 4 September 2011): www.ibo.org/ibap/conference/documents/JaneViner-IBDiploma-ExtendedEssayLibraryProgram.pdf

Williams, D and Coles, L (2007): Evidence-based practice in teaching: an information perspective, in *Journal of Documentation,* 63 (6), pp812-835.

Part B
Aspects of Growth and Development

Chapter 10

The 'growth' of the IB diploma: critical perspectives on balance, depth and 'development'

Tristan Bunnell

The growth of the DP

The extent of 'growth'

The International Baccalaureate (IB) has come a considerably long way since Alec Peterson, a key 'architect', writing almost exactly 40 years ago at a time when there were just 22 authorized schools operating in 14 countries, commented that there was already every reason 'to suppose that this experiment will prove successful' (Peterson, 1972: 31). By August 2011 there were almost 3300 IB schools, including over 2300 offering the Diploma Programme (DP) (IB, 2011a). The IB looks set on serving 2.5 million children in 10,000 schools by 2020. We might expect at least 40 percent of these to be in the USA alone, whilst 63 percent will be state-funded and just five percent will be 'international schools' (Beard and Holloway, 2010). The projection is therefore to expand by a *further* 6800 schools over the coming decade, adding at least 5000 more DP schools (*ie* an extra 200 percent growth).

The exact growth of the DP thus far has been well documented (see, for instance, Bunnell, 2008; Tarc, 2009; Hill, 2010) but it is worth considering a few salient facts. The number of schools following the DP increased 53 percent between 2005 (when there were 1335, including 143 November session schools) and 2009 (2025, including 192 November session schools). In other words, the number of schools following the programme grew by an average of 15 per month between 2005 and 2009. The number of candidates examined in the May session increased from 1217 in 1975 to 105,000 in 2010. Looking at the number of schools entering candidates for the May examination session during the 35-year period between 1975 and 2009, there were 23 years that saw double-digit growth. The figures for number of candidates entered (again, 1975 to 2009) reveal even more impressive growth. Only five years over this period had less than double-digit growth.

There is thus no doubting that the DP has been a 'successful' experiment, certainly as measured by numerical growth. However, raw data such as these mask significant details. Take, for instance, the three main working languages of the DP. In 2009 the vast majority of schools (88 percent) were following the DP in English, 10.6 percent in Spanish, and a miniscule 1.4 percent in French

(IB, 2011b). The growth has involved much *breadth*, involving more schools in more countries (Ecuador, for instance, now has almost 50 DP schools) and among a greater diversity (90 percent of DP schools in the USA are publicly funded, for example) compared with the private international school-dominated beginnings of the DP. Yet one can critically question the level of *balance* and *depth*. Take subject choice, for instance. In the May 2010 examination session exactly one-third of all students sat a history paper, and 85 percent sat a group 3 subject, yet only one percent was examined in music. Thirty-one percent sat biology.

Thirdly, consider geographical distribution. The growth in the USA has been especially dramatic, and exactly one-third of DP schools in 2011 are now located there. However, 55 percent of all IB schools in the USA are located in just eight states. Walker (2005a: 5), talking specifically about growth in North America, noted that 'if we exclude the MYP schools in Québec the remaining distribution is not very impressive'. It has previously been critically noted that 62 percent of students who undertook the May 2005 higher level (HL) history examination sat the optional 'history of the Americas' paper, whilst only 0.7 percent took the 'history of Africa' paper (Lewis, 2006). My own concerns over the growth of the DP in the USA (geographical, assessment, political and organizational) have been discussed in detail elsewhere (Bunnell, 2011a).

What these figures seem to show is that the DP is growing in breadth (*eg* students can now be examined from a choice of nine group 3 subjects) but this growth (both in terms of geographical distribution and subject choice) lacks a degree of balance and depth. This situation was somewhat inevitable; 'no one could claim that the expansion has been planned, that it has followed a careful pattern or that it has reflected any particular set of IBO priorities' (Walker, 2004: 2). But it is an important issue requiring discussion. The official monograph, *A Basis for Practice* (IB, 2002), makes clear the core principles of the DP. It states that 'from its inception, the development of the Diploma Programme was based on three fundamental principles'. The first principle states 'the need for a broad general education', while the third states 'the need for flexibility of choice among the subjects to be studied, within a balanced framework'. Two of the key wordings that stand out here are 'broad general education' and 'a balanced framework'. George Walker, in his introduction to a remarkably candid book (recently published by the IB) about challenges facing the IB, writes of the beginnings of the DP: 'Here, at last, was an international programme balancing breadth and depth that satisfied the universities.' (Walker, 2011: 4). This chapter will now critically explore in more detail a number of issues regarding the balance and depth of the DP. Unless otherwise acknowledged, all data included in this chapter have as their source the IB website (www.ibo.org).

Perspectives on growth

Growth and balance

The May 2010 examination session revealed enormous *breadth* in terms of subjects on offer yet little real *balance*. A total of 104,999 candidates were entered for the May 2010 examination session, for instance, but fewer than half (47,723) were entered for the full diploma (with the remaining entries accounted for by 32,090 certificate candidates, 1326 retakes and 23,860 anticipated candidates) (IB, 2011c). In total, 85,129 students undertook a group 3 subject, showing that a large number of students took *two* group 3 subjects (*ie* with the second acting as their sixth choice). History was by far the biggest subject taken (aside from English A1): 34,751 students sat history at either higher or standard level. Economics was the second most popular group 3 subject (with 13,749 candidates). However, only 1175 candidates were entered in May for computer science (in group 4). More significantly, in May 2010 the group 6 arts subjects combined had only 16,542 entries (including film studies with just 907 student entries, and music with 2,827).

As can be seen, twice as many students sat a history examination in May 2010 as took all four arts subjects combined. The assessment implications of this will be explored later. The four pilot subjects (dance, sports exercise & health science, text & performance, and world religions) had 495 entries, whilst the 15 school-based syllabuses had 770 student entries. The November 2009 session saw just 72 candidates entered for computer science (compared to 1858 in history) whilst this examination session revealed that theatre arts is almost obsolete as an examination subject (just 161 candidates entered). The school-based syllabuses are also seemingly obsolete there, attracting a mere 49 candidates. The November session also shows that twice as many students were entered for biology as for physics.

It is clear from these figures that group 6 for many students involves another group 3 subject rather than an arts subject, or another group 4 subject. The 105,000 candidates in May 2010 sat a total of 354,054 subjects. The group 3 subjects accounted for 24 percent of these and group 4 accounted for a further 20 percent. Group 6 subjects accounted for just 4.7 percent of the total subjects. In other words, when given a *free choice* the majority of DP students reject the arts and prefer instead a second group 3 (especially history or economics) or a further group 4 subject (especially biology). This discrepancy has widened slightly over the past five years. The May 2006 examination session saw 23 percent of the students sit a group 3 subject, and five percent took a group 6 subject.

The issue of 'imbalance' can be further applied. The May 2010 examination session saw a continuation of the gender imbalance (it is usual for 55-56 percent of candidates in this session to be female). Interestingly, the November session generally turns out to have a 50-50 split (though in fact 2007 saw more boys than girls entered). The May 2010 examination session continued the trend where almost half of all EEs were in group 3 subjects (mainly history), but fewer than three percent were mathematics-based. The November 2009 session similarly showed that 47 percent of EEs were in group 3 subjects. The May 2010 examination session revealed that only 0.12 percent of schools follow the DP in French (this figure was 1.33 percent in November 2009), which questions the efficiency and cost of producing May session examination materials in this language.

Growth and depth

The DP in May 2011 had a presence in 137 countries. At first glance, therefore, the DP seems thinly spread around the world. However, this figure masks two significant facts. Firstly, the DP is heavily concentrated *across* the world; almost exactly half (49 percent) of schools are located in just three countries (USA, England, and Canada). Interestingly, Ecuador (with 47 schools) now has more DP schools than the whole of Africa combined (46 schools), or the Middle East (32 schools). Secondly, the DP is heavily concentrated *within* the world; in October 2010 just eight states of the USA (California, Florida, Texas, Virginia, Colorado, New York, Georgia, and North Carolina) accounted for 16 percent of DP schools worldwide (362 schools).

Hence, we can identify two very distinct growth trends; the DP is becoming more concentrated in some areas, and isolated in others. One can make more sense of this polarization using Pareto Analysis, a marketing tool that adopts the so-called 'Pareto Rule'; 20 percent of customers account for 80 percent of sales (Westcott, 2009). The distribution of a product's customers, over time, tends to be quite concentrated. A few customers usually start to account for a large proportion of total sales. In May 2011, a Pareto Analysis of the raw DP examination statistics reveals that the top 28 countries (accounting for 20 percent of the 137 countries in total) accounted for 84 percent of total schools (1915 to be exact). This gives rise to an '84-20 Rule'. In this respect, the DP is more heavily concentrated among its key customers than even the 'Pareto Rule' states. Eighty percent of DP schools are located in just one-sixth of countries. Alternatively viewed, 115 countries in May 2011 accounted for just 20 percent of schools.

The May 2010 examination session revealed another *breadth versus depth* issue. Although it involved candidates claiming 206 nationalities, the three biggest (American, British, and Canadian) accounted for exactly two-thirds of all candidates (58 percent were American citizens). Only 11 nationalities had more than 1000 candidates involved, whilst 53 nationalities had less than a dozen students involved. The location of the candidates revealed a further discrepancy. The USA 'housed' 56 percent of all the candidates and Canada a further nine percent. In total, two-thirds of all those who sat the May 2010 examinations were based in schools in North America. At the other extreme, 48 countries had fewer than 50 students involved within their borders. The issue of the IB becoming increasingly North America-centric is controversial but needs discussing. The November 2009 session revealed that although 94 countries were involved, close to half the candidates (3862 out of 7685) were located in Australia, Argentina and Singapore. At the other extreme, 42 countries had fewer than ten students involved.

The issue of 'depth' can also be applied in terms of how many students take the DP examination. The strategic planning document (IB, 2006: 9) had noted: 'Today, we know that 48 percent of IB World Schools offer the DP to less than half their students.' Walker (2005a) highlighted the fact that the median figure in the North American region was just 43 students. The May 2010 examination session continued the trend where only one-quarter of schools enter more than 80 students, and 40 percent enter less than 30 students. It is equally common for about 12 percent of schools to enter fewer than ten students, which questions the financial viability of such a move.

The implications

An effective school

The IB has openly talked of the impact it wants the DP to have on the school. The IB identifies three major contributions it can make to education (Walker, 2004). Firstly, it offers programmes and assessment. Secondly, it facilitates a school offering an international education. Thirdly, the IB has the capacity to help schools to become more *effective*. Walker outlined his view of an 'effective school' as one, *inter alia*, where children are keen to learn and are prepared for the next stage of learning; that is valued by the local community; where teachers engage in study and research; that makes the best use of its location and facilities and that has satisfied parents. This view placed a responsibility on the IB (in terms of both programme development and school authorization) to facilitate schools' provision of a suitable and purposeful learning environment: 'the IBO has an obligation to make the partnership possible.' (Walker, 2004: 8). What was being iterated here is that the IB offers a relationship to schools and aims helps them to become *effective* learning institutions.

In particular, Walker (2004: 3) further asserted that: 'An effective school uses whatever buildings it has to the best effect.' The notion that an effective DP school makes 'best' (full?) use of its facilities is an important one. There is evidence that many DP schools could focus more on the use of their resources, especially in terms of their arts and computer laboratory facilities. One of the world's undisputed leading DP schools is Sevenoaks School in Kent, England. The May 2010 examination session saw ten students there awarded the maximum 45 points. A total of 130 had taken economics and a further 99 took history. At the other extreme only 37 students had taken a group 6 arts subject (18 took visual arts, 12 took theatre arts, and two took music). These figures seem to imply an 'imbalance', which might, in practice, be leading to an 'ineffective' allocation and usage of resources (an area that needs further research). The question arises, for instance: 'to what extent do DP schools make full use of their music and drama facilities?'

A quality programme

Commentators are beginning to talk openly about the impact that growth is having *on* the DP (see Bunnell, 2011b). George Walker stated that 'quality' should be judged in terms of consistency and reliability (Walker, 2005b: 5-6). The IB prides itself on providing consistent and reliable assessment of the DP, with good reason.

The number of DP students who achieve the maximum 45 points averaged just 78 students between 2006 and 2009. The figure for May 2009 was 86 students out of a total entry of 35,181. In percentage terms, the number of 'full point' students has been highly consistent, with the years 2007, 2008, and 2009 producing an almost exact same figure (between 0.18 and 0.19 percent). This was in spite of a 40 percent increase in the total number of candidates over the period from 2006 to 2009. The proportion of candidates who 'pass' (*ie* are awarded the diploma by obtaining a minimum of 24 points and meeting a number of other conditions) has also remained highly consistent, with the maximum difference being just two percent (it was 80.34 percent in 2006, and 78.71 percent in 2009). The corresponding figures for the November examination session are equally consistent. The DP 'mean scores' and 'mean grades' worldwide further substantiate the level of consistency. The DP mean score over five years deviated by just half of one grade (the highest was 30.09 in May 2005 and the lowest was 29.51 in May 2009). The corresponding figures for the mean *grade* worldwide were also very close (for instance 4.78 in May 2005 and 4.66 in May 2009).

However, there is public concern about the effect that growth is having (and could have) on assessment. One IB school head has expressed concern at the 'Gadarene rush' to attract schools (Toze, 2008: 6). Another has accused the IB of being 'intoxicated by quantitative growth' (Mott, 2009: 19). This issue, of a 'headlong rush', surfaced in Seville (13-16 October, 2009) at the World Conference for Heads of IB Schools. Here 530 delegates met, and expressed concerns regarding quality being compromised. The Academy of International School Heads (AISH) held a special gathering in Seville in November 2009 to express a number of concerns, including 'the overall integrity of the exam process' (Betts, 2009: 4). A statement from AISH was officially handed to the IB. Toze had sent out a letter to members of AISH, which began by saying that 'In recent years, we have become increasingly concerned about the accuracy of IB grades', and went on to question the standard of marking of DP examinations. Toze further questioned the wide variations in average grades between subjects, and 'some stark anomalies in component results' (Toze, 2008: 6). He stated that in May 2006 the world average grade for HL Pilipino was an extraordinary 6.82

out of 7 (even though the average score for group 2 subjects that year was 5.21), and added: 'I am also sure that the drive for expansion has created a number of other issues ... [including] imbalanced demands on good IB schools to provide trainers, markers, curriculum leaders and evaluation visitors.'

An 'impact' programme

The strategic planning process (IB, 2004) saw the IB view its growth beyond merely school and student numbers (number growth: N), looking also at the ease by which the 'experience' of an IB education can be implemented (ease of implementation: E), and the extent to which the programmes 'make an educational difference' (difference factor: D). The emergence of a somewhat controversial 'impact function' (best explored through a speech by George Walker, 2005a) where impact is a function of N, E, and D, was an attempt by the IB to *measure* the impact of growth. Moreover, it allowed the IB to move beyond seeing growth merely in terms of the number of programmes, schools authorized, or students involved.

The 2004 strategic planning process made reference to a situation of 'critical mass', a concentration of about 50 schools (see Oliver's 2006 interview with Monique Seefried, then President of the IB Council of Foundation) where 'things start to happen'. Presumably this involves economies of scale and wider word-of-mouth marketing; the DP gets more publicity and the average costs of operation fall, thus promoting further growth. In other words, growth has its own internal momentum. Therefore a concentration of schools within a region of the world, or within a country, can be beneficial. Furthermore, a 'critical mass' of schools is more likely to be able to make an 'impact'. However, in May 2011 just seven countries each had over 50 schools, although another four had almost this number. Moreover, there was a solitary DP school to be found in 40 countries and fewer than ten DP schools in 103 countries. The average number of candidates per school has increased from 40.6 in 1975 to 61.2 in 2009, yet still falls short of the 80 students seen by Walker (2005a: 6) as constituting a 'critical mass of influence within its school'.

Conclusions

Taking forward the notion of 'impact'

For the vast majority of DP students, group 6 does not involve an arts subject. Instead, it most probably involves either a second group 3 subject (especially history or economics), or a second group 4 subject (especially biology). Indeed, many students probably take both history and biology but no arts subject. Although the DP may conceptually be imagined as a hexagon, with six equal subject areas surrounding the core, the operational truth is that each subject area is of slightly different size and 'value', with group 6 in particular being a very small element of the hexagon. The May 2010 examination session shows a definite history bias whilst both examination sessions reveal a marginal role played by group 6 arts subjects (especially with regard to music and film studies). There is certainly a substantial history bias in terms of EE. This is problematic for the simple reason that to the casual observer the concept of the DP being a 'balanced' programme seems unreal, whilst even the idea of it offering 'breadth' can be questioned.

This allows taking a different perspective on growth. The IB itself has attempted to move away from merely seeing growth (as inherently 'good') in numerical terms. The 'impact function' was a prominent feature of discussion and presentation by George Walker (IB Director General 1999-2006) but has had little mention since 2006. It seems time to resurrect the notion of an 'impact function' but within a much broader framework of analysis. A major weakness in considerations to date has been the emphasis placed on how growth is allowing the IB to *make an impact* (externally-oriented impact) rather than how growth is *having an impact* on the IB itself (internally-oriented impact). This huge growth is placing enormous infrastructure and institutional pressure on the IB, and is also bound to change the relationship the IB has with its schools (who may start seeing themselves as remote customers). Growth is also placing pressure on maintaining quality (*ie* reliability and consistency of assessment), and is seemingly causing some level of concern. It seems time to take forward the notion of 'impact', seeing it as both positive and problematic.

Taking forward the notion of 'development'

One way of taking this issue forward is through making a crude distinction between 'growth' and 'development'. The 'impact function' model that appeared in 2003 struck me, as an economist, as very similar to the Human Development Index (HDI), an annual database published by the UN Development Programme. Here, the progress of countries is plotted using three key sets of data: life expectancy, GDP per capita, and literacy rates. Figures for GDP per capita can, very crudely, be identified as an indication of 'economic growth' whilst the combined index might perhaps offer a better insight into 'economic development'. Applying this to the 'impact function' one can argue that figures for expansion in number of programmes (N) is a measure of 'growth', whilst the combination of N, E and D provides an insight into the 'development' of the DP. Hence, the 'impact function' might be alternatively viewed as a 'development index' and here we have the basis for a multi-dimensional view of growth. Expansion in terms of 'balance' and 'depth' could be added to the 'impact function', perhaps as variants of number growth (N). This needs more discussion. The aim of this chapter is not to formulate a new 'impact function' but to point out that 'growth' of the DP does not necessarily equate to 'development'. Alternatively, the term 'progress' could be used: in other words, the DP is *growing*, but is it *progressing*?

The strategy document *From Growth to Access* (IB, 2006) saw impact being viewed from a 'development', or 'progress', perspective. Within the discussion about how a situation of 'critical mass' created internal growth momentum, it was stated that 'it is possible to create a critical mass of schools where growth is more easily sustained, student numbers increase rapidly and the impact on the national educational debate is significant' (IB, 2006: 11). This document also referred to 'mission impact' and implied that a form of 'technology impact' exists. George Walker revealed a further dimension of 'impact' when he pointed out that 'the IB has made an impact in North America: it is written about by journalists, spoken about by politicians and weighed and generally welcomed by universities' (Walker, 2005a: 3). This might be deemed the 'political impact'.

There is also scope for a perspective on the 'sociological impact' of growth of the DP. The geographical distribution of the DP could lead to negative conclusions of a more social and moral nature. Firstly, both the areas of concentration (*eg* mid-Atlantic USA) and isolation (*eg* sub-Saharan Africa) might experience excess demand, and therefore competition for places. This could become a source of tension and resentment, causing social disharmony and unhappiness. In the USA the DP has come under considerable local political attack since 2003 (initially by parents), being viewed as a 'foreign' programme and an unnecessary and expensive one (see Bunnell, 2009). Secondly, the DP could emerge as an economic positional good; a vehicle for expressing superiority and perpetuating economic advantage (see Bagnall, 2010). This model for social and moral tension and conflict fits well within the framework of 'social limits to growth', as articulated by the British economist Fred Hirsch in 1976 (see Bunnell, 2011c).

Taking forward the research

There are three issues concerning growth and impact of the DP on the schools that need further exploration and research. Firstly, it has been asserted that a concentration of 50 DP schools in a region brings about 'critical mass', in other words 'things start to happen'. Yet we know little about how this actually impacts on schools. What advantages (presumably economies of scale) ensue? It seems important to research this issue given the fact that in 40 countries one 'IB World School' operates (in May 2011) in a totally monopolistic position. While this may seem advantageous for the school (in that it has little or no local competition), it is likely adding to the cost of training teachers in that the school has to send them to workshops on another continent. Secondly, we are told that a concentration of about 80 students also brings about 'critical mass'. Yet again, we know little about the benefits and advantages of such a situation. The May 2010 examination session revealed that only one-fifth of schools enter 80 or more students; a significant proportion (almost half) entered fewer than 30. This seems another important issue needing to be taken forward. Would DP schools benefit from operating in 'clusters' of schools sharing facilities? Thirdly, and inter-connected, the notion of an 'effective DP school' needs substantial discussion and research. I have highlighted in this chapter a 'group 3/group 6 imbalance' in subject choice that exists in many schools. How prevalent is this situation? To what extent do DP schools utilize and make 'full use' of their resources? Is it perhaps time to reconsider the role of group 6 as a 'free choice' subject area? Is it not time to consider the role of the arts in the (broad and balanced) IB Diploma Programme? What we have now is a situation where growth, and its impact, needs to be viewed in a totally different way. It seems time to take forward the concept of an 'impact function' but within a wider scope of analysis, seeing growth as not necessarily equating to 'development'.

References

Bagnall, N (2010): *Education Without Borders: Forty Years of the International Baccalaureate 1970-2010.* Saarbrucken: Verlag Dr Muller.

Beard, J and Holloway, S (2010): *Head to head: A session for IB Heads of School.* 25 March 2010, Singapore. Online (last accessed 8 July 2010): www.ibo.org/ibap/conference/archive/2010/documents/JeffBeardandSallyHolloway.pdf

Betts, B (2009): AISH attempts advocacy over IB concerns, in *The International Educator*, 24 (2), p4.

Bunnell, T (2008): The global growth of the International Baccalaureate Diploma Programme over the first 40 years: a critical assessment, in *Comparative Education*, 44 (4), pp409-424.

Bunnell, T (2009): The International Baccalaureate in the United States and the emerging 'culture war', in *Discourse: Studies in the Cultural Politics of Education*, 30 (1), pp61-72.

Bunnell, T (2011a): The Growth of the International Baccalaureate Diploma Program: concerns about the consistency and reliability of the assessments, in *The Educational Forum*, 75 (2), pp174-187.

Bunnell, T (2011b): The International Baccalaureate in the United States: from relative inactivity to imbalance, in *The Educational Forum*, 75 (1), pp66-79.

Bunnell, T (2011c): The International Baccalaureate and 'growth scepticism': a 'social limits' framework, in *International Studies in Sociology of Education*, 21 (2), pp157-172.

Hill, I (2010): in M Hayden (ed), *The International Baccalaureate: Pioneering in Education (The International Schools Journal Compendium, Volume IV)*. Woodbridge: John Catt Educational Ltd.

IB (2002): *A Basis for Practice: The Diploma Programme.* Cardiff: International Baccalaureate.

IB (2004): *Strategic Plan of the International Baccalaureate Organization (April 2004).* Online: www.ibo.org/mission/strategy/documents/sp2004.pdf (last accessed 29 August 2011).

IB (2006): *From Growth to Access: Developing an IBO access strategy (September 2006).* Online: www.ibo.org/mission/strategy/documents/FromGrowthtoAccess.pdf (last accessed 29 August 2011).

IB (2011a): *IB Fast Facts.* Online: www.ibo.org/facts/fastfacts/index.cfm (last accessed 29 August 2011).

IB (2011b): *The IB Diploma Programme Statistical Bulletin: May 2009 examination session.* Online: www.ibo.org/facts/statbulletin/dpstats/documents/May2009Statisticalbulletin.pdf (last accessed 29 August 2011).

IB (2011c): *The IB Diploma Programme Statistical Bulletin: May 2010 examination session.* Online: www.ibo.org/facts/statbulletin/dpstats/documents/May2010Statisticalbulletin.pdf (last accessed 29 August 2011).

Lewis, C (2006): International but not global: how international school curricula fail to address global issues and how this must change, in *International Schools Journal*, 25 (2), pp51-67.

Mott, P (2009): IB Part 2, in *The International Educator*, 24 (2), p19.

Oliver, A (2006): Access all areas, in *IB World*, 48, pp10-11.

Peterson, A (1972): *The International Baccalaureate: An Experiment in International Education* (First Edition). London: George G Harrap & Co Ltd.

Tarc, P (2009): *Global Dreams, Enduring Tensions: International Baccalaureate in a Changing World*. New York: Peter Lang.

Toze, D (2008): Concerns about IB exam results undermining confidence in program, in *The International Educator*, 23 (2), p6.

Walker, G (2004): *Helping to create an effective school. IBLA regional conference: Buenos Aires: 26 November 2004.* Online (last accessed 29 August 2011): www.ibo.org/dg/emeritus/speeches/documents/ibla_nov04.pdf

Walker, G (2005a): *Looking back and looking forward: the next 30 years. Plenary Address to the IBNA Annual Regional Conference, Montréal, Québec, Canada, 9 July 2005.* Online: www.ibo.org/dg/emeritus/speeches/documents/ibna_jul05.pdf (last accessed 29 August 2011).

Walker, G (2005b): Research and the IBO strategic plan, in *IB Research Notes*, 5 (2) pp11-13. Online: www.ibo.org/programmes/research/publications/documents/notesjuly05.pdf (last accessed 29 August 2011).

Walker, G (2011): Introduction: past, present, and future, in G Walker (ed) *The Changing Face of International Education: Challenges for the IB*. Cardiff: International Baccalaureate, pp1-18.

Westcott, R (2009): Pareto Analysis, in *Quality Progress*, 42 (1), pp22-23.

Chapter 11

Growth of the international school market in China and its potential implications for the IB

Barry Drake

Introduction

Much has been written in the last decade about the intriguing growth in the number and variety of international schools, and many researchers believe future expansion will be exponential in specific areas of the world – particularly Asia. This chapter seeks to add to the discourse through a consideration of the conundrums posed by changes to the international school market in China (PRC) and by offering some thoughts on the impact such developments may have on the International Baccalaureate (IB). The basic challenge may be stated simply. Until very recently government regulations, as well as a restricted expatriate and domestic middle class demand for international education, have combined to hinder the growth on the Chinese mainland of the international school market in general, and the expansion of IB programmes in particular. This historic landscape is set to change dramatically in the very near future.

Defining an international school

The absence of a clear and unambiguous definition of an international school significantly inhibits any discussion on the current and future size of the international school market worldwide, let alone as it relates to a country such as China. This is not, of course, a new dilemma. Indeed the debate on the nature of international schools has engaged the minds of many educators for upwards of 30 years without, it has to be said, having made a great deal of progress. In 1997, when this author was completing his PhD in international education, he noted that there was 'considerable divergence of opinion over what makes a school "international" (Gellar, 1981; Matthews, 1989; Jonietz and Harris, 1991; Hayden and Thompson, 1995) as, indeed there is over the relationship between an "international school" and "international education" (Belle-Isle, 1986; Hill, 1994; Hayden and Thompson, 1995)'. What most of these writers agreed upon was that it 'would be dangerous to assume that a school which designates itself "international" will, by definition, deliver an international education. Nor can it be asserted with any degree of conviction that "international education" can only be provided, *de facto*, by an "international school"' (Drake, 1998: 4). From the perspective of 1997, at least, it seemed that any attempt to create a single definition of an international school was fraught with difficulties and, perhaps, destined to failure.

Some writers attempted to tackle the challenge by creating taxonomies of international schools based on a variety of broad observable features. Leach made, perhaps, the first published attempt to classify international schools using this approach (Leach, 1969), which was later expanded upon by Sanderson (1981) and (Pönisch, 1987). Matthews (1988) offered a further set of criteria and posited that international schools could effectively be located in two broad domains: those that were market driven and those that were ideologically driven. Gellar (1993) and Hayden and Thompson (1995) have suggested that this view is a rather narrow one since, clearly, market driven international schools may at the same time be ideologically driven. Hill (1994) continued the debate by insisting that it was necessary to distinguish between international and national schools. An international school, Hill claimed, was one where 'students and staff are representative of a number of different cultures and ethnic origins, where the IB and/or a number of different national courses are offered and where the ethos is one of internationalism as distinct from nationalism'. For many writers at the end of the 20th century this notion seemed to hold the key to an acceptable definition of an international school. 'For surely an "international school" must provide an "international education" .... however an "international education" cannot simply mean an international academic curriculum such as the IB or IGCSE but in the words of Peterson (1987) is a programme in which international understanding is developed.' (Drake, 1998: 9)

With the substantial growth in the number and style of international schools around the world in the first decade of the 21st century, attempts to define the concept of an international school have become ever more challenging. Wylie, for one, suggests that the term 'international' is in fact unhelpful since '[s]chools have called themselves "international" without paying attention to what it means' (Wylie, 2008 reflecting on Gellar, 2002). One potential way forward, Wylie suggests, is to accept Gellar's proposal that there had been a paradigm shift by 2002 and that two types of 'international' schools could subsequently be distinguished: those that were internationally-minded and those that were not (Wylie, 2008).

Regretfully, many of the attempts made to date to chart a clearer understanding of the international school movement have been predicated on 'value judgements' rooted in late 20th century Anglo-centric idealised constructs of a 'genuine' international school (Ritter, 2011) rather than on the reality of current practice. In these circumstances, there remains no universally accepted set of criteria to help define, list and analyse the international school movement.

Whilst this debate remains of intriguing academic interest, there is a more important concrete reason to reach a common understanding of what an international school is. A working definition is clearly essential to scaffold analysis of the growth of the market and the potential impacts of such growth. In this context the Council of International Schools (CIS) offers practical support to researchers by providing a list of registered international schools based on a screening system for schools wishing to be added to their database and website. The criteria used by CIS continue to hold to the concept of international schools providing education grounded in international understanding:

> CIS Membership is conferred on a school that:
>
> 1. Clearly demonstrates international mindedness and actively promotes international awareness in its students.
> 2. Applies the CIS code of ethics.
> 3. Is willing to undertake an external school improvement process.
> (CIS, 2010)

Given the very specific nature of these criteria 'one must assume that some schools are included ... whose claims to international school status must be dubious, while other "true" international schools might not be listed' (MacDonald, 2006: 196). CIS's website currently lists 642 international schools registered with the organisation, a total considerably lower than the number listed by ISC Research Ltd who use a very different definition of an international school. As one of the leading providers of data on international schools, ISC have adopted a very broad practical definition: 'ISC has no involvement in determining standards in international education. The aim is simply to provide comprehensive, up to date data about the English-medium international school world. If a school delivers a curriculum to any combination of infant, primary or secondary students, wholly or partly in English outside an English speaking country, then it is included in ISC systems.' (ISC, 2011a). ISC systems are value-free in that users are free to apply their own criteria to filter lists of schools using any combination of geography, age, range, size, curriculum, examinations, membership of international school associations and so on. Given the flexibility such data provides for researchers, the following analysis will draw heavily upon information provided by that group.

Growth of international school numbers

Whilst ISC figures, based on the criteria articulated above, are invaluable they do need to be handled with some caution in that:

> a) they intentionally avoid making value judgements as to whether any given school deserves to be placed on their lists as a 'genuine' international school, other than by the application of their broad criteria. This imperative inevitably leads to significantly higher figures for the total numbers of current and projected international schools than would be recorded by organisations using much more restrictive sets of criteria, such as those described above for CIS;
>
> b) the ISC figures do not include other types of international schools who deliver the curriculum through languages other than English (such as

French, German, Japanese, Korean): 'The 400 French and 120 German international schools generally deliver the curriculum in French or German and are therefore not included in ISC figures.' (Brummitt, 2011b).

What does the current and future landscape look like in terms of numbers? The international school worldwide 'family' has been estimated to have grown from around 50 schools in 1964 to approximately 1000 in 1995 (Hayden and Thompson, 1995). Eleven years ago the number had grown to 2584 (ISC, 2011b) and by 2010 there were 5676 schools, 43 percent of them offering international curricula (ISC, 2011a). The ISC website notes that the number of international schools had grown again by May 2011 to 5788 and further predicts that there will be 11,000 schools with five million students by 2020 (ISC, 2011b). Clearly any paper discussing the growth of international schools will inevitably be providing out of date figures by the time it goes to press. The growth rate articulated above is remarkable, but a further word of caution is required. When writers were discussing the number of international schools in existence in the late 20th century it is likely that they were using a more restricted and value laden set of criteria by which to define an international school than the definition in use by ISC in more recent times. The utilisation of such significantly different qualifiers could distort perceived growth rates.

How does China fit into this growth model? The ISC website in July 2011 listed 306 international schools plus a further 164 in Hong Kong (ISC, 2011c). Of these schools 90, or 32 percent, offered full or part of an international curriculum (ISC, 2011b), ISC also records that there were 63 IB schools in China, 23 percent of the total (Brummitt, 2011a). In Hong Kong there were 49 IB schools or 33 percent of the total number of international schools (Brummitt, 2011a). The ISC forecast for the worldwide international school growth rate is that, by 2020, numbers will have virtually doubled from the 2011 position. The raw percentage growth rate calculated for the period is 90 percent. Extrapolating from this forecast to the international schools market in China, the indications are that there would be at least 581 international schools in China by 2020 and that the number in Hong Kong would grow to 312. The same unadjusted ISC percentage growth projection applied to the number of IB schools would suggest a rise in China to 120 schools by 2020 from the current 63. This would be an increase of 57 new schools, and a further 44 new IB schools for Hong Kong could be projected.

However, China's international school growth rate is likely to be even more marked than the world growth rate. How does one explain this? Tristan Bunnell has recently adapted Walt Whitman Rostow's model of economic growth to the IB and suggested that the organisation is moving towards the Rostovian stage 5: the age of high mass consumption (Bunnell, 2011). Applying Bunnell's approach to the growth of international schools worldwide, and to China in particular, one might argue that whilst Hong Kong is already at stage 5, the rest of China is operating on the cusp of stages 3 and 4: between the 'take off' and the 'drive for maturity' stages. In this phase it would be natural to expect faster rates of growth for certain sectors of the economy than would be the case in stage 5. The phase that currently China finds itself in typically sees levels of poverty significantly reduced and rising standards of living. To apply ISC world growth projections to China and Hong Kong without making any adjustments to account for differing economic contexts can only present, at best, a low-end forecast. Indeed, ISC itself acknowledges that its forecasts for growth in China are 'very conservative' (ISC, 2011a) as, according to ISC, already in 2011 one thousand schools have begun registration to commence operations as international schools in China. Even this pales into insignificance compared to the 3000 international schools that a government spokesperson alluded to at the 2006 Alliance for International Education conference in Shanghai (Brummitt, 2007: 38).

The changing profile of international schools

It might have been difficult to reach agreement on an academic definition of what an international school was in the late 20th century, but all who worked in these schools knew what they were! They were generally small, family orientated, non-profit making institutions, often set up by parents (Hayden and Thompson, 2011: 86) catering to a largely transient expatriate population with 80 percent of the student body being expatriate (ISC, 2011a). They employed largely expatriate teachers, teaching a curriculum in English (or sometimes in other languages such as French or German) drawn from the 'home country', though with a few 'pace setters' experimenting with 'new' (at the time) and exciting international programmes such as the IB.

How has this profile changed? In some parts of the world international schools still cater exclusively for expatriate children, but the student clientele profile in most international schools is being ever more shaped by children from the local middle class families (ISC, 2011b). These days the typical international school is likely to have only 20 percent expatriate children and 80 percent local students (ISC, 2011a). Furthermore, the new international school market is increasingly characterised by proprietary, profit making, organisational structures (single, or corporate ownership), often part of a larger regional or worldwide educational group such as GEMS or Cognita (Hayden and Thompson, 2011: 86). As far as learning and teaching are concerned, the IB has established itself as the curriculum provider of choice for most of the international school market still catering to expatriate children but, in some parts of the world, the IB remains under-represented: in China, for instance, schools offering the IB account for only 23 percent of the total number of international schools on the mainland (Brummitt, 2011a). Other international curriculum structures being aggressively marketed in China are the Cambridge International General Certificate of Secondary Education (IGCSE) and international A level programmes, as well as the AP programme and various Australian and Canadian curriculum options. Despite all the differences described above that contribute to the changing international school landscape, the one constant is the teaching body. International school teachers are still being drawn in the main from the USA, Canada, the UK, Australia and New Zealand (Hayden and Thompson, 2011).

In discussing the range of international schools now available in China, one is immediately reminded of how dangerous it is to generalise about anything in a country so vast and disparate. There is really not one China but many. There is really not one Chinese culture but a number of interlocking cultures, and so on. Consequently, all attempts to offer crude generalisations about the organisational models that characterise the international school market in China are sure to miss their mark. The challenge is magnified by the inclusion of Hong Kong in such a discourse.

The Hong Kong educational market has already reached a higher stage of development characterised by Rostow as high mass consumption, and is further defined by a predilection to conspicuous consumption (Bagwell and Bernheim, 1996) which, amongst other things, encourages increasing proportions of local Chinese families to place their children in international schools, partially because fees are so high (to be further discussed below). Hong Kong has the full range of international schools and arguably more 'internationally minded international schools' (Gellar, 2002: 31) than any other city in the world. At the top end of the market in reputational terms (including Canadian International School, Chinese International School, Discovery College, the English Schools Foundation, Hong Kong International School and Renaissance College) the schools are large, non-profit-making, employ mostly expatriate teachers, have a student body that is mostly local, and virtually all are now ideologically committed to IB programmes. There is in fact little variety available to parents in the Hong Kong market. A number of international schools linked to a home nation curriculum exist: Korean, Japanese, Australian, French, German-Swiss, but a number of these also have adopted the IB. Virtually all of the international schools in Hong Kong have been created as stand-alone educational institutions. The major exception is the English Schools Foundation (ESF), which represents one of the largest power blocks within Hong Kong and is set to become an increasingly important voice in the IB movement. The ESF has five large secondary schools offering the Diploma Programme and IGCSE/GCSE, nine primary schools offering the IB Primary Years Programme (PYP), one special needs school, two independent schools (linked to ESF but run semi-independently) offering all three IB programmes (PYP, MYP and DP), and four kindergartens (ESF, 2011). A recent development reflecting new directions in educational organisation on the mainland is that of the franchised Harrow boarding school due to open in the near future.

On the mainland the international schools are, like the economy, at a different stage of Rostovian development to those in Hong Kong. The demand for international schools in the past was limited both by the size of the domestic middle class and by the restrictions on foreigners living and working in China.

As the economy was opened up, so a number of the older style international schools made their appearance to cater for the transient expatriate population. There are still relatively few international schools in the country. Bunnell notes, for instance, that '[t]here are as many IB schools in Buenos Aires as there are in the whole of China' and that '[t]here are more MYP schools in Chicago than in China' (Bunnell, 2011: 172). This situation is set to change.

Currently no single organisational model dominates the international school market. Instead there is a very wide spectrum of types of international school, but the key features of the new landscape are size and the dominance of profit-making imperative. In terms of size, whilst many of the older style international schools catering for expatriate populations remain small, there is an understandable tendency in a country such as China towards the economies of scale to be gained from 'size'. Of course everything is much bigger in China, but many of the international schools catering for both expatriates and local children fit into the large school category, and some of the new educational organisations are enormous. Take for instance the China Bilingual Technology and Education Group, which announced earlier in the year that applicants for its two schools had doubled from 4800 to 9600 for school year 2010-11. The school operates two K-12 private boarding schools with a total enrolment of 10,000 students! The schools are located in Shanxi and Sichuan Provinces and 'provide students with an innovative and high quality education with a focus on fluency and cultural skills in both Chinese and English' (GlobeNewswire, 2011).

Regarding the issue of 'for profit' schooling, ISC estimates that two thirds of the international schools in mainland China are owned by private Chinese individuals and business groups (Brummitt, 2011a). The other third are foreign owned and include a handful of schools that are non-profit making trusts such as Western Academy of Beijing, International School of Beijing, Shanghai American School, International School of Tianjin or nominally non-profit making such as Wellington School in Tianjin. The vast majority of the 306 international schools currently listed by ISC (ISC, 2011c) have been established, at least in part, as business ventures. Risking the danger of over-generalising, one might identify two broad categories of schools: firstly those offering international education to largely expatriate children. Subsections of this spectrum would include old style international schools, and new style entrepreneurial international schools including the developing niche market in franchising British private school models such as Dulwich, Wellington and Harrow. The second broad category would be local schools offering English language education and/or a foreign curriculum (including AP, A level and the IB) delivered in English to Chinese, and occasionally foreign, students in stand-alone or sections of local schools. Here also the spectrum is extensive, ranging from highly ideological enterprises such as Alcanta International College with its United World College personnel connections and aspirations, to prestigious national schools such as the Beijing National Day School, China Bilingual

Technology and Education Group, and organisations such as U-Link who have established Cambridge International A level centres at a number of locations around China. The government itself helps delineate the two categories of schools by laying down a legal framework by which foreign-owned international schools in China can offer places to expatriate students only, while schools owned by locals can offer places to both local and expatriate students.

Yamato and Bray described the educational landscape they saw in Shanghai in 2006 in the following terms: '[i]n particular, international schools and international divisions of Chinese schools catered respectively for a) internationally mobile English language families, b) returning expatriate Chinese whose Chinese language skills were limited and whose children found total Chinese immersion too stressful and c) overseas Chinese seeking a Chinese international education.' (2006: 72). What they did not describe in 2006 was the burgeoning demand from a growing Chinese middle class who increasingly wish to have an English language education for their children; nor were the needs identified of other expatriate nationalities whose first language is not English but whose families find themselves in China as a result of increasing economic globalisation (discussed further below).

What is driving this growth in China?

The answer to this question, received wisdom suggests, lies in the worldwide growth of the middle class, with some estimates suggesting that 'by 2030 1.2 billion people in developing countries – 15 percent of world population – will belong to a "global middle class", up from 4000 million today' (World Bank 2007, cited in Bates, 2011:1). Given its size and the pace of its prodigious recent economic development, it is highly probable that a significant proportion of this new middle class will be located in China. Already the Chinese economy ranks number 2 in the world, having moved up from fourth place in 2006 (Hutton, 2006). It seems set to overtake the USA during the next decade to become the world's largest economy, and most analysts have concluded that the 21st century will be dominated by the Chinese (Hutton, 2006). What has happened in China has been little short of astounding, and the enormity of some of the bald statistics generated by such growth is difficult to internalise. For instance, between 1981 and 2001 alone the proportion of the Chinese population living in poverty fell from 53 percent to eight percent, and that involved 400 million people! (Hutton, 2006: 7).

With so many people emerging from poverty and beginning to have access to hitherto unknown wealth, the platform for an emergent and powerful Chinese middle class was established. It is currently estimated that 23 percent of the Chinese population can be defined as middle class, up from 15 percent in 2001. By 2020 one forecast indicates that there will be 700 million people in the Chinese middle class, representing 48 percent of the 2020 predicted population (Euromonitor International, 2011). As with other countries in the world whose economies have gone through this Rostovian stage of growth, it is inevitable that the new middle class in China will seek to seize every opportunity that presents itself to provide better educational opportunities for their children; especially given the cultural premium placed in China on planning for the long term and on education in particular. Already China has seen its middle class wealth grow to the point where there is sufficient demand to reconfigure the international educational market away from being one dominated by a foreign elite to one that affords conspicuous opportunities for the aspiring *nouveau riche* (Bates, 2011) and allows affluent middle class families access to 'quality education in a wider range of schools (which is) ... a commodity now within their means, given the prevalence of one-child families ... and increasing income levels' (Forse, 2010: 72).

As a result of such developments worldwide there have been significant changes in the profile of students attending international schools. In the early days of the international school movement 80 percent of the students were expatriate children. Today these proportions have been reversed and only 20 percent of students are expatriate, with the other 80 percent being local students (ISC, 2011a). This trend is being replicated in China. What is it that attracts the new middle classes of China, including Hong Kong, to the international school market? Amongst other things, such education is seen as a stepping stone to tertiary education, particularly overseas (Forse, 2010: 71). Moreover, some '[p]arents in China's new middle and upper classes ... [send] their children to receive private school education to give them an advantage in China's increasingly competitive workforce' (GlobeNewswire, 2011). Other parents are attracted by the perceived quality of learning and teaching to be experienced in international school education (ISC, 2011b). Certainly many parents feel that international education offers a better model than national education. Then Minister of Education in South Australia Greg Crafter suggested that international curriculum, worldwide, is meeting a shortfall in local systems inviting schools to go 'international' to provide students and teachers with the opportunity to grow in a way that is simply not available within the national system (in Wylie, 2008: 6), while Forse claims that many Chinese learners are anxious to benefit from a 'liberal education in English-speaking international schools which will best equip them for the type of career to which they aspire' (Forse, 2010: 72). Furthermore, others including Jabal (2010: 75) argue that middle class parents may well 'believe that the global currency of international qualifications (*eg* the International Baccalaureate) makes its graduates more marketable than those schooled in the local curriculum' (Lowe 2000, cited by Jabal, 2010) or that middle class parents are concerned with the direction of public education (Bruce 2004; Dowson *et al*, 2003, cited in Jabal, 2010). Finally in both Hong Kong, and to a lesser but growing extent mainland China, the middle and upper classes are active exponents of Veblen's conspicuous consumption (as noted above) and, as MacDonald suggests, 'experience shows that many clients actually view price as an indicator of quality and therefore higher prices can actually increase the appeal of an international school in the eyes of some customers' (2006: 205). International education may well be pursued by the middle and upper class in Hong Kong, and increasingly in China, because it is expensive and admission for one's child at one of the more prestigious schools ostentatiously locates the family's place in society.

Living proof of these rationalisations can be seen in Hong Kong, at virtually all the top international schools. Take the ESF as an example. Though the organisation began as providers of British-style international education to largely expatriate children, the majority of places at the schools are now held by local children. At least 50 percent of the students are now local Chinese. 'Of the Chinese families that take up the school spaces, approximately 10 percent are ethnically Chinese and "purely local", carrying only Special Administrative Region (SAR) travel documents and never having living abroad. Another 30 percent of the total enrolment consists of overseas Chinese who went abroad for study, work or foreign passports, leading to the handover of rule from the British to the Chinese in 1997. Still another 10 percent are Eurasian, normally with one Chinese parent and with either local or overseas backgrounds.' (Forse, 2010: 60). A similar point is made by Jabal (2010: 75).

Demand is clearly driving supply and, in a part of the world where there is no shortage of entrepreneurs (at least in the 21st century), the potential profitability of education as a business is helping to shape the new international school landscape in China, as it is in Asia in general as well as in the Middle East (MacDonald, 2006). 'Increasingly entrepreneurs recognise that the public's dissatisfaction with one-size-fits all schools is more than just fodder for political debates. It is a tremendous business opportunity.' (Lips, 2000, cited in Bates, 2011:1).

Challenges posed by this growth

One might first ask if these growth rates are sustainable. MacDonald postulates that: 'Though the reasons for growth have not been proven, it seems reasonable to assume that international school growth rates and international trade growth rates are correlated to a degree, as international schools are clearly a natural stepchild of international business and provide a vital piece of international business infrastructure.' (MacDonald, 2006: 206). If this argument is valid then, as the growth of international trade begins to level off in the future, surely the demand for international schools will eventually slow down? In Hong Kong, where both the general state of the economy and the international school market is at a higher stage of Rostovian development than mainland China, one might imagine that the growth in demand for international school education would indeed be set to slow down in the near future. However, as Forse has posited, the Hong Kong middle and upper classes see international school education as superior to that offered in the local system, and the demand for places in the territory's international schools shows no sign of abating (Forse, 2010). On the other hand, as mainland China is at an earlier stage of Rostovian development there would appear to be many more years of growth ahead. Moreover, depending on how the Chinese government responds to increasing demand for access for local students to international schools that are currently reserved for expatriates, mainland China could experience an even greater boost to demand of the sort that has occurred in Thailand and Hong Kong where locals are allowed into all international schools (Hayden and Thompson, 2011).

If one accepts that the growth in international schools will be sustained in both mainland China and Hong Kong for some time to come, then one of the biggest challenges facing international schools, and in particular that section of the market that provides IB programmes, will be the recruitment and training of suitably qualified teachers. As ISC notes, the biggest challenge facing international schools worldwide today is '[n]ot only to meet the demand of students, but also to maintain the high quality standards that most international schools currently hold' (ISC, 2011b): 'Currently there are 250,000 fully qualified teachers working in international schools and that number is anticipated to rise to close to 500,000 by 2020 to meet the demand of increased student intake and additional new schools.' (ISC, 2011b). Herein lies the fundamental challenge of recruitment, retention and training. Where are these additional teachers going to come from and what are the specific issues for China?

ISC has forecast a 90 percent growth rate in the number of operational international schools worldwide between 2011 and 2020 to a projected 11,000 (ISC, 2011a). ISC has further estimated this growth would require a 96 percent rise in the number of international teachers available to staff these schools by 2020 (ISC, 2011a). ISC statistics indicate a raw average of 45 teachers employed per school. Applying these unadjusted average world forecasts to China and Hong Kong would suggest that the number of international schools operating in China by 2020 might grow to 581 from the current 306 (www.iscresearch.com/international-schools-around-the-world/). Similarly, in Hong Kong the number of international schools could be expected to grow from 164 today (ISC, 2011d) to 312 by 2020. Whilst once again some caution needs to be exercised in calculations that treat China and Hong Kong as if they are likely to experience the same growth patterns, it is interesting to note that using the basic, unfiltered ISC growth figures, such developments described above would call for 12,375 new international school teachers in China to service the estimated 275 new schools that would come on line by 2020. In Hong Kong 6660 new international school teachers would be needed to staff the 148 new schools anticipated by 2020.

Whilst such growth in the demand for international school teachers may seem like another very real business opportunity for recruiting organisations such as Search Associates, CIS and International Schools Services (ISS), there is a very real challenge here given the general international teacher supply problems (Hayden and Thompson, 2011) and the current difficulty in persuading large numbers of international school teachers to opt for employment in mainland China. These recruitment challenges would certainly be compounded by a) the need for specific curriculum training in those schools offering programmes such as the IB, AP and A level; and b) the need to offer sensitivity training for international school teachers destined to work in the new breeds of international schools where leadership and organisational cultures, let alone approaches to learning and teaching, may be radically different to that experienced as the 'norm' in the country of teacher recruitment or in the more traditional international schools (Hayden and Thompson, 2011; Drake, 2004; Ritter, 2011).

Challenges for the Diploma Programme

To drill down further on the challenges presented to the IB in the areas of recruitment and training, some fine tuning of the figures above is required. The IB is generally believed to be experiencing a 14 percent annual growth rate (Bunnell, 2011), which is higher than the ISC forecast annual growth for international schools in general. Applying the 14 percent compound growth rate to China would mean the number of IB schools on the mainland would grow to 205 by 2020 from the current 63 schools; an increase of 142 schools rather than the 57 schools noted above (the figure derived from an application of ISC unadjusted percentage growth rates). Such an expansion would require 6390 additional IB teachers! In Hong Kong, applying the same 14 percent growth rate would lead to 159 IB schools by 2020 – a rise of 110 requiring 4950 additional teachers. Further adjustments to these figures may well be needed for, as has already been noted, China is moving through a period of substantial economic growth and this will inevitably lead to greater expansion in the number of operational international schools than indicated by the raw figures above. Certainly the adjusted estimate of 11,340 additional IB-trained teachers needed to staff new IB schools alone on mainland China and in Hong Kong must be seen as a lower end figure, and if the 1000 new schools identified by ISC come on stream by 2020, let alone the possible 3000 new schools, the figures for new international school teachers required for both IB and non-IB schools in China and Hong Kong will, of course, increase substantially. Extrapolating from these projections, if 3000 new schools do come on stream to add to the 306 in place in July 2011, and the IB continues to maintain rather than increase its current 23 percent market share, then the number of IB schools on the mainland could reach 691 by 2020 – requiring 31,000 IB-trained teachers! The IB has naturally, as part of its strategic thinking, begun to plan for the increased future demand for training courses and quality assurance programmes by providing online facilities, outsourcing of workshops and accreditation visits and the like, but it is to be hoped that IB personnel have given due consideration to the true extent of the challenges generated by China's growth to a system that is already screaming overload.

Caveats do, however, need to be made regarding the potential growth of the IB in China. For a variety of reasons the IB has not made the same sort of expansion into China (or indeed the Middle East) as it has in other parts of the world (Bunnell, 2011). How do we account for this? It is perhaps useful to consider Gellar's (2002) concept of dividing international schools into those that pursue international understanding and those that do not, to help understand the apparent reticence of many Chinese founders of new international schools to adopt the IB. It could be that the majority of entrepreneurs establishing new schools in mainland China do not find philosophical affinity with the IB programmes and/or are wary of potential cultural dissonances with IB programmes that could create tensions for their schools (Drake, 2004). 'It is argued that the IB is overtly international at the content level but thoroughly "western" at the epistemological level' says Van Oord (2007). Moreover, as Hayden and Thompson argue: 'The institutional learning environment appropriate for the promotion of international-mindedness includes the centrality of an experiential learning approach to the development of the values associated with international education as promoted by many international schools. Indeed, the prevailing style of learning/teaching to be found in international schools worldwide is undoubtedly what might be described as a western liberal student-centred, constructivist approach which, while familiar to many of those recruited to teach in international schools, will pose challenges for those trained in a context where a more teacher-centred, didactic approach is the norm.' (2011: 89)

Another plausible factor inhibiting the uptake of the IB in mainland China's international schools is the current dominance of entrepreneurial structures. 'Though one would hope schools are ideologically driven, striving to manage their educational programme ahead of all else, those familiar with international schools (especially schools governed by business orientated boards or owners) might tend to agree with Richards' (1998) assessment that many schools articulate a philosophy grounded in the ideals of international education but remain, in reality, quite "market driven".' (MacDonald, 2006: 201). Even with the best will in the world '[t]ensions exist between pragmatism and ideology in the enactment of international education' (Wylie, 2008:14). In a culture of managing the bottom line it could be that many school owners in China reject the additional costs involved in delivering IB programmes, especially in those areas that may seem to the entrepreneurs to be interesting, but unnecessary, bolt-ons to the basic educational programme being offered. Such thinking could certainly apply to experiential or service learning programmes that lie at the heart of the IB. The IB may, in fact, be happy to accept a smaller expansion of its programmes in China than it is experiencing elsewhere in the world. However, if the IB is to maintain one of its current imperatives to develop 'greater influence among a broader body of students and a deeper scope of activity' (Bunnell, 2011: 170) then it will have to engage more pro-actively with the Chinese educational market and help persuade all concerned, through effective cost-benefit analysis, of the value of service and experiential learning and the like. Whatever the case, the IB will certainly have to accept the very practical challenge posed to its quality assurance frameworks by schools opening up in mainland China, which may wish to obfuscate their commitment to the IB's philosophical core in pursuit of profitability or, indeed, the accommodation of differing cultural perspectives.

This may well be more of a challenge than it might first appear, given the impact that international education and experiential service learning, in particular, can have on local culture and its value systems (Drake, 2004). International education, at least of the sort provided in those international schools promoting international understanding, inevitably impacts upon student value systems (Mattern, 1990; Ellwood and Davis, 1991; Bartlett, 1992; Charleson *et al* 2011). Whether or not values are being deliberately taught, they are a shared part of any community and will be passed on (Fail, 2011). Bernstein argues that schools are agents of cultural change and that all schools, irrespective of their context, are engaged in the socialisation of their pupils (1975: 37-8, cited in Wylie, 2008: 10). It would clearly be disingenuous to claim that values are not being 'taught' in international schools. What of the values espoused in the IB learner profile? What of the values inculcated through service learning? (Charleson *et al*, 2011; Brian and Drake, 2007). Clearly a value system is at the heart of both the informal and formal curriculum in IB schools, and many would argue that this system has a distinctly western liberal orientation. How far have Chinese entrepreneurs made conscious decisions as to which curriculum model they will buy into and, in doing so, have rejected the IB model as likely to produce unwelcome cultural tensions or the potential to divert student attention from the 'real' job of getting the results required to ensure entry to top universities worldwide? Where possible tension between philosophy and pragmatism exists, it could well be that the Chinese entrepreneurs choose pragmatism; hence the relatively low uptake on IB programmes on the mainland.

There has always been a tension between, on the one hand, the IB's mission to promote international education, international understanding and a particular western liberal set of values and, on the other hand, the IB providing a 'global quality-assured and branded certification process to an elite group of candidates' (Bunnell, 2011: 168-9). Such tensions have been exacerbated by the commercialisation of education around the world, which developments in China are set to further complicate. As noted above, the vast majority of international schools in China are run as business operations and with hundreds, perhaps thousands, more Chinese international schools coming on stream in the next ten years that will be established along the same organisational lines, this development must significantly impact the IB and its relationships with its schools. Bunnell noted in 2011 that the IB has already metamorphosed into a 'global brand' with the characteristics of 'other symbols of hyperglobalization' (2011: 166). One impact of this corporate development is that schools will increasingly see themselves as 'customers' rather than members of an elite international school fraternity. It is inevitable, given the 'commercialisation of education' in China, that schools will wish to locate their relationship with the IB within a business practice framework: in terms of, for instance, service providers and customers with the *leitmotiv* surely being 'customer satisfaction'; 'I am paying the bill, therefore I demand the appropriate service'. For after all, as Matthews and Sidhu note, '[m]arketised expressions of international education are ultimately disengaged from notions of a global public good' (2005, cited in Bates, 2011:17).

The sheer size of this potential China growth factor must increase the challenges for the IB. If the number of international schools in China were to stay at the current level then, perhaps, the IB would not need to be so concerned about the 'demands' of Chinese IB schools. But as noted above, that simply is not going to happen. Size and exponential growth are surely part of the new defining features of the Chinese market.

If ISC projections for future growth of international schools in China are correct, and there appears to be no reason why they should not be, then it will be a relatively short time before the Chinese cohort make up the largest group of international schools worldwide as well as providing an increasingly important proportion of the total number of IB schools worldwide. Education will continue to be seen as an exciting business opportunity in China, as it is elsewhere in the world. Chinese 'edupreneurs' know that 'learning and profit are not mutually exclusive' and will continue to 'strike a balance between being cost-conscious and providing high-quality learning experiences. If they cut costs to the detriment of quality, they [know] they will lose customers' (Lips, 2000). However, they will certainly see international education through their own particular cultural and business lens, and will have a clear idea of their specific customer-service-provider needs, which the IB will be forced to accommodate if it wishes to develop its share of the China market. The China schools will certainly represent a coherent power block that cannot be ignored, particularly if they unite through a broader version of the current ACAMIS group (Association of Chinese and Mongolian International Schools: an organisation for the international schools that currently serves the expatriate population). Furthermore, within this larger power block it is possible to envisage sub-power blocks emerging similar in size to some educational organisations such as the ESF in Hong Kong. The parallel groups on the mainland might be franchised schools such as Dulwich and Wellington, or schools connected to international educational organisations such as GEMS, whilst the sheer capaciousness of some of the national schools running international programmes may also propel them into such sub-power blocks.

Conclusion

In many of the traditional centres of international school power, such as the IB Heads and Regional Committees, there remains a rose-coloured-spectacled approach to remembering the past. The landscape fondly recalled is that of an idyllic, tranquil, rural, 'European' countryside, with low level, simple cottage-style housing, neatly arranged around the village square. Everything ordered, and in its place. Everyone known to each other, in a secure, enriching environment shaped by a warm, caring community of like-minded individuals. That landscape has been replaced, many would argue, by a bleak, menacing megalopolis, characterised by high-rise accommodation inhabited by 'others' who do not share the same histories or cultures. The new landscape encapsulates stress, ill-considered haste, unrestricted growth and a total absence of coherent town planning! For many the mourning, indeed grieving, over the lost past continues.

It is time to move on and accept that the international landscape has irrevocably changed, and to seize the opportunities presented by new challenges. Indeed, one is reminded of the major inhibitors to late 19th century progress in China. At a time when Japan was steaming ahead with modernisation, in China far too many people continued to subscribe to the Confucian logic which held that the 'golden age' lay in the past, rather than in the future. In such circumstances reception to innovation was at best lukewarm; China failed to make the parallel progress being made in Japan and, as a result, succumbed to rampant western imperialism. The future development of international schools in China will clearly provide both the IB and China (including Hong Kong) with a range of important challenges. Neither the organisation nor the country can afford to take these challenges lightly. As with 19th century China, what is needed for progress to occur is acceptance of the belief that the 'golden age' lies not in the past but in the future (Wright, 1978). The Chinese have always taken the education of their children very seriously. It is vital that they play a significant part in selecting the architecture that will shape the future of international schooling and international education in their country, rather than allow some postmodern, culturally imperialist, model to be foisted upon them. The IB on the other hand must actively engage with the Chinese educational market, and seek to understand why its programmes are under-represented there at present and whether more could, or should, be done to persuade Chinese entrepreneurs of the advantages of a genuinely international education. Conversely, the IB may have to moderate some of its existing philosophical imperatives in order better to 'ride the Chinese wave' but, even without seeking to enhance their market share, the IB will need to envision its future in China very carefully and, one hopes, plan strategically in order to manage the inevitable tensions caused by issues of size, cultural dissonance and organisational style. This can only be done effectively if the Chinese are engaged as equal partners.

References

Bagwell, L S & Bernheim, B (1996): Veblen: effects of conspicuous consumption, in *The American Economic Review*, 86 (3) p349: ABI/INFORM Global.

Bartlett, K (1992): Defining international school education: a proposal for the future, in *International Schools Journal*, 23, pp45-52.

Bates, R (2011): Introduction, in R Bates (ed), *Schooling Internationally. Globalisation, internationalisation and the future of international schools.* Abingdon: Routledge.

Belle-Isle, R (1986): Learning for a new humanism, in *International Schools Journal*, 11, pp27-30.

Bernstein, B (1975): *Class, Codes and Control: Towards a Theory of Educational Transmissions.* London: Routledge and Kegan Paul.

Brian, D & Drake, B (2007): Taking students out of their comfort zones, in *is Magazine*, pp29-31.

Bruce, N (2004): Don't plan to bring home the bacon with ham-fisted reforms, in *South China Morning Post.* Hong Kong, 18 December 2004.

Brummitt, N (2007): International Schools: exponential growth and future implications, in *International Schools Journal*, XXVII (I), pp35-40.

Brummitt, N (2011a): Personal communication with Nick Brummitt, 29 June 2011.

Brummitt, N (2011b): Personal communication with Nick Brummitt, 11 July 2011.

Bunnell, T (2011): The International Baccalaureate; its growth and complexity of challenges, in R Bates (ed), *Schooling Internationally. Globalisation, internationalisation and the future of international schools.* Abingdon: Routledge, pp165-181.

Charleson, C, Moxley, T and Batten, D (2011): 21st century learning: community and service in the MYP, in M Hayden and J Thompson (eds), *Taking the MYP Forward.* Woodbridge: John Catt, pp95-118.

CIS (2010): *2010-11 School Membership Criteria.* Revised October 2010, Petersfield: Council of International Schools.

Drake, B (1998): *The Development of Effective Pastoral Care in an International School.* University of Bath: PhD.

Drake, B (2004): International education and IB programmes: worldwide expansion and potential cultural dissonance, in *Journal of Research in International Education*, 4 (2), pp189-205.

Downson, C, Bodycott, P, Walker, A and Coniam, D (2003): *Continuing Education Reform in Hong Kong: Issues of contextualization.* Hong Kong: Education Policy Analysis Archives, p11.

Ellwood, C and Davis, M (1991): An international curriculum for the middle school years, in *International Schools Journal*, 27, pp46-55.

ESF – English Schools Foundation (2011): Online: www.esf.edu.hk/ (last accessed 30 August 2011).

Euromonitor International (2011): Online (last accessed 21 July 2011): http://bbs.chinadaily.com.cn/viewthread.php?tid=674086

Fail, H (2011): Teaching and learning in international schools: a consideration of the stakeholders and their expectations, in R Bates (ed), *Schooling Internationally. Globalisation, internationalisation and the future of international schools.* Abingdon: Routledge, pp101-120.

Forse, C (2010): Fit for purpose? Why Chinese families choose international schools in Hong Kong, in J Ryan and G Slethaug (eds), *International Education and the Chinese Learner*. Hong Kong: Hong Kong University Press, pp59-72.

Gellar, C A (1981): International Education: Some thoughts on what it is and what it might be, in *International Schools Journal*, 1, pp21-26.

Gellar, C A (1993): How international are we?, in *International Schools Journal*, 26, pp5-7.

Gellar, C A (2002): International education: a commitment to universal values, in M Hayden, J Thompson and G Walker (eds), *International Education in Practice*. London: Kogan Page, pp30-9.

GlobeNewswire (2011): News Release, 25 January 2011. Online (last accessed 4 September 2011): www.msnbc.msn.com/id/41257664/ns/business-press_releases/t/china-bilingual-new-student-applications-double---school-year/

Hayden, M C and Thompson J J (1995): International schools and international education, in *Oxford Review of Education*, 21 (3), pp327-345.

Hayden, M C and Thompson J J (2011): Teachers for the international school of the future, in R Bates (ed), *Schooling Internationally. Globalisation, internationalisation and the future of international schools*. Abingdon: Routledge, pp83-100.

Hill, I (1994): *The International Baccalaureate: Policy Process in Education*. University of Tasmania: PhD thesis.

Hutton, W (2006): *The writing on the wall. Why we must embrace China as a partner or face it as an enemy*. New York: Free Press.

ISC (2011a): *The changing face of international schools: historical growth, current overview and future prospects*. ACAMIS presentation at the CIS Administrators Conference, March 2011.

ISC (2011b): February newsletter.

ISC (2011c): Online: http://iscresearch.com/ (last accessed 30 August 2011).

ISC (2011d): Online: www.iscresearch.com/international-schools-around-the-world/ (last accessed 30 August 2011).

Jabal, E (2010): Being, Becoming, and Belonging: Exploring Hong Kong-Chinese student experiences of the social realities of international schooling, in J Ryan and G Slethaug (eds), *International Education and the Chinese Learner*. Hong Kong: Hong Kong University Press, pp73-88.

Jonietz, P L and Harris, N D (eds) (1991): *World Yearbook of Education 1991: International schools and international education*. London: Kogan Page.

Leach, R J (1969): *International schools and their role in the field of international education*. Oxford: Pergamon Press.

Lips, C (2000): Edupreneurs: a survey of for-profit education, in *Policy Analysis*, 386: pp1-29. Online: www.cato.org/pubs/pas/pa386.pdf (last accessed 4 August 2011).

Lowe, J (2000): Assessment and educational quality: implications for international schools, in M Hayden and J Thompson (eds), *International Schools and International Education*. Sterling VA: Stylus Publishing, pp15-28.

MacDonald, J (2006): The international school industry: Examining international schools through an economic lens, in *Journal of Research in International Education*, 5 (2), pp191-214.

Matthews, J and Sidhu, R (2005): Desperately seeking the global subject: international education, citizenship and cosmopolitanism, in *Globalisation, Societies and Education*, 3 (1), pp49-66.

Matthews, M (1988): *The Ethos of International Schools.* University of Oxford: MSc thesis.

Matthews, M (1989): The uniqueness of international education, in *International Schools Journal,* 18, pp24-34.

Mattern, G (1990): The best of times, the worst of times and what to do about it on a Monday morning, in *International Schools Journal,* 19, pp35-47.

Peterson, A D C (1987): *Schools across frontiers.* La Salle Illinois: Open Court.

Pönisch, A (1987): *Special Needs and the International Baccalaureate. A study of the Need for and Development of Alternative Courses to the International Baccalaureate.* University of Oxford: MSc thesis.

Ritter, J (2011): Personal communication with a Senior Associate of Search Associates International Teacher Recruitment, 6 August 2011.

Ryan, J and Slethaug G (eds) (2010): *International Education and the Chinese Learner.* Hong Kong: Hong Kong University Press.

Sanderson, J (1981): *International School: The 'Mobile' Pupil and his Educational Needs.* University of Oxford: MSc thesis.

Van Oord, L (2007): To westernize the nations? An analysis of the International Baccalaureate's philosophy of education, in *Cambridge Journal of Education,* 37 (3), pp375-390.

Wright, M (1978): *The last stand of Chinese Conservatism: The T'ung-Chih restoration, 1862-1874.* Stanford: Stanford University Press.

Wylie, M (2008): Internationalizing curriculum: Framing theory and practice in international schools, in *Journal of Research in International Education,* 7 (1), pp5-20.

Yamato, Y and Bray, M (2006): Economic development and the market place for education: dynamics of the international schools sector in Shanghai, China, in *Journal of Research in International Education,* 5 (1), pp57-82.

Chapter 12

Assessment in the IB diploma: the role and potential of e-marking

Keith Allen

As noted elsewhere in this volume, the International Baccalaureate's *Annual Review* 2009 announced that 'fast moving technology will enable us to continue to provide high quality services to schools in ... assessment' (IB, 2010a). It is evident to many involved in IB diploma assessment that the move towards e-marking is also extremely fast-moving, but its impact on the quality of assessment is much less clear.

IB assessment principles

IB documentation (see, for instance, IB, 2004) emphasises that the primary aim of assessment is to support and encourage appropriate teaching and learning in the classroom. The same paper clearly states that 'assessment of the DP is high-stakes, criterion-related performance assessment' (p 12). As the number of students grows, the task of maintaining quality in this system magnifies. For the May 2010 examination session, the number of subject registrations was 374,840 (IB, 2010b), leading to approximately one million papers to mark.

The high-stakes nature of the DP requires high standards of reliability and validity. As Carolyn Adams, IB's Assessment Director, has often explained, one of the key issues is to maximise reliability whilst retaining – or increasing – educational validity (*eg* Adams, 2011). The 'validity of an assessment is the extent to which it actually measures what it is stated to measure. The term reliability is used to define the accuracy of measurement resulting from an assessment, and how likely it is that the same result would be produced in slightly different circumstances' (IB, 2004). Reliability and validity are often in tension. Assessment protocols with high reliability include multiple-choice tests and mathematical problems where marks are only given for the answer – not for the methodology. But these are low on educational validity in an IB context as they relate poorly to the underlying objectives of learning. Higher validity comes from opportunities for students to demonstrate their understanding through theory of knowledge (ToK) essays, for example. But ToK essays tend to have lower reliability – in the sense that different assessors might grade them differently. In a wide-ranging review of literature on the reliability of assessment, Meadows and Billington state: 'There is an assumption on the part of the public that the marks awarded to candidates in high stakes examinations ... are (with only the occasional exception) highly reliable... Yet there is a long history of research findings to the contrary.' (2005: 4).

In attempting to improve reliability, the IB uses a hierarchical system of assessment. The principal examiner is responsible for the markscheme and other guidelines, and is assisted by team leaders in setting the standard. Assistant examiners are then expected to follow the guidelines. Assessment depends on the expertise of the senior markers (who set the standard), the clarity of communication to and with assistant examiners, and quality control systems to check marking standards (IB, 2004). But as the number of students taking IB examinations has grown, the system has received criticism. Tristan Bunnell (2011) reports that the Academy of International School Heads expressed concern over 'the overall integrity of the exam process'. As Bunnell points out, at one level IB grades have been remarkably consistent over the years and closely match those predicted by schools. Between 2006 and 2008, for example, 43 percent of grades were exactly as predicted by schools and 90 percent were within one grade point. This consistency at the macro level can, however, mask inconsistencies within the system. Anecdotally, we often hear complaints from teachers about the marking or moderation of individual components. In addition, achieving consistency when the number of papers marked was 300,000 (as in 2008) is not to say that the systems and processes can provide consistency when that number doubles or trebles. And, as noted by Bunnell (2011), signs of dissatisfaction have been growing over the last four years. There is clearly a challenge here. Growth makes individual anomalies harder for the IB to see. Yet schools see them just as clearly as they did in the past.

Growth requires an increase in the number of examiners. For a long time, the global distribution of IB examiners has been seen as an asset. Despite the associated logistical challenges, the examiners are more likely to reflect the global nature of the diploma itself. In 2004, the IB reported that it had 'about 4,000 examiners' (IB, 2004). Data on the IB's website in 2011 refer to 'over 10,500 examiners and moderators' (IB, 2011b). That represents an annual growth rate of 15 percent and, extrapolating, suggests a need for 1600 additional examiners for 2012. If there were also an attrition rate of 15 percent (considered by some to be a conservative estimate), the IB would be looking to hire and train in excess of 5000 new examiners per year by 2016. This is a significant – but extremely important – task. Finally, it is worth noting that DP assessment operates within a tightly-constrained timeline. Six weeks after the date of the last examination, the results are released. The challenge is for a lot of highly-accurate work to be undertaken in a tight time frame.

IB interest in onscreen marking

For some time, the IB has been investigating the possibility of shifting from paper-based marking to e-marking (or onscreen marking) as part of the strategy to maintain or increase reliability within a rapidly expanding context. In a 2007 presentation, George Pook, IB's then Assessment Director, reported that the organisation was working on e-marking, e-assessment and e-coursework (IB, 2007). In relation to e-marking, he reported on a planned trial whereby 400 scripts from the November 2008 examinations would be double marked by different sets of examiners – once in paper form and once onscreen. I have not been able to find a report on the outcome of this trial. The IB's research agenda for DP assessment (IB, 2011a) also states that 'recent advances in technology have led to a number of potential new approaches to the way in which the assessment is undertaken, examined and administered, the most significant of which involves the move from a conventional, paper-based, approach to an electronic one'. The document also lists four enquiries underpinning research in this area:

- How to improve reliability whilst maintaining validity
- The extent to which the change from moderation to seeding (discussed further below) impacts reliability
- What are the challenges facing a change to electronic moderation of internal assessment?
- How can the IB use digital technologies to change the way that students are assessed?

It will be interesting to see reports of these research enquiries as they are completed.

IB onscreen marking

In 2009, the IB launched an electronic examination marking system with Oxfordshire-based RM Education plc, using a product known as *Scoris* (Bunnell, 2011). For 2011, thirty seven percent of scripts were marked using the system. In 2012, the proportion will be 70 percent; in 2013, this will rise to 97 percent (Adams, 2011). The essence of the system is as follows:

- Scripts are scanned onto the computer system at a handful of global centres. Paper copies are retained for reference, but scripts are then distributed to examiners online.
- *Scoris* gives examiners a view of the paper and tools to annotate/mark it. When marking is complete, the marks are stored on the RM computers.
- For approximately one week after the examination, the only people marking the papers will be the principal markers (chief examiner and senior team leaders, for example). Their marking is to set the standard.
- Assistant examiners are then given access to five pre-marked papers. The assistant examiners can hide the principal markers' grades if they want, but the aim is to use these scripts for training.
- After reviewing the training scripts, examiners are then given a number of pre-marked scripts. But on this occasion, they cannot see the principal

examiners' grades. These are 'standardisation' scripts.

- If assistant examiners allocate marks on the standardisation scripts that are within a predetermined tolerance of the principal markers', they are allowed to mark scripts that have not been pre-marked. If not, they must undergo further training with one of the principal markers. After that training, they are given another batch of standardisation scripts. If they 'pass', they can mark scripts that have not been pre-marked. If not, they are rejected from the list of markers.

- When given access to scripts that have not been pre-marked, examiners will also, occasionally, encounter 'seeded' scripts. To the assistant examiner, these are indistinguishable from the others. However, they have been pre-marked by the principal markers. If the marks given by the assistant examiner fail to match those awarded by the principals (allowing for a certain tolerance), the assistant examiner is required to engage on a retraining schedule (seeing the principal examiners' grades for the seeded script, returning to a set of standardisation scripts, and so on).

- In cases where the assistant examiners repeatedly fail to grade seeded scripts with adequate conformity, all of their scripts will be re-marked by other examiners.

- These processes remove the system of moderation that has occurred in the past with paper-based assessment.

Introducing changes of this kind has installation costs. In Hong Kong, the estimated cost of introducing e-marking was HK$200 million (US$25 million) (Hong Kong Legislative Council, 2010). But in terms of running costs, it is assumed that e-marking is less expensive than paper-based assessment. The sections below consider a number of issues related to the IB's e-marking system.

Other organisations' experience of onscreen marking

The IB is not the first organisation to move into this type of marking system. Cambridge Assessment started to investigate onscreen marking in 1999 (Cooze, 2011). The reported advantages of online marking were identified as:

- reduced administration for examiners
- increased security through the reduction of mailings
- the anonymity of scripts
- greatly enhanced monitoring of examiners

The Hong Kong Examinations and Assessment Authority adopted onscreen marking in 2007, basing their experience on online marking that had occurred in 'some 14 to 15 cities and provinces in the Mainland'. They decided to have all marking done at a handful of centralised marking stations to 'enhance security and supervision of the marking process', adding that 'overseas experiences had shown that onscreen marking conducted by markers at their chosen location was unsatisfactory' (Hong Kong Legislative Council, 2010). Hence, their approach was compatible with the first stages of the IB system (scanned scripts being marked onscreen), but their quality assurance system was to monitor examiners whilst marking rather than seeding.

Comparing experienced examiners working onscreen and the same examiners working on paper, Johnson et al (2009) report a trial where 12 experienced GCSE English literature examiners marked 90 scripts on paper and 90 onscreen. Six examiners marked batch A on paper and batch B onscreen. The others marked batch A onscreen and batch B on paper. The mode of marking 'did not present a systematic influence on marking reliability'. The authors, however, express some notes of caution. For example, the e-markers were all highly experienced examiners and they were not under the same sort of time pressures as occur during an examination session. The data also reveal significant differences between examiners – some consistently harsh, some consistently lenient. Johnson et al (2009) report that this is 'a positive finding since within-marker variation is more difficult to deal with than between-marker variation', adding that 'this type of variability reinforces the continued need for procedures ... to reduce between-examiner variation levels' (p 12). Some authors present slightly different perspectives. Paek (2005) reports that 'tests with extended reading passages remain more difficult on computer than on paper' while Kurniawan and Zaphiris (2001) found that reading on paper was 10-30 percent faster than onscreen for adults, and suggested that onscreen marking may be more onerous.

Another comparative investigation is reported by Geranpayeh (2011). Certificate in Advanced English (CAE) writing scripts were marked by eight examiners on paper and onscreen. The results showed the mode of marking had no impact on grades. But again this investigation only used experienced examiners and, although the intention had been to mark 100 scripts by each method, one batch of four examiners only managed to mark 13 scripts in common. It is difficult to see how well these results can be extrapolated. This dip into the literature suggests that e-marking has significant advantages, but that there are still questions relating to the relative difficulty of online marking and the most appropriate systems for quality assurance.

Issues relating to examiners

As noted earlier, the IB employs more than 10,000 assessors. The effectiveness of these examiners underpins the quality of assessment. In ideal circumstances, reliable examiners would be retained for a number of years and newly-recruited individuals would have effective training to induct them into the system. In the move to e-marking, examiner satisfaction with the new system will be fundamental. In the *Annual Review 2009*, one examiner is quoted as saying: 'I thought it was wonderful – I hope I never have to go back. There were no papers to lose, no papers to mail, no papers to sort. The software was responsive and fast. Best of all, it added up the points correctly every time!' (IB, 2010a). Statistics from IB show that, when surveyed after the May 2010 examination session, 43 percent of examiners who had used the online system reported it as 'straightforward to use' and 23 percent said it was 'enjoyable'. In contrast, three percent said it was 'complicated' and seven percent that it was 'cumbersome' (Adams, 2011). Whether examiners who had dropped out of the system during the introduction of online marking were included in these statistics is unclear.

Further statistics show that only one-third of examiners agreed that they 'generally liked e-marking and found it straightforward to use'. Another one-third generally liked it but had some reservations. Nineteen percent indicated that they took a while to get used to it, but were comfortable with it by the end. Twelve percent found it more time-consuming than paper marking and two percent did not like it. Cooze (2011) reports that 'it was clear ... that there was considerable examiner apprehension about the shift to onscreen marking' within Cambridge Assessment. This is echoed in Geranpayeh's (2011) study, with 50 percent of examiners reporting that they felt apprehensive or worried by the new system and the observation that 'long periods onscreen caused problems for some of them'. Nevertheless, 'their confidence in their marking accuracy grew with practice'. Misgivings reported to me by IB examiners echo many of these points. Amongst the most common reactions are concerns over the additional time taken onscreen, the difficulties associated with long onscreen sessions, and reduced opportunities to be able to take scripts to a place where the examiner feels comfortable marking. There are also stories of experienced examiners being 'failed' by the seeding programme, of higher than usual drop-outs and of, consequently, other examiners having many more scripts to mark. How examiners view the electronic system needs to be closely monitored.

Moreover, the e-marking system has technological requirements. A teacher from West Africa has told me that colleagues are dropping out from examining due to the instability and unreliability of their internet connections. A colleague from central Europe reported that his school IT set-up was inadequate for e-marking. Another reported problems in parts of South Asia. It seems likely that the move to e-marking will lead to a shift in the geographical distribution of examiners. This is sad in many ways. Having the opportunity to become an examiner has been seen as extremely valuable professional development for DP teachers, allowing them to provide better guidance for their students. It would be contrary to the mission of the IB if this opportunity were denied to teachers in remoter settings or from schools with smaller IT budgets. Increased attrition rates of examiners puts much greater strain on the training programmes for new recruits and on the need for quality assurance. It may also lead to legal challenges if examiners are 'dropped' and they can substantiate cases of unfair dismissal by demonstrating that the quality assurance systems were flawed.

As stated earlier, the IB uses a hierarchical system of assessment, the foundation of which is to have a clear set of notes (such as markschemes) to guide assistant examiners. This top-down approach is ameliorated by opportunities for dialogue between assistant examiners and team leaders. But in its extreme form the system could lead to the de-professionalisation of examiners as they are required to follow pre-ordained rules: the 'infallibility approach'. Within the UK a hierarchical assessment system is the norm and is set out in the code of practice for examining bodies (Meadows and Billington, 2005), but it is not the only possible model. Meadows and Billington report on suggestions for the development of a 'community of practice' as an alternative model (2005: 53-55). Under this concept, the 'application of the markscheme ... is a social construct negotiated by members of the community'. There are suggestions that embracing others into a community of practice may enhance examiner retention. They suggest (p 55) that the introduction of e-marking can enhance this development – and it is not hard to see how, with the same scripts being available for multiple examiners and the near-instant communication systems of the web.

Meadows and Billington also point out that with hierarchical assessment systems and prescribed markschemes, assistant examiners tend to mark down unexpected but correct answers (2005: 42). If the entire cohort of examiners were allowed to see the draft markscheme as soon as the paper has been completed, their comments could all be fed into the refinement of the examiner guidelines. Processes akin to this seem to be underway for UK-based GCSE and A level examinations, where assistant examiners meet online for standardisation. Going one step further in the context of the DP, if IB teachers were encouraged to submit their comments on the papers within a few days – rather than within 28 days – those comments could also be fed into the processes for clarifying the markscheme.

Using online systems, there are many greater opportunities for effective collaboration between examiners and teachers than under the paper-based system. As Meadows and Billington also suggest, 'the process of reaching a consensus regarding the best mark for a script may serve a useful training function, improving the accuracy with which examiners apply the marking scheme' (2005: 50). Online marking could be used to transform marking to incorporate inputs from a variety of sources. This may disrupt the hierarchical principle, but it suggests other advantages may accrue.

Issues relating to reliability

There would seem to be at least three major sources of unreliability in assessments: the test itself, candidates' behaviour on the day of the assessment, and the reliability of ascribing a grade. It is the last of these that is relevant in discussions on the introduction of e-marking. Clearly, reliability is linked to the scale used for assessment. Reliability data in a situation with binary outcomes (*eg* pass/fail) are likely to be higher than where outcomes are on a scale stretching over 100 or more marks. For the IB diploma, the emphasis is on reliability at the grade level, *ie* on the A-E scale for ToK and the extended essay (EE), and on the 7-1 scale for subjects (IB, 2004). The same paper continues by stating that 'the aim is to have at least 95% confidence that any final subject grade is "correct"' (p 13). Ninety five percent confidence is impressive but, at the statistical level, it may be misleading. Research cited in Meadows and Billington shows that even 98 percent reliability leads to up to 15 percent of students being awarded different grades by two examiners, and reliability of 90 percent generates 40-50 percent of students with disputable grades (2005: 68). We must appreciate that valid assessments contain inherent unreliability. But, for the IBDP, we can console ourselves with the thought that a typical DP student's work will be assessed by more than 20 separate examiners and that many inconsistencies will become balanced out.

The literature seems to contain many divergent estimates of reliability of marking. These are hard to compare as the range of grades is often not specified. But figures in the range of 0.5-0.75 are not unusual (Meadows and Billington, 2005). Should the IB publish reliability data, information on variances and tolerance limits and so on? The data suggest that, although this may be useful for some, many others will have difficulty in interpreting the data. It has also been suggested that publication of uncertainties may generate greater problems in a litigious society where grades influence high-stakes outcomes. In 2004, the IB's systems for ensuring reliability focused on 'the use of detailed markschemes, assessment criteria, moderation procedures' to reduce marker bias (IB, 2004). Under the paper-based system, an examiner's marking was 'acceptable' if the correlation coefficient between the examiner's marking and the moderator's assessment of the same scripts was at least 0.9 (IB, 2004). If the value were lower, the scripts may have been re-marked by a more reliable examiner.

Byrne (1979) compared inter-marker reliability across subjects at the UK's Open University. The research found – perhaps not surprisingly – that reliability was highest for mathematics, followed by the physical sciences. The other extreme was populated by assessments from the arts, social sciences and educational studies. It was also clear that, irrespective of subject area, essay questions presented the greatest reliability problem. Essay-style assessments can be argued as having high validity, but it is hard to generate a reliable markscheme that can be cascaded down a hierarchical structure of markers without broad tolerance levels – and consequent grade uncertainty. One solution is to double-mark assessment components with lower levels of reliability. The time cost of this is negligible with e-marking, as individual scripts can be marked simultaneously by two assessors, but the financial cost could be significant. Nevertheless, the IB must have data to indicate which assessment components are susceptible to the greatest challenges to their reliability. These would include components where grade changes during paper-based moderation has been most common, those eliciting most enquiry on results requests from schools, those awarded wider tolerance limits in e-marking and those where most assistant examiners failed to match the gold standard of seeded scripts under the e-marking regime.

In particular, there are regular complaints from schools about ToK and EE grading. It is not coincidental that these are assessment components with inherently low reliability *and* the only IBDP grade outcomes where only one examiner is used. Introducing double-marking for all of these should be considered, although this could be restricted to scripts where the school's predicted grade is two or more grades different from the examiners. It should also be noted that these are two components that are not constrained by the six week timeline for the main examinations, allowing more time for double-marking. But such changes may require a philosophical shift. If the flag of assessment is firmly nailed to the mast of a hierarchical system (the principal examiner knows best) a move towards the consensus-favouring approach of double-marking may be contentious.

A second approach for assessment components with broad tolerance levels is to ensure that moderation also occurs. When assistant examiners encounter a seeded script, their marks are compared with those of the principal examiners. If assistant examiners are within the tolerance limits, they are allowed to continue to mark. But if the tolerance limits are broad, assistant examiners may be awarding marks that are some distance below – or above – those given by the principals. However, the data from the comparisons could easily be used to generate a moderation coefficient. If, for example, the assistant examiner is consistently harsh in grading by ten percent, all of that examiner's grades could be increased by the ten percent margin. This combination of seeding and moderation would be relatively easy to introduce in an e-marking scenario.

The reliability of marking has also been shown to be susceptible to – amongst other things – 'contrast effects' (Meadows and Billington, 2005), when the mark awarded to a script is influenced by the standard of preceding scripts. There is no reason to suspect that e-marking would increase the likelihood of this. Indeed, the fact that scripts will be randomly selected from the total collection may reduce contrast effects. But it is also possible to build in a statistically-generated checker. For example, if a script is awarded a mark significantly different from those before, this could trigger a re-mark by a different examiner. Other forms of bias identified by Meadows and Billington (2005) include those related to the gender, race, ethnicity or name of the candidate. This bias will be eliminated by e-marking as scripts are anonymous. On one other aspect, e-marking also clearly reduces errors. Examiners are no longer required to add up their marks and/or transfer the marks to a summary sheet. Meadows and Billington (2005) report that a startling 70 percent of GCSE examiners made arithmetic or transcriptional errors of this kind.

In summary, the shift to e-marking may impact reliability, but has the potential for the introduction of double-marking, moderation factors, checks of contrast effects, and so on. Some of these have cost implications, but they should be investigated as part of the strategy to increase school's confidence in the grading system. Under the paper-based system of marking, the IB had to hire an army of temporary assistants to receive, sort and check scripts – including the arithmetic of examiners. These roles are lost with e-marking. Hence, the judicious use of double-marking may be affordable. It is likely to lead to greater satisfaction with grades.

Issues relating to quality assurance

The quality assurance component of the IB's online system introduces the notion of seeded scripts in place of moderation. Cambridge Assessment is also reported to be considering seeding 'to either supplement, or replace, monitoring by Team Leaders' (Cooze, 2011). What are the key impacts of this change? With paper-based marking, the moderation sample for each assistant examiner was nominally set at 15 percent of the total allocation although, for examiners allocated more than 133 scripts, this percentage fell to a maximum of 20 (IB, 2004). Examiners were requested to submit samples from a full range of marks, but it is unclear whether this was always the case in practice as samples may have had to be sent off before examiners had completed all their marking.

Research has suggested that, when seeing the first examiner's marks, the moderator is influenced by those marks and tends to support them (Meadows and Billington, 2005). If the moderator cannot see the first examiner's marks, the second marking diverges from the first by a larger extent. In other research, the Welsh Joint Education Committee (WJEC, 2004) conducted an e-marking pilot where senior examiners re-marked assistant examiners' scripts without seeing the first marks given. The investigation involved an examination paper with an objective markscheme. Nevertheless, the senior examiners' marks showed greater variation in this blind trial than under the normal moderation procedure (where the first marker's annotations and grades are visible). The report concluded that 'there is a clear difference between asking a senior examiner to mark blind and requiring them to make a professional judgement about the appropriateness of an assistant's marking'. On the one hand, this suggests that an electronic system – where the first marks awarded are hidden from second or subsequent markers – may be better at supporting 'the standard' than moderation, as moderators may have been swayed by the first marker. But it may also indicate that the moderator had appreciated that the initial markscheme did not cover all the bases and consequently awards a 'compromise' mark that better reflects the student's performance. If this were true, it provides a challenge to the hierarchical system of marking.

In reporting on their investigation into onscreen marking, Johnson *et al* (2009) reveal the diversity of marks awarded by examiners. As part of the investigation, the most senior markers set the 'gold standard' and other 'experienced' examiners were compared with them. One script rated 29.5 by the senior examiners was awarded 13.0 by an experienced junior examiner. Another outlier was awarded 19.0 by the senior examiners, but 30.0 by the junior examiner. If this diversity were replicated within the IB's e-marking system, either a high proportion of examiners would fail against seeded scripts or the tolerance levels would have to be set extremely broadly. The research by Johnson *et al* (2009) suggested that inter-marker variability was high, but individual examiners showed consistency across their marking. Performance of this sort can easily be standardised through moderation. How well the seeding system can pull examiners into line remains to be seen.

Seeding requires the application of tolerance limits: the extent of variation permitted between an assistant examiner's marking and the gold standard. Meadows and Billington (2005) cite tolerance limits within the UK's GCSE marking system of 20 percent (for art), five percent (for English) and six percent (for computer studies). How this compares with the IB's tolerance limits would be interesting to discover. It is inevitable, of course, that strict tolerance limits are more likely to lead to examiners 'failing' the seeding test. In contrast, loose limits would hide inconsistencies between examiners that could, in theory, have been compensated for by moderation.

The e-marking system adopted by the IB also requires clear information for assistant examiners on the standards to employ. In many ways, this is relatively unchanged from the paper-based approach. But there are two significant differences. Firstly, under e-marking the principal examiners have immediate access to the full range of scripts. During the first week after the examination, they can examine a wide cross-section of scripts in order to refine their markscheme. This was impossible with the paper-based system. It raises the potential for more thorough modification of the markscheme prior to its use by assistant examiners. On the other hand, the new system appears to reduce the opportunities for assistant examiners to debate interpretations of the markscheme with their team leaders. In other words, it has become increasingly hierarchical. As suggested earlier, a strict hierarchical system can produce high degrees of standardisation if the markscheme is clear and tolerance limits are tight. But these features bring with them the possibility of reducing assistant examiner professionalism and of higher attrition rates of examiners.

Issues related to training

'The training of examiners is a crucial component of any testing programme since if the marking of a test is not valid and reliable, then all of the other work undertaken earlier to construct a "quality" instrument will have been a waste of time.' (Alderson, Clapham and Wall, 1995). In their comprehensive review of assessment, Meadows and Billington draw attention to the need for intensive training of examiners (2005: 30-34). They cite research showing that training is much more important than any specific entry qualifications for examiners, such as years of teaching. Research into training suggests that the goal of training is consistency rather than uniformity (Meadows and Billington, 2005: 51), although this was within a context of moderation. Moderation allows standardisation of consistent but divergent examiners. The seeding system requires greater initial conformity.

Following their early trials into e-marking, Cambridge Assessment decided that training of examiners was crucial and decided on 'practical face-to-face' training for all examiners (Cooze, 2011). The system in Hong Kong was similar. But this is impracticable for IB with its geographic distribution of examiners. Cambridge Assessment ESOL had the opportunity of gradually inducting some of their examiners into e-marking due to the year-round nature of their testing. For IB examiners, such opportunities are reduced. It would seem possible, however, to set up well-structured, realistic training sessions for IB examiners by using old scripts in, for example, February and March or September and October. The e-marking system adopted by the IB seems to have great potential in this area. With thousands of scanned and marked scripts available online and the opportunity to hide the previous marks and annotations, the potential for requiring new markers to grade pre-marked samples during training is clear.

Issues relating to script distribution

The IB's e-marking system randomly distributes scripts to examiners in small batches. This has a couple of implications. Although the system has features to allow e-markers to move around the script, it does not allow examiners to return to previously-marked scripts to cross-refer. When I was examining, I found it useful to go back to previous scripts on occasions. For example, when looking for the possibility of collaboration or when suddenly realising that I may have misinterpreted the way that a student had expressed an idea. The batch system of IB onscreen marking does not permit markers to return to review previously marked scripts. Nor does the scattering of scripts from a centre across different examiners make it feasible, in ToK essays for example, to detect possible collaboration between students. It also remains to be seen how the scattering of a school's scripts across different examiners affects systems for providing feedback to schools.

Future opportunities for e-marking

Johnson *et al* (2009) reported that 'technology offers the potential to broaden educational assessment beyond what traditional methods allow'. Will e-marking facilitate the development of a wider range of assessment instruments and hence greater validity? There is already a proposal to use e-marking for visual arts in place of the current system of assessment by a visiting examiner (Adams, 2011). How might that change the opportunities for students to develop and demonstrate their abilities? Could other assessment components be amended in light of the opportunities provided by e-marking? It has been suggested that a key advantage of e-marking is 'that examiners' marking tendencies can be monitored more comprehensively and effectively online ... allowing senior examiners to intervene in the marking process if necessary' (Jordan *et al*, 2011). It is possible to introduce statistical triggers to identify cases where intervention is advisable. Triggering when an examiner rates a seeded script outside the tolerance limits – as the system includes – is one way. But there are others too. As suggested earlier, consistent under- (or over-) grading – even if marked within the tolerance limits – could lead to the introduction of conventional moderation coefficients. The statistical monitoring of examiners as they progress through batches of scripts can also, potentially, lead to more sophisticated comparisons between each examiner and the 'standard'. For example, does examiner A tend to be more lenient on assessment criterion X than does the principal? If so, a moderation factor could be applied specifically for that criterion.

Another often-cited possibility is to allocate different components of an examination to different sets of examiners. For example, some may focus on questions 1-4, others on 5-8. Or where students have a choice of essay titles, one batch of examiners may be asked to mark only question 1, others question 2, and so on. Schemes such as these may increase reliability as examiners became 'experts' in assessing a narrow range of questions. Examiners would then no longer be influenced by the candidate's performance on other questions (the 'halo effect'). Whether this a significant difference – and whether it would lead to more or less appropriate grades – is a moot point.

Overview on e-marking

As the IB recognises, 'any issues relating to IB assessment must be discovered and action taken to remedy them before they have an impact on candidates' results' (IB, 2011a). The e-marking system introduced by the IB relies heavily on the hierarchical approach to grading. Examiners need appropriate levels of IT facilities, and the process requires clear markschemes and other guidance for assistant examiners as well as appropriate tolerance limits. The system also introduces a new quality assurance system in replacing moderation with seeding. It is probably too early to make judgements, but there are concerns over each of these features. On the other hand, the system does raise the possibility of better statistical oversight of the assessment process, enhanced assessment tasks and the reduction in possible bias.

All of these changes are taking place on a fast time-scale and go alongside the continuing rapid growth in the DP. Whether the time-scale allows issues to 'be discovered and action taken to remedy them before they have an impact on candidates' results' needs careful consideration. Only time will tell the value and impact of online marking. Will it cope with the growth in numbers? Will the pre-marking by the principal markers be consistent? Will it lead to either unsatisfactorily high degrees of tolerance or greater examiner attrition? Will the changes lead to assessment procedures with greater educational validity? These are important questions upon which the future of our students depends. I recall a meeting in Malaysia in 1997, where a friend told me that he did not want his school to be at the cutting edge of technology because you could be injured there. He wanted to be behind the cutting edge. Whilst e-developments within the DP may well be pointing in the right direction, there are voices suggesting that their introduction should be evaluated more carefully. This view is reflected, for example, in Malcolm McKenzie's question towards the end of Walker's excellent *Changing Face of International Education* (2011): 'Might there be some value in a moratorium on growth, a fallow period for reflection and regrouping?' (2011: 170)

References

Adams, C (2011): *Assessment: Rigour and Consistency. Meeting the Challenge.* Presentation to IBSCA Summer Conference, 8 June 2011, London, UK.

Alderson, J C, Clapham, C and Wall, D (1995): *Language Test Construction and Evaluation.* Cambridge: Cambridge University Press.

Bunnell, T (2011): The Growth of the International Baccalaureate Diploma Program: Concerns About the Consistency and Reliability of the Assessments, in *The Education Forum*, 75 (2), pp174-187.

Byrne, C (1979): Tutor-marked assignments at the Open University: A question of reliability, in *Teaching at a Distance*, 15, pp34-43.

Cooze, M (2011): Assessing Writing tests on Scoris: The introduction of online marking, in *Research Notes*, 49, pp12-15.

Geranpayeh, A (2011): The impact of online marking on examiners' behaviour, in *Research Notes*, 49, pp15-21.

Hong Kong Legislative Council (2010): Panel on Education Background Paper LC Paper No CB(2) 182/10-11(02).

IB (2004): *Diploma Programme assessment: Principles and practice.* Geneva: International Baccalaureate.

IB (2007): *Developments in Diploma Programme Assessment (Academic, technical, structural)* Presentation given by George Pook, Assessment Director, at IB Africa, Europe and Middle East (IBAEM) Conference.

IB (2010a): *Annual Review 2009.* Geneva: International Baccalaureate.

IB (2010b): *The IB Diploma Programme Statistical Bulletin: May 2010 examination session.* Cardiff: International Baccalaureate.

IB (2011a): Research Agenda for Diploma Assessment. Online (last accessed 15 July 2011): www.ibo.org/informationfor/mediaandresearchers/researchers/documents/ResearchAgendaforAssessmentWebsiteversion.pdf

IB (2011b): Online: www.ibo.org/informationfor/examiners (last accessed 18 July 2011).

Johnson, M, Nádas, R, Bell, J F and Green, S (2009): *Marking essays on screen: an investigation into the reliability of marking extended subjective texts.* Paper presented at the AEA-Europe conference, Malta, 5-7 November 2009.

Jordan, S, Hughes, G and Betts, C (2011): Technology in assessment, in *Research Notes*, 43, pp2-6.

Kurniawan, S H and Zaphiris, P (2001): *Reading online or on paper: Which is faster?* Proceedings of HCI International 2001. Mahwah, NJ: Lawrence Erbaum Associates.

McKenzie, M (2011): Conclusions: Reflections and refractions, in G Walker (ed), *The Changing Face of International Education: Challenges for the IB.* Cardiff: International Baccalaureate.

Meadows, M and Billington, L (2005): *A Review of the Literature on Marking Reliability.* National Assessment Agency, London, UK.

Paek, P (2005): *Recent Trends in Comparability Studies.* PEM Research Report 05-05.

WJEC (2004): *CMI/CMS 2004 Pilot Investigation.* Cardiff: Welsh Joint Education Committee.

Part C
Contexts for the IB diploma

Chapter 13

Taking forward the IB diploma in India: context and challenges

Gillian Ashworth

The IB diploma in India – an overview of the historical and current contexts

Amidst the vastly rich history, culture and traditions which India can so readily boast, the adoption back in 1976 by a boarding school up in the hill stations of south India of the then fledgling International Baccalaureate (IB) Diploma Programme (DP) may well have struggled to impact on the consciousness of most, when set alongside Amitabh Bachchan's several Bollywood premieres of that year, or Peter Lever's 7-46 in the England-India Delhi cricket test match.

In educational terms, however, the decision by Kodaikanal International School to join a small cadre of schools worldwide in adopting and trialling the DP marked a watershed moment in educational terms, pronouncing as it did the arrival in the country of an alternative to highly traditional educational methods and experiences. Not that Indian students were the intended recipients of this shiny new programme, however: 'the IB diploma was founded to meet the needs of international students living abroad' and 'the original intended consumers of the IB diploma [were] international students completing the IB diploma (outside of their home country) with the intent to return home for tertiary studies' (Guy and Switzer, 2010: 67-68). Such was largely the case at Kodaikanal.

Thirty-five years later, however, some 77 schools around India are authorised to deliver the programme (IB, 2011b), with the number more than doubling in four years from 35 in 2007 to 77 in 2011 (IB, 2011b). Meanwhile the queue at the IB's door for future authorisations shows no signs of diminishing. Indian students, studying both within and outside of the country, currently make up the largest nationality group registering for the DP from within the Asia-Pacific region (Guy and Switzer, 2010: 62-63), and while many within India itself continue to use the DP as a passport to university abroad, an increasing number are looking to continue on to universities within the country. This all collectively represents a landscape significantly different to that in which the DP arrived, and has presented challenges that an IB undergoing no less change itself over that same period has sought to respond to in various ways. The landscape seems well set to continue to shift, however, and the DP to grow in the country: what role, then, might the DP be playing within India in the future, and what may be the nature of some of the challenges that arise?

The Indian teaching context from Grades 10 to 12: the '+2' years

The DP takes its place within the Indian educational context during what are known as the '+2' years between Grade 10 and university entry. That context comprises state schooling administered by non-governmental educational boards around the country such as the Council for the Indian School Certificate Examinations (CISCE), and the Central Board of Secondary Education (CBSE). Students within Indian state schools make their way through somewhat traditional educational methods of rote learning and memorisation towards competitive and high stakes externally-assessed board examinations set at the end of Grade 10, performance in which is used to determine the pathway taken in the +2 years. Access to university is achieved or otherwise via further board examinations at the culmination of Grade 12, with responsibility for the conduct and administration of their respective board examinations in Grades 10 and 12 falling to the individual educational boards.

Educational pathways and progress are thus highly dependent on performance in the board examinations, the resultant stress of which on students can quickly be gleaned from a 'board exam' search on the website of a publication such as the *Hindustan Times*, and its resultant eclectic mix of stories of anxiety, helplines being set up to counter such pressures, and even the occasional depressing account of a teenage suicide. Newspaper reports (*eg* Dore and Seshasayee, 2011; Indo-Asian News Service, 2009) suggested stress and unhealthy competition formed important factors in a significant decision by one of the major boards, the CBSE, to make its Grade 10 board examinations optional for the first time in 2011, with students able alternatively to opt for school-based examinations – a landmark decision within the context of Indian state education. Students opting for this route formed a minority, and it remains to be seen whether the move represented the beginning of an important longer-term trend to be followed with increasing acceptance and enthusiasm across the Grade 10 spectrum.

One factor influencing the choice of many, meanwhile, lay in the necessity to take the board examination if an intention existed to attend a junior college in the +2 years between Grades 10 and 12. Students for this phase may remain at their existing schools and work towards the Grade 12 board examinations, but in states such as Maharashtra (which includes Mumbai), Karnataka (where Bengalaru/Bangalore is situated), Andhra Pradesh (including Hyderabad), and Orissa the possibility exists of attending 'junior colleges' (sometimes referred to as 'pre-university colleges' (PUCs)), entry to which is determined via application, and performance in the Grade 10 board examinations. Either pathway forms a relatively narrow route to university entrance, with choices on offer comprising courses in commerce/business management, or in sciences (with particular emphasis on physics and engineering), or medicine, or in humanities/social studies-type courses (which may be termed more as 'liberal arts' courses elsewhere) – with scope not existing to mix any components within these three streams. Such courses are thus 'all very compartmentalised', to quote one IB diploma coordinator, and specialisation choices are made early.

Who takes the DP in India, and why?
Thus currently stands the nature of Indian state education prior to and during the +2 years, and one may be forgiven for wondering how the significantly contrasting nature of the DP might not only have found a foothold within such a context, but also now be expanding at such a rate. The short-term answer lies, as is the case in much of the Asia-Pacific region, in the opportunity it offers as 'a passport for University studies abroad' as Judith Guy and John Switzer illustrate in their 2010 paper (*The Migratory Trends of International Baccalaureate Diploma Students in Asia Pacific: Going Global?*), using transcript request data and research from the likes of Doherty (2009: 77, cited by Guy and Switzer 2010: 60) who argued that 'upwardly mobile consumers in Asia are strategically deploying the IB diploma to facilitate routes for transnational mobility'. With regard to India in particular, Guy and Switzer cite a 'western' degree and the 'social cachet' of 'sending children abroad to study at tertiary level' (2010: 66) as significant 'pull' factors influencing the desire to pursue university studies abroad, with the DP providing the means to achieve that goal.

The DP has in many ways therefore represented a bespoke solution for a niche market within the country, in the light of which there can be little surprise that it is found mainly in the domain of private schools levying significant fees, and exists to all intents and purposes as an entity separate from the Indian state school system and the types of aspirations found there. Equally unsurprising in the light of this is the fact that its student clients tend to originate from a limited economic stratum within the country.

Student and parent perceptions of the DP
While talk of a 'passport to university abroad' on grounds of 'social cachet' and the like may imply somewhat mercenary motives for taking the DP route, students and their parents are neither unaware nor unappreciative of the wider educational and holistic benefits that also emanate from student involvement in the programme. Both if asked may well cite the opportunity offered for experimentation with a range of subjects and discovering where one's potential really does lie to be realised in time, in contrast to the imposition at this stage of highly-specialised courses in the state system, and a consequent need to make effective life decisions at age 16.

Pronouncements may also be readily offered on the intrinsic value of the programme's holistic approach of educating the 'whole person', on specific elements such as the theory of knowledge (ToK) component, extended essay (EE) requirement and development of research skills, on exposure to a wider range of cultural experiences, and so on – all of which may act as further 'pull' factors of the programme. One student, sandwiched in her DP experience between Indian Grade 10 board examinations and a hoped-for place at a university in Mumbai (though with a 'safety net' abroad in hand if that failed to work out as hoped), waxed eloquently on the opportunity the DP gave her to 'explore myself' by engaging in activities absent from the purely Indian experience – oral assessments, the evidently much-loved and certainly oft-cited ToK, and the ability to question (initially found 'annoying' after 13 years of rote learning!), along with developing independent learning skills, and fairer assessment with students not being judged only on a final examination and the memorisation of textbooks in the run-up to that.

The latter meanwhile hints at some of the 'push' factors cited in relation to the choice of DP as opposed to state alternatives for +2: the 12th grade board examination that counts for everything at the end, the frantic learning of textbooks in the lead-up, and of possible infrequent teacher indifference in between, with regular student absence and time felt better spent on reading up on textbooks and learning with a private tutor instead. Not that DP students are immune to this by any means: similarly to Erika Elkady's experience in Dubai (2011: 185), it is common practice for Indian students also to avail themselves of private tuition outside of school, and weaning students off such tuition during a DP course in which final assessments pepper the programme cycle rather than just occurring once at the end is a task similar in magnitude and nature to that once undertaken by Sisyphus with his rock.

University challenges

It cannot be denied that the ultimate aim of many DP students in India is university abroad, nor that the programme largely caters at present for the more economically fortunate. While the programme globally may have progressed to a stage where '[t]oday over half of the 2000+ IB diploma programme schools are state schools' (Guy and Switzer 2010: 59), the state system in India remains largely unaffected by its neighbourly presence. Given the aspirations of many of its students, meanwhile, one might be forgiven for assuming India's universities remain similarly untroubled, particularly given their continuation of the traditional approach generally found throughout Indian educational establishments. In line with substantial efforts globally by the IB in the field of university recognition of the DP, however, significant efforts have been made to build bridges with universities around the country, and to facilitate better access for students wishing to remain in the country to pursue their tertiary studies.

These efforts meanwhile appear to be leading to a growing trend of DP students with aspirations of progressing to university within India subsequent to completion of the IB diploma. Priyamvada Taneja, IB university liaison officer within the country and co-author of the recently-published *Guide to University Recognition in India* (Taneja and Switzer, 2011), estimates from transcript data derived from the IB's information system (IBIS) that 30-40 percent of current

DP students may well want to attend Indian universities, and that the number is rising. Should it continue to do so – and if accessibility to such universities continues to widen, then it appears inevitable that it will – this would have significant implications for the DP in terms of potential growth rates, and of the associated challenges.

Recognition for the DP as an entry qualification to universities within India arrived in 1983, in a letter from the Association of Indian Universities (AIU) to the Deputy Director-General of the IB, which stated that:

> Resolved that the International Baccalaureate Diploma Examination awarded by the International Baccalaureate Office, Geneva, Switzerland, be recognised as equivalent to a pass in the +2 stage of the new pattern of education (10+2). (AIU, 1983)

This was confirmed in a further letter to the IB from the AIU in December 2010:

> 'International Baccalaureate Diploma' awarded by the International Baccalaureate Organization, Geneva, Switzerland, has been equated with +2 stage (Grade 12) qualification of an Indian board since 1983. Students intending to join Indian universities after completion of their IB qualifications are eligible to pursue Bachelor's degree programme at Indian Universities. (AIU, 2010) (all cited in Taneja and Switzer, 2011)

The reality of engaging with Indian Post-18 institutes has been less straightforward than the statements might suggest, however. Admissions policies can vary, the universities deal in percentages and not the IBDP's 1-7 final grades, and DP results come out too late to count in the application process. The IB shows considerable flexibility in countering these issues, supplying students aiming at Indian university entry with a percentage equivalency for each 1-7 grade along with both the transcript of results and a 'no-objection' Migration Certificate – mandatory for Indian university entry – stating that a student, having studied in the DP, has the IB's permission to study and appear for examinations 'of any board, university or college in India'. In regard to specific entry requirements, students needing to complete courses in three sciences for their intended university course can apply to the IB to take a 'non-regular' diploma allowing them to include three sciences among their six subjects. Where university admission is complicated, meanwhile, by the misalignment in the timing of university admissions decisions and publication of IB results (as in the case of Delhi University, for example), predicted grades can be used as the grounds for such decisions in the cases of DP students.

Moreover the decision has already been taken to offer the core elements of the DP (ToK, CAS, and the EE) as individually-recognized stand-alone courses for the first time to students embarking on the DP in 2012. It is these that students must complete in order to be eligible for the Migration Certificate, which is needed for entry to university, and this requirement currently necessitates all students with aspirations of Indian university entrance undertaking the full DP, including three subjects studied at higher level. It represents an overall package that can be a daunting prospect for some students. The effect of the change, however, will be to enable students to undertake six subjects at standard level while still completing the core components requirement, and hence be eligible for the Migration Certificate and university entrance. 'The decision to allow DP courses students to experience this integral part of the diploma supports the IB's continued dedication to its "access agenda"', states the IB (2011c). It may well help to alleviate the currently considerable demands levied on the DP student with aspirations to Indian university entrance, enabling a larger number to tackle the programme successfully and subsequently to access a university.

Nonetheless, while some bridges have been built between the IB diploma and Indian university entry, others remain projects in the making. In particular, a swathe of prestigious professional institutes – the aspirations of many among the cream of academically high-flying Indian students – remain largely unaffected by the entry of students from the DP. The Indian Institutes of Technology (IITs) and National Institutes of Technology (NITs) to which would-be engineers aspire, along with other major professional institutes such as the top law universities and medical or dentistry colleges, all use highly competitive entrance examinations, which take place in April or May of each year requiring a high level of knowledge of particular content, and intense revision to acquire it. Both study requirements and timing of entrance examinations thus make these difficult university choices for DP students, few of whom as a consequence tend to find their way into them.

The DP has therefore yet to make meaningful contact with a prestigious and significant element of Post-18 educational establishments in India, and with the high-flying students who populate their undergraduate courses – and, consequently, with a significant number of those forming the academic cream of India's youth looking to make a contribution in key professional areas to a country very much on the move in a number of socio-economic ways.

The main challenges faced by the DP for the future

The story of the IBDP within India since its introduction has been one of considerable success in many ways, given its rate of expansion and future prospects of continuing in similar vein; the challenges that exist or seem set to arise in the future are in many ways the products of such success. A number relate to growth and its implications, while others will arise from the gradual diversification from the traditional role of the DP in India as a passport to university abroad to something increasingly educationally relevant within the country itself, as growing numbers of Indian DP students seek to remain and to invest their futures here. Three particular areas might be identified in which challenges either exist already, or may be anticipated to arise in future. Aspects of India's educational landscape undoubtedly give rise to some challenges, including the need for promoting the programme among universities, schools, students and parents; an additional need exists to prepare effectively to respond to potential developments in that educational landscape in the future. Yet a further area of challenge might be seen in the need to maintain the programme's quality and integrity in the face of exponential growth, while overall the IB might ponder too its own accessibility in a context of state schooling that operates within straitened means, and consequent perceptions of economic exclusivity that do not perhaps sit entirely comfortably with its declared mission and vision for education around the world.

Challenges relating to India's educational landscape
Continuing promotion of understanding and acceptance of the programme on the part of Indian universities

Significant inroads have been made into providing access to Indian universities through the substantial recognition work that has been carried out, and continuing promotion of the IBDP is needed to help develop that further. In particular, while many universities will engage with the DP, this engagement frequently remains at the level of percentages and grades, with rather less of a premium placed on the elements of understanding, skills, and holistic development that prove so valuable to DP students at university and beyond. Meanwhile the entry demands made of DP students do not always enjoy equivalency with those levied for students following alternative access paths. This can be seen in the requirement for students to engage in the full diploma to acquire Indian university entry, leaving DP students mandatorily tackling substantial undertakings in the forms of the core components (EE, ToK and CAS requirements); these are additional to discrete subject study, and not similarly required of students engaged in alternative programmes of study where the focus can largely remain on the demands of the subject-specific courses. Where additional elements do exist elsewhere, such as with the requirement in the state system for 'Socially Useful Productive Work' (SUPW), the expectations of engagement do not equate to those levelled by CAS in the DP, and quality (or lack of this) will not impede subsequent university entry. This is unlike the case with the DP, where a failure to fulfil CAS requirements prevents the award of the diploma itself, which prevents in turn the university entry for which the diploma is needed.

Clearly, therefore, there remains a need to promote recognition not only of the programme *per se* with the universities, but also of its nature and worth in different ways for students looking to continue their studies at university, and of the actual value of achievements in different elements as relative to what is attained overall in the course of pursuing other possible pathways. Continued coaxing is also needed in terms of the equivalency of demands made of students entering from different pathways. Wider awareness in this respect within universities should better support the student opting for the DP when aiming subsequently at an Indian university, and lessen any possibility that students could possibly be disadvantaged by the fact they have opted for the DP when their aim is university entry within India. That said, much depends on the willingness to engage by the universities and colleges themselves – a factor outside of the IB's scope of influence – and the question does arise as to how much incentive exists for that to happen when demand outstrips capacity to the extent seen every year in any good Indian university. As noted by Guy and Switzer (2010: 67), concerns relating to 'quality and accessibility to a highly competitive tertiary sector' have represented a significant 'push' factor influencing the choice of so many DP students within India to go to university abroad. Such is even more the case with the prestigious technical institutes and other professional colleges, meanwhile, and it is difficult to see a way around the current scenario in which a DP student still determined to access these institutions must spend an additional year subsequent to completion of their DP course on revising the textbooks and content necessary for undertaking college entrance tests in the following April/May test sessions.

While promotion and recognition efforts must continue, therefore, the DP does not form a naturally comfortable fit with the nature and expectations of state education in India, and it seems likely that changes in this respect may happen only over time – perhaps as educational perceptions within the country gradually change more. Increasing evidence does exist of serious debate on this point, however, from a variety of sources such as on the one hand Dr Shaym Menon, Professor of Education at the University of Delhi, who has stated that:

> Good schooling facilitates a wide spectrum of learning possibilities including intellectual-process skills, social skills, physical abilities and aesthetic sensibilities. What a board manages to assess through its 'written-examination-of-two-three-hours-at-the-end-of-the-term' format is, however, only a narrow band of skills, mostly those related to memorisation of information. On the other hand, a school-based evaluation system, if done well, can effectively focus on the entire spectrum of learning with its 'continuous and comprehensive' format. (Menon, 2010)

Meanwhile, elsewhere came the approving thoughts of 'Ajit', a reader of *The Hindustan Times*, in response to the move by the CBSE board to make the Grade 10 board examinations optional from 2011: 'Mockery is when kids pass by "mugging up" subjects and no understanding and others killing themselves under pressure. Even after years you shudder from the trauma that the schooling caused you.' (Chopra, 2010). There do thus seem to be murmurings of support for reform in education – towards an approach perhaps rather closer to that of IB programmes – from various stakeholders along the educational spectrum, and perhaps in time greater alignment between the Indian educational context and IB programmes may be achieved more from the progression of the former, rather than being wholly dependent on the need for promotion and conciliations from the latter.

Responding effectively to Indian educational developments

Any reform bringing greater alignment with the IB programmes, or increasing the benefits for students of taking those programmes, will itself bring further challenges for the IB, largely in the form of further, and perhaps accelerating, growth. Nor may one such reform be too far away, with current human resource development minister Kapil Sibal being widely reported in newspapers as talking of a 'large revolution' in the educational sector in India, and expending efforts on one particular proposed piece of legislation that, should it come to fruition, could have very profound implications for the DP in India. This takes the form of *The Foreign Education Institutions (Regulation of Entry And Operations) Bill*, 2010, introduced by Minister Sibal into the Indian parliament, Lok Sabha, on 3 May 2010, with the aim of permitting the setting up of campuses in India by foreign institutions, in a bid to 'facilitate quality education in India itself and reduce the flow of Indian students abroad' (IANS, 2010). The Bill itself is not without opposition, nor is it a foregone conclusion, but it has progressed sufficiently far at this stage to suggest a likelihood of its provision coming into being within the next few years. This would see the arrival of foreign university campuses with a range of courses on offer (quite possibly including the professional courses currently so difficult to access for DP students), and to which the DP may form a rather more familiar entry path.

The idea of foreign university courses in itself would not in fact be a new one. The London School of Economics and Political Science (LSE), for instance, already offers business and related courses within the country in a number of colleges such as Russell Square International College, an educational institute set up by the promoters of the Ecole Mondiale World School (the first school in India to be authorized for all three IB programmes) and sharing premises with the school. Students can study for a diploma in economics or in social sciences, both designed by LSE, with successful completion providing access to a further two years of study leading to a bachelor's degree in the fields of economics, management, finance and the social sciences, awarded by the University of London.

Thus some opportunities already exist for pursuing foreign university degree courses within colleges in India. Nonetheless, should the scenario of foreign university campuses solidify into reality, a potentially dramatic increase in the range and availability of courses on offer would seem inevitable. This would be especially the case if some of the names initially speculated upon, which have included leading university players in both the UK and US, really were to establish operations within the country, and were to provide actual campuses in addition to courses. In such a context the value of the DP as a university entry qualification could only rise, and some of the access arguments for opting against a DP education in the +2 years could disappear – all hypothetically leaving the DP an attractive +2 option for an increased potential consumer base – including state schools and colleges offering +2 pathways, as well as the students within them. The way would thus be open to a further possible surge in demand for the DP, bringing with it challenges in maintaining the quality of programme implementation – particularly in providing sufficient training opportunities for teachers, addressing pressures arising from the need to attain highly in a still competitive tertiary sector, and the use of predicted grades in determining entry into parts of that sector. What, meanwhile, might be the role played in implementation quality by the MYP, indicated in annual data collected by the IB as providing the best preparation for students entering the DP in terms of ultimate DP achievement levels, but still playing something of a bit part within India as a whole?

Ensuring quality in DP implementation in India

Professional development challenges

The growth of the DP renders the question of training a key one, with the main group of programme deliverers likely to comprise local teachers recruited from the rather different traditions of state education. Teaching an IB programme requires training in IB philosophy and practices, as well as subject-specific content, and calls for teachers who in India may be much more used to a lecture-style approach and teaching through a textbook to develop quite different understandings and methodologies, and to apply these in the classroom. Much of the development of teachers is likely to be relatively gradual – initiated at a workshop, but far from completed there – and there will be a need for ongoing support and training in order to ensure and maintain quality of implementation of the programme.

The picture is further complicated by significant cost implications for schools availing themselves of official IB training and, while support is increasing in the form especially of guidance and exemplar materials available via various sources such as the IB's online curriculum centre (OCC), there is scope to argue for a greater level of 'face to face' support of different kinds. This too is increasing, via an expansion of in-school DP workshops offered by the IB, while organisations such as SAIBSA (the South Asian International Baccalaureate Schools Association) supplement official IB training events with an annual 'jobalike' day that allows teachers from all the IB schools in India to come together to share ideas, and receive training from volunteers who often work as IB workshop leaders, examiners and school visitors in addition to their roles as DP teachers within some of the schools. The IB teacher award, a recent development offered in conjunction with a number of university postgraduate programmes worldwide (IB, 2011f), also provides professional development for IB teachers by encouraging reflection on their practice within an academic context. Both capacity for these events and activities, and what can be achieved in a limited timeframe, are necessarily limited, however, and continuing growth in the number of teachers entering DP teaching will not be accommodated by such events in their current form. The need to consider how to meet likely training needs in the future, and cost implications of these, very much represents a challenge for the IB, if programme quality is to be maintained as expansion continues within the country.

Preserving the integrity of the programme – pressures and possibilities

A slightly different kind of challenge in terms of ensuring programme quality may lie in the pressures for high achievement that form part of the Indian educational experience in any case, but which are brought more sharply into focus by the levels of achievement demanded by Indian universities, and the use of predicted grades to determine university entrance.

Final IBDP grades emanate from specific assessment tasks and types, with some types of internal assessment potentially lying open to temptation and possible manipulation within an environment so heavily results driven, and where the use of tutors is so widespread. Students point for instance to a required mathematics portfolio, where a 'perfect storm' almost of 'push' and 'pull' factors conspire to bring about a situation in which, judging from the words of some, irregular practice is closer to the norm than is the alternative: students in the first instance compelled to opt for a higher level mathematics course that may stretch or even prove beyond their capabilities; needing to succeed in it as highly as possible for the purposes of university entry; a requirement for a portfolio of work that they may be unable to manage, and for which teacher support is quite radically restricted; the ready supply of private tutors...

In the case of predicted grades, meanwhile, there exists the added complication that, unlike the situation with final grades, predicted grades must emanate in part at least from in-school assessment, giving rise to possible questions over consistency of assessments used from school to school, and in the internal application of criteria to those assessments each time. Meanwhile one may suggest that internal assessments may *per se* stand more likely to be compromised than are final, often externally-examined, assessments.

The competitive nature of access to tertiary education, and of public examinations in general, is unlikely to change a great deal. Hence maintaining programme integrity in the face of significant growth, prevailing pressures for achievement and use of predicted grades undoubtedly represents a challenge to be considered seriously as the DP expands within the country.

Addressing MYP take-up rates to enhance student achievement in the DP

The IB has in recent years collected and published figures suggesting that students graduating into the DP from its MYP achieve more highly than do students entering the programme from alternative courses. The statistics are not decisive, but are displaying a consistent trend to support the theory that the

MYP offers the most effective preparation for success in the DP. As part of the PYP-MYP-DP school continuum, the MYP does contain a number of elements designed to prepare MYP students for the diploma, such as the criterion-related assessment system, extended research project in the form of the personal project, mandatory community and service requirement, and the focus on developing critical thinking skills. Recent years have seen a more conscious effort to align the two programmes in a manner aimed at rendering the earlier programme an even more effective preparation for the later one, via the 'MYP: Avoiding the Gap' project (IB, 2009).

The degree to which the MYP may influence higher achievement in DP within India, however, is somewhat limited by the fact that while 77 schools have been authorised to offer the DP, the number for MYP currently stands at eight and, while future growth prospects are also on the up, the rate of acceleration is somewhat less notable. Despite the fact that highest achievement plays such a major role in the national psyche, the use of the MYP to enhance achievement in DP is a concept yet to take any real root and thus, as a pathway to the DP and a preparation for that programme, the MYP overall plays a limited role within India.

Yet developing the MYP within the country may be an effective way of expanding IB understanding among students, parents, and teachers, as well as enhancing quality and achievement within the DP. Thus the MYP might – in addition to its major attraction in its own right of offering a quality educational experience for students within its target age range (11-16) – also have a role to play in helping to sustain the quality of the DP within a context of significant growth.

The challenges in doing so, however, and in making greater headway in establishing the MYP in India, are far from insignificant. The programme is, in the first instance, arguably a more complex proposition for the average classroom teacher to implement than is the DP. It is perceived in the author's experience as a somewhat more daunting proposition than the DP by many teachers charged with the task of delivering both. Indeed the quality of implementation, and considerable investment in professional development and planning time needed to achieve this for MYP in schools, are cited by some as *the* major obstacles to greater MYP expansion within the country. Fundamental concerns seem to exist over the highly teacher-dependent nature of the MYP, and perceived costs involved in acquiring sufficient quality of understanding to lead to effective delivery of the programme – and then sustaining this by retaining teachers newly-armed with powerful tools potentially enabling them to seek out any higher bidders in schools elsewhere. All appear to represent key factors in a reluctance in many schools within India to take on the MYP.

Allied to those concerns are perhaps more traditional ones relating to the absence of externally assessed examinations, the prevailing mindset on which around India seems unlikely to undergo radical transformation at any point soon. India has a long tradition of investment in this type of assessment, and firm beliefs are held in its ability to sidestep issues of bias and possible unfairness through central administration and marking – not insignificant considerations in such a competitive and high stakes local educational context, where suspicions of bias (or potential susceptibility to it) can be rife. It is not difficult in this context, therefore, to understand the hesitation over a programme and assessment model that is so teacher-dependent. Students and parents often additionally point to the lack of examinations in MYP as undermining to some extent its value as a preparation for the DP where examinations assume a significant role in final assessment and grades, and the view that an Indian state education up to the Grade 10 board examinations is actually better preparation for the DP than is the MYP is not uncommonly heard.

If the trends apparent in the data collected by the IB are correct in suggesting that the MYP does represent the best preparation for the DP, then a clear need exists for wider promotion of that fact. Even so, the prevailing status and perceptions of externally-assessed examinations probably means to all practical intents and purposes that, if MYP is to spread its influence over a wider area of India, expectations in regard to these may well need to be accommodated in one way or another. Whether that will be achieved via the optional online assessment currently being mooted for MYP from 2015 – the nature of which remains at the time of writing under wraps – is still to be seen.

In the meantime, a number of those schools offering the MYP also offer within its framework a set of International GCSE (IGCSE) examinations in order to meet expectations of and demands for externally assessed examinations at the end of Grade 10. Commissioning of a serious investigation into how the content, nature, and demands of IGCSE syllabuses and examinations might be integrated properly within the MYP framework could thus prove of value – particularly given the prevalence of IGCSE in many other parts of the world in which the MYP also makes its home. The question of MYP/IGCSE integration is a repeated one in the author's experience of workshops and school visits involving teachers charged with delivering both, and of working in a school using both. Theoretically at present, MYP/IGCSE schools attempt to deliver IGCSE content within an MYP framework, though how far in practice actual integration may be taking place as opposed to one programme being implemented at the expense of the other is not always easy to discern, to say the least.

It is the reality that many more schools within India (300+, currently) offer the IGCSE than offer the MYP – with a number nonetheless implementing PYP and DP on either side of the IGCSE. Responses as to why the middle of the IB's programmes is so callously eschewed will generally encompass a perceived need for examinations, and difficulties of integration – along with questions as to the necessity and potential success of so doing. Investigating how proper integration of the two might be achieved, therefore, and providing specific guidance, might result in more schools becoming more open to the possibility of adopting the MYP, alongside the IGCSE as the externally assessed examinations that are likely in India to remain perceived for some time to come as far too important to dispense with. Meanwhile, moves evidently afoot by IGCSE provider Cambridge International Examinations (CIE) to promote elements such as the concept of the 'Cambridge Learner', and aspects targeted at providing students with better preparation on the IGCSE side specifically for students subsequently entering the DP, could conceivably serve to usurp the wider benefits of the MYP. They could also nullify arguments for adopting or continuing with the MYP in India – all of which further points to a need for the IB to give some attention to the status of the programme and its future prospects within the country.

Costs involved in ensuring quality in MYP implementation, and concerns over externally-assessed examinations, would appear to represent the two major obstacles to greater MYP growth in India. It may, meanwhile, find itself coming under further pressure from developments in the IGCSE sector. For the sake of development of the MYP itself in India, therefore, these all represent issues that seem well worth addressing. The particular context of an expanding DP, however, and the potential of the MYP to reinforce quality of implementation and encourage higher achievement there, might form further good reasons for promoting and further expanding the role of the MYP within India.

Fulfilling a mission, and increasing the programme's relevance within the local context

A number of practical challenges thus exist for the DP – or may do so in the future – in its journey through the Indian timescape. One additional challenge might, meanwhile, be found in reference to the IB's mission for education in general. The IBDP has grown substantially within the country, in a manner rather mirroring its global progress. Elsewhere, however, it has evolved from a programme with an original purpose of 'facilitating routes for transnational mobility of a cosmopolitan middle class' (Doherty 2009, cited in Guy and Switzer, 2010: 60) to its present situation in which '[t]oday over half of the 2000+ IB diploma programme schools are state schools' (Guy and Switzer, 2010: 59). The IB itself meanwhile has a stated aim to 'create and provide access opportunities so that more students are able to benefit from a high quality, international educational experience', and a model to go along with that, indicating particular aspirations of 'living our mission' and 'widening influence' (IB 2011a); elsewhere on the IB website lies the assertion that graduates of the DP should 'share a commitment to community service and civic engagement to "make a difference" in their local and global community'. (IB, 2011d).

Yet, within India, IB programmes are of relatively little relevance to those most likely to invest their futures in this country, and potentially to 'make a difference' in their local communities. IB programmes – along with their philosophies and practices – have yet to make any kind of real inroad into state schools, and hence into the consciousness of the vast majority of Indian schoolchildren. Meanwhile a dearth of IB students exists in many of the main professional institutes – a point of particular relevance in a country where such professions will be so integral to its continuing socio-economic development, and where professional courses and careers assume greater importance among the aspirations of students and their families than might be the case in many other places.

Instead the programme still lies very much open to perceptions of economic exclusivity and a limited role as a passport abroad, catering largely to a boutique audience, and found chiefly in the domain of private schools levying significant fees, with its student clientele consequently originating in the main from a particular socio-economic background within the country. Occasional exceptions may exist in the form of colleges such as the Mahindra United World College in Pune, where economic means are not an essential criterion for access to the DP. Such exceptions are few and far between, however and, even here, dependent on wealth in the form of a private benefactor of the means and inclination to fund the school, or the existence of, for instance, United World College scholarships.

The scenario of migratory DP students itself is not one confined to India, as Guy and Switzer clearly illustrate, but rather transcends much of the Asia-Pacific region. Nor can its causes within India – with their roots in a context of 'constrained' tertiary provision that limits options within the country for Indian students in general, and thus provides a powerful 'push' factor encouraging those with the means to do so to look at tertiary education abroad – be attributed to an IB that has sought very positively to engage with the educational scenario existing in the country, as Taneja and Switzer's *Guide to University Recognition in India* states: 'The IB is committed to supporting the large proportion of students who wish to remain in India for their undergraduate studies and to creating pathways to enable more students to consider this option.' (2011: 5). Ultimately, however, it has limited powers in a context in which little compulsion exists for radically oversubscribed Indian universities to overly concern themselves with the needs and fates of DP students who want to stay.

Nor will wider access to Indian universities in itself tackle perceptions of economic exclusivity, so long as IB students at school level are to be found within private high fee-paying institutions in the first place. The question arises, therefore, of what the IB might be expected and able to do in terms of considering ways of 'enabling more students to experience and benefit from an IB education regardless of personal circumstances' (IB, 2011a), as is the stated aim of the IB Board of Governors. Quite apart from questions of the differing educational experiences and expectations that exist between a traditional Indian education and an IB education, costs relating to authorisation, annual fees and so on – along with the need for ongoing professional development – would very likely prove prohibitive for any independently-minded state educational institutes willing to go against the flow and announce a willingness to take on an IB programme. Nor does the IB, a not-for-profit organisation, possess the means – or consent of its fee-payers, for that matter – to start lavishing significant largesse on individual beneficiaries within the state educational system of any individual country.

In promoting access in general, the IB seeks to engage with 'like-minded donors, schools, universities, non-governmental organizations, and ministries' (IB, 2011a), and in the absence of concrete details as to what may already be happening in terms of such engagement within India, it is difficult to suggest concrete approaches to it. One can thus only wonder about possible engagement with players and potential partners within India, such as the CBSE board that has recently made its Grade 10 board examinations optional and begun increasing the emphasis placed on the more IB-like concept of 'comprehensive continuous evaluation' (CCE), while overseeing in the classroom the replacement of reproducing a textbook with science projects, and testing of students 'on projects, discussions and participation in class and their other skills' (Dore, 2010).

Existing educators within the country might also be useful sources of information and suggestions on educational developments within the country. Members of the IB Educator Network (IB, 2011e) around the region, meanwhile, might be willing on occasion to carry out their own piece of community service, by offering some voluntary support to projects involving the introduction and implementation of an IB programme within an individual school context, set up in order to begin to establish an IB presence in the state sector.

Whatever may already be happening, however, the fact remains at present that IB programmes in India are found almost exclusively in the domain of high fee-paying schools and colleges, and tend to be the preserve of students from within a particular economic stratum of society – with a consequence being a perception (justified to a large degree at present) of IB being economically exclusive. One might feel that, 76 schools after the DP's first foray into the country, this represents something that does now need to change, especially in view of the IB's wider educational mission and proclamations on access. If there is a desire for IB education to be of greater relevance to the lives of the vast majority of Indian children who come from economic strata other than those of the rich, therefore, this represents an area requiring some serious consideration in the future and thus a further challenge within India for the IB.

Conclusion

Bob Dylan, when singing that the times they are a-changin', probably did not have India especially in mind, but a-changin' they most certainly are in this country, and potentially quite significantly within its educational context – among other areas. It is clear that the IB, undergoing significant expansion and change of its own, is working extremely hard to respond to those changes, and to increase its relevance both in regard to the number of schools now offering IB programmes (and the DP in particular), and to a wider range of students than simply those seeking a 'passport to university abroad'.

As has been seen, the future for the IB looks set to present a diversity of challenges, with on the one hand potentially significant DP growth to be managed and provided for, with all of the attendant issues of maintaining programme integrity and quality throughout that process. On the other hand, there exists a situation of perhaps insufficient growth, where the programme largely remains the preserve of private sector students from economically advantaged backgrounds, and is perceived as relevant to a limited consumer base with an often pragmatic goal of facilitating for themselves a range of additional university options abroad. Growth of the DP may thus be occurring at a notable rate, but its relevance to students from a wider range of economic backgrounds is not doing likewise – something that sits uncomfortably with the IB's overall educational mission and commitments to access.

Many challenges await, therefore, in a context that looks inevitably dynamic and potentially highly productive and constructive for the IB, if it can meet those challenges effectively and maximise the opportunities to 'live the mission' and 'widen influence'. Exciting times appear to lie ahead for the IB in India – though it would do well to heed the wise words of India's very embodiment of the learner profile. As Mahatma Gandhi once said: 'The future depends on what we do in the present.'

Acknowledgements

Personal thanks are due to Priyamvada Taneja (IB university liaison officer in India), Leena Francis (college counsellor, Ecole Mondiale World School), Sudeshna Sengupta (DP coordinator, Ecole Mondiale World School), Monica Sarang (MYP coordinator, Ecole Mondiale World School), Kavita Sukhani (IGCSE coordinator, Ecole Mondiale World School), Nitin Padte (deputy head of secondary, Ecole Mondiale World School), and assorted students, ex-students and parents of Ecole Mondiale World School.

References

AIU – Association of Indian Universities (1983): Letter to the Deputy Director General of the IB, 17 August 1983.

AIU – Association of Indian Universities (2010): Letter to IB Headquarters, 14 December 2010.

Chopra, R (2010): 10th boards now history; all pass, in *Hindustan Times*, 29 May 2010. Online: www.hindustantimes.com/News-Feed/india/10th-boards-now-history-all-pass/Article1-550038.aspx (last accessed 12 June 2011).

Doherty, C (2009): The appeal of the International Baccalaureate in Australia's educational market: a curriculum of choice for mobile futures, in *Discourse: Studies in the Cultural Politics of Education*, 30 (1), pp73-89.

Dore, B (2010): Classrooms brace for change, in *Hindustan Times*, 29 September 2010. Online: www.hindustantimes.com/News-Feed/mumbai/Classrooms-brace-for-change/Article1-605844.aspx (last accessed 20 June 2011).

Dore, B and Seshasayee, H (2011): Help just a phone call away, in *Hindustan Times*, 11 February 2011. Online (last accessed 23 June 2011): www.hindustantimes.com/News-Feed/mumbai/Help-just-a-phone-call-away/Article1-660997.aspx

Elkady, E (2011): The MYP and its cultural context: a reflection from Dubai, in M Hayden and J Thompson (eds), *Taking the MYP Forward*. Woodbridge: John Catt Educational Ltd, pp180-189.

Guy, J and Switzer, J (2010): The Migratory Trends of International Baccalaureate Diploma Students in Asia Pacific: Going Global?, in *Journal of the World Universities Forum*, 3 (5), pp59-74.

IANS (2010): Foreign university bill introduced in Lok Sabha, in *Thaindian News*, 3 May 2010. Online: www.thaindian.com/newsportal/politics/foreign-university-bill-introduced-in-lok-sabha-lead_100357819.html (last accessed 17 July 2011).

IB (2009): *Middle Years Programme: Coordinator's Notes*. Cardiff: International Baccalaureate (November 2009).

IB (2011a): *Access and Advancement*. Online: www.ibo.org/accessandadvancement/ (last accessed 3 August 2011).

IB (2011b): *Country information for India*. Online: www.ibo.org/country/IN/index.cfm (last accessed 20 August 2011).

IB (2011c): *Diploma Programme: Coordinator's Notes*. Cardiff: International Baccalaureate (May 2011).

IB (2011d): *IB Diploma graduates: prepared for success in university and life beyond*. Online: www.ibo.org/recognition/DPgraduates/ (last accessed 3 August 2011).

IB (2011e): *IB Educator Network (IBEN)*. Online: www.ibo.org/iben/ (last accessed 4 September 2011).

IB (2011f): *International Baccalaureate Teacher Award*. Online (last accessed 1 September 2011): www.ibo.org/programmes/pd/award/

Indo-Asian News Service (2009): Exam stress: students taking memory pills, in *Hindustan Times*. 6 March 2009. Online: www.hindustantimes.com/News-Feed/teens/Exam-stress-students-taking-memory-pills-smoking/Article1-386944.aspx (last accessed 23 July 2011).

Menon, S (2010): Board exams are ineffective tests of skills, in *Hindustan Times*, 25 May 2010. Online: www.hindustantimes.com/board-exams-are-ineffective-tests-of-skills/Article1-548315.aspx (last accessed 19 June 2010).

Taneja, P and Switzer, J (2011): *The International Baccalaureate: Guide to University Recognition in India*. Singapore: International Baccalaureate Asia Pacific.

Chapter 14

The internationalisation of Dutch secondary education: the IBDP and the Dutch international secondary schools

Boris Prickarts and Theo Brok

Introduction

This chapter takes as its focus how the International Baccalaureate (IB) Diploma Programme (DP) has taken forward a group of Dutch schools – the Dutch International Secondary Schools (DISS). Issues to be considered include how important the IBDP has been in increasing the variety and innovation of secondary education in The Netherlands, what kind of consequences of the internationalisation of Dutch education can be distinguished, what can be expected for the future, and what are the desired government policies towards these consequences (and how do we know). With regards to the last point, there is a question as to whether finding out (*ie* the research undertaken) adopts a defensible methodology in the light of issues surrounding the internationalisation policies. Some of the evaluative research undertaken focuses on narrow policy questions, while the changes that may come about as a result of these policies may relate to much wider structural questions concerning inclusion and exclusion in education.

This suggests that a different approach and methodology is required. Concepts such as those of structures may not be observable. In turn this suggests that we need to adopt a realist methodology (Bhaskar, 1978: 5) that allows for the possibility that while structures may not be seen, they generate real effects. This is in contrast to methodologies employed to advise the Dutch government on policy. In particular, some of this research has relied on an eclectic mix of questionnaires and interviews but with a narrow focus.

In this chapter, we will describe the cross-fertilisation of the IB, the DISS and the Dutch secondary education system. We will also explain why we believe the Dutch government's role and research provide opportunities, as well as risks, in terms of inclusion and exclusion in education. The focus will be on the new IBDP policy (IGO Archives, 2011) as a case in point. Lastly, we aim to assess the extent to which the IBDP and Dutch government policies and research can be expected to lead to desirable outcomes for secondary students in The Netherlands.

The structure of this chapter is as follows:

- The IB, DISS and the internationalisation of Dutch secondary school education, 1979-2011.

- The role of the Dutch government and its research in internationalising Dutch secondary education: the new IBDP policy (IGO Archives, 2011).

- Conclusion: are the IBDP and DISS moving towards a shared 'land of values'?

DISS, the IB and the internationalisation of Dutch secondary school education, 1979-2011

The DISS is part of the DIS (Dutch International Schools) who, through DISS and DIPS (the Dutch International Primary Schools) provide government-sponsored secondary and primary international education in The Netherlands. In 2011, the DIS cater for the educational needs of over 5000 Dutch and foreign students whose parents temporarily work in The Netherlands (DIS, 2011: 20). The development of the DIS is very closely connected to the economic crisis of the 1970s and 1980s, and the development of the IB. In 1979 the Dutch Minister of Education, Van Kemenade, looking for ways to attract foreign multinationals with appropriate schools for the children of their employees, hosted the first European Ministerial Conference on the IB in The Hague, which in 1982 inspired three Dutch secondary school leaders to set up the first three international secondary departments (Van Elderen, *et al*, 1996: 5) in their schools in Eindhoven, Hilversum and Oegstgeest.

Before the DIS started, two other types of international education – in terms of management and governance – existed in The Netherlands: privately funded international education (including British, French, German, American), and European international education (the European School, sponsored by the European Union). The start and development of the DIS was stormy. Issues such as the legal status of the DIS ('what are we legally?'), its membership ('who are we?'), its Dutch language and culture programme requirements ('what do we offer and why?'), and the government's financial contribution to it ('who pays for us?') caused years of intense controversy and discussion. DIPS followed the secondary example in 1984. Between 1984 and 1988 five other secondary schools joined (Arnhem, Groningen, Maastricht, The Hague and Rotterdam), bringing the total of secondary students to over 1100 in 1988 (IGO Archives, 1992-1994, Appendix II). The number of primary and secondary DIS locations grew to 11 in the next 20 years, also including Amsterdam (2003), Almere (2005 and 2006) and Enschede (2008). A rapidly increasing number of internationally mobile parents were interested in the primary and secondary DIS for their children. They were attracted by the fact that all DIS provide English-medium international education at a relatively low cost. All but one of the secondary DIS (Almere) offer the IBDP as their pre-university programme. All but one of the secondary DIS (Rotterdam) moved from offering the International General Certificate of Secondary Education (IGCSE) to offering the IB Middle Years Programme (MYP) to their 11-16 year old students. All but one of the primary

DIS offer the International Primary Curriculum (IPC). The IB Primary Years Programme (PYP) is offered at one primary DIS (Hilversum). The DIS (primary and secondary) have never adopted a policy of all schools offering the same international education programme, thus leaving the schools free to choose which to adopt.

In 1989 the Dutch government sent a letter to Parliament (TK, 1988-1989: 2) stressing the need for continuation of the DIS. In that letter the Dutch State Secretary of Education, Ginjaar-Maas, defined as three eligibility requirements for admission that students should be either:

- foreign students who will reside in The Netherlands for a defined term while their parents are employed in the country; or
- Dutch nationals who have had at least two years of international education while their parents have had employment overseas; or
- Dutch nationals who are planning to be educated overseas, for at least two years, due to their parents' employment outside The Netherlands.

The extra funding costs of the DIS needed to be contained. The DIS had to be aimed at expatriates. Opening up the DIS for all Dutch students was financially not feasible.

In the course of the 1980s however, in the slipstream of the development of the DIS, it became clear that many Dutch, often professional middle class parents, whose children did not meet the DIS eligibility requirements were also interested in international education. An increasing number of Dutch schools regarded the MYP – and later the IBDP – as very compatible with 'broadly established, nationally organised top-down innovations such as Basic secondary education and the Second Phase' (Oonk, 2004: 83). In Hilversum in 1989, this trend marked the birth of internationalised, government-sponsored, predominantly Dutch-English, bilingual education (TTO or *TweeTalig Onderwijs*). TTO went on to be developed at the DIS locations initially, but rapidly spread to many regular Dutch schools after the mid-1990s, making it one of the most well-developed in Europe (Fruhauf *et al*, 1996: 177-187). The Dutch government *de facto* recognised TTO, when it published the policy document 'Exceeding Boundaries' (*Grenzen Verleggen*), stating: '… it has to be open to everyone, it needs to correspond to the final examinations, which, after all, remain Dutch, and it should not involve additional costs.' (TK,1991-1992; p 29-30). The further development of TTO is very closely connected to the recession at the beginning of the 1990s, reductions of the education budget, and the trend towards more deregulation and autonomy for schools. All the main Dutch political parties regarded deregulation as the way to create a wider variety of better schools (Lucardie *et al,* 1992). (The Social-Democratic (PvdA), Liberal (VVD) and Christian Democratic (CDA) parties published their relevant policy documents in 1992-1993, respectively called 'Enlargement of

Autonomy at Primary and Secondary Schools' (*Autonomievergroting in het primair en voortgezet onderwijs*); 'Choosing Autonomy' (*Kiezen voor autonomie*), and 'The School to the Parents' (*De school aan de ouders*).) The Dutch government, under the influence of neo-liberalism (Weenink, 2005; 77), left (quality) regulation of TTO, and its links with the DIS, to the schools themselves. In 1993 the DIS reacted by publishing 'The DIS and Internationalising Education' (*IGO Scholen en Internationalisering*), followed by TTO schools, in 1997, formulating their own quality standards for the first time. The Dutch State Secretary of Education in 1994, Cohen, summarised the position of the government quite well, when he said: 'I admire and respect the DIS. However, because their education doesn't correspond to the Dutch final examinations, and it is not open to everyone, it seems bound to remain a restricted service. …I expect and hope the DIS' experience with language education, multicultural education, mixed ability classes and community service programmes will be an enormous inspiration to the development of TTO schools.' (IGO Archives,1992-1994).

Most recent estimates are that the DIS, together with the private international schools, the European School and the TTO schools, cater for the educational needs of well over 25,000 Dutch and foreign primary and secondary students (Innovatie Platform, 2009a: 5; DIS, 2011).

The role of the Dutch government and its research in internationalising Dutch secondary education: the new IBDP policy (2011)

The new IBDP policy (2011)

In 2004 two Members of Parliament urged the Dutch government – supported by a Parliamentary majority – to:

- acknowledge the international reputation, monitoring of assessment and university access opportunities of the IB Diploma Programme, an international secondary school programme;
- consider the limited access to the IBDP of diplomats' children and children from abroad only;
- bring the IBDP within reach of normal Dutch children; and
- enable schools to offer the IBDP as a regular programme.

In 2005 the Education Minister asked its main Advisory Body, the *Onderwijsraad*, to research this proposal in more detail and advise. Their conclusion, in 2006, was that the IBDP should be accessible to 'cosmopolitan' students only; students who aim for an international career and future (Onderwijsraad, 2006; 9). The Minister decided in favour of the introduction of a so-called IBDP pilot at government sponsored schools for a period of four years, starting in 2007. With this decision, she wanted to increase diversity and innovation (EK, 2006: 5-6). The advice of the *Onderwijsraad* to restrict the IBDP to 'cosmopolitan' students only was dropped. As a result, six DISS locations (Amsterdam, Arnhem, Eindhoven, Groningen, Hilversum and Oegstgeest) were allowed to enrol a maximum of 20 students each, who:

- must be 16+ year-olds, so they are able to use the Dutch and English language at an advanced level;
- must be taught Dutch at the highest IBDP (language A1) level;
- are able to make use of an existing legal financial aid arrangement (WTO) only;
- are able to access the IBDP only on the condition that extra costs are not subsidised by the government;
- must go to experienced DISS/TTO schools with higher secondary and pre-university education; and
- must have a higher secondary education diploma or a certificate of successful completion of their penultimate year of pre-university education.

In March 2011 the Education Minister decided that the IBDP pilot was a success (IGO Archives, 2011). In her opinion, evaluative research had shown that Dutch students were transitioning well from regular Dutch schools to the IBDP, their high Dutch language level was being maintained and they were achieving good results. She announced the intention to formally subsidise the entrance of 'regular' (*ie* resident) Dutch pre-university students to the IBDP at a 'regular' (*ie* non-DIS, which is slightly higher) subsidy level from 31 July 2012. The Minister wrote that the extra funding costs of the DIS still needed to be contained because they should be aimed at expatriate children only. Opening up the extra funding of the DIS for all Dutch students, not only pre-university students but also primary and middle school students, is still not financially feasible. Yet non-cosmopolitan Dutch pre-university students can now look forward to being legally allowed entrance to the IBDP at a similarly relatively low tuition fee.

The role of the Dutch government and its evaluative research

On the one hand, when the Dutch government developed the DIS and formulated its IBDP policy, it acted like a 'guardian'. It responded to international and national demands by setting some real boundaries and formulating clear and informed regulations in order to guard or minimise the number of losers. Access to the extra funding of DIS and the IBDP pilot is restricted to those who really need it, so public funds are not spent wastefully, to the detriment of the educational opportunities of others. The Dutch government clearly searched for the preservation of national social cohesion and a sense of national identity, of which equality of opportunity for all Dutch students is one element.

On the other hand, the Dutch government's involvement is also limited, especially in terms of financial and educational governance and accountability. Acting like a 'player', it accepts no extra financial responsibility and leaves internationalisation of Dutch schools to the networks that exist. Access to the IBDP from 31 July 2012 is not restricted any more to those who really need it. The Dutch government has been playing along with, and has been being driven by, global educational market concerns, thereby maximising education as a commodity. It has also focused on competitiveness and integration of Dutch elites into the global economy, of which equity of opportunity for global elites is one element.

The evaluative research upon which the Education Minister based her new IBDP policy (2011) involved a government-sponsored research group called E&S, and a privately (McKinsey & Co) and publicly sponsored think-tank called the *Innovatie Platform* (platform for innovation). The aim of E&S (Keersemaker, 2009a and 2009b) was to research the question: 'To what extent do the IBDP pilot experiences of the school leaders and the pilot students generate reasons to change the IBDP pilot policy in order to achieve its intended aims and objectives?' This research had a narrow focus in the sense that it mainly evaluated (experiences with) the IBDP pilot only (Keersemaker, 2009a and 2009b: 3), and in the sense that it was not so much concerned with the wider question of whether it attracted the 'right kind' of students. E&S used semi-structured interviews with all the school leaders of the DIS IBDP pilot schools, and web-based qualitative questionnaires to obtain data from a little over half (52 percent) of the IBDP pilot students.

The epistemic underpinnings of the research methods of E&S seem to be that an object of human scientific research (*ie* the effects of an educational experiment on the economy and educational system of a society) can be reduced to individuals (*ie* interviewees). This type of 'methodological individualism' (Bhaskar, 1978: 5) can be seen as ignoring a crucial aspect of the reality of all social phenomena: they all operate in a wider social context. Therefore, this poor and superficial conception of the social threatens to play down the fundamental role of relations (between individuals, groups and structures – and the natural world – and the relations between them). As a result, the explanatory power of the E&S research approach lacks depth and breadth. It therefore seems to fail to address wider societal issues concerning inclusion, exclusion and equality. And what is more, the ontological underpinning of E&S research methods seems to be an underlying – static (*ie* non-dynamic) – belief that all people apply instrumental reason (wherever and whenever). The result of this assumption is that underlying (class) relations and structures were overlooked. E&S chose an empiricist 'toolkit', so it researched only observable phenomena (using questionnaires with a limited scope).

The Innovatie Platform, with four Chief Executive Officers as the steering committee, carried out evaluative research (Innovatie Platform, 2009b) aimed at researching the question: 'How can the [reputation of] international education in The Netherlands be improved to attract more significant international businesses and talent to The Netherlands?' This is not a disinterested question about wider societal issues such as access opportunities to international education, but is a government-driven question within a narrow frame for evaluative research, *ie* about how to attract (the children of) global elites. The Platform started by formulating a new (proto-scientific) idea that in a globalising world more students (Dutch and foreign) need to participate in international education in The Netherlands (Innovatie Platform, 2009b: 20). It then made no serious attempt at discerning generative structures or mechanisms at work except, perhaps, by pointing at a 'rapidly globalising, knowledge-working elite which needs us to catch up with them' (Innovatie Platform, 2009b: 4). So, without informed theory, the Platform went about collecting data from sources of various kinds, to justify ways to expand the current Dutch international education system.

Conclusion: are the IBDP and DISS moving towards a shared 'land of values'?

The IB initially 'took the DIS by the hand', when at the end of the 1970s and into the 1980s it inspired a growing number of schools either to adopt the IBDP (and later the MYP) or to internationalise their curriculum. The IB in general, and the new IBDP policy in particular, have been very important in increasing the variety of (international) secondary education in The Netherlands over the last 30 years. The DISS later 'took the IBDP by the hand', when in the course of the 1990s and the 2000s it helped with blurring the notion of private and public international education and the notion of international and intercultural education. The DISS, and also increasingly the TTO schools, have been very important in classifying and framing (Bernstein, 1971) relations between and within curriculum contents. These contents are aimed at reconciling education for education's sake (and the love of scholarship) with education for acquiring a competitive edge in the knowledge economy (and the performative treadmill). As we have seen in this chapter, however, the internationalisation of Dutch secondary education, the new IBDP policy and the evaluative research that justified it can result in anything between an elitist (global) market-driven and therefore instrumentalist international curriculum, and an equitable, contextualised, value-driven and therefore holistic international curriculum. In this chapter we have attempted to outline certain 'internationalisation risks' in terms of inclusion and exclusion, and the potential outcome of moving students towards a land of narrow, individualised values.

Much will depend on the role of the Dutch government and the kind of research with which it would inform its decisions. The Dutch government has been operating more like a player than a guardian (Prickarts, 2010). The Dutch government 'plays along with' global educational trends, accepts no extra financial responsibility for the extra it is facilitating, and leaves internationalisation of Dutch schools to the networks that exist. Yet, at the same time, the new IBDP policy shows that the government is setting and 'guarding' real boundaries and formulating clear and informed regulations aimed at redistributing collective social capital (Bourdieu, 1974).

The desirable outcome for secondary students in The Netherlands would be that they, including the less advantaged students, are facilitated to access elements of good quality international programmes such as effective language education and intercultural education. The good quality of the international programmes, including the IBDP, needs to be clearly defined and rigorously monitored. The desired government policies should challenge schools to formulate and share clear underpinning principles and values of their programmes along these international lines. And 'international' could be surprisingly 'national': DISS commit to addressing the differences between the students' own culture and that of the local community (Jackson, 2005). In other words, schools also need to be challenged to couple the individual and the social. Researchers in international education policy therefore need to look for agents, their agenda, curriculums, structures and cultures that may not be seen but which generate real effects (Archer, 2010). These include values, generating not only visible and intended consequences but also hidden and unintended consequences. Here is hope that the DISS, the IBDP, researchers and the Dutch government will keep on 'holding hands' and squeeze hard when a scenario of Dutch international schools becoming like expensive, elitist, market-driven, bastions of upper middle-class power looms large. Less advantaged students, such as immigrants, should increasingly be able to benefit from the opportunities that come with access to government sponsored international education.

References

Archer, M S (2010): Routine, Reflexivity, and Realism, in *Sociological Theory*, 28 (3), pp272-303.

Bernstein, B (1971): On the classification and framing of educational knowledge, in M F D Young (ed), *Knowledge and Control: new directions for the sociology of education*. London: Collier Macmillan.

Bhaskar, R (1978): On the possibility of Social Scientific Knowledge and the Limits of Naturalism, in *Journal for the Theory of Social Behaviour*, 8 (1), pp1-28.

Bourdieu, P (1974): The school as a conservative force: scholastic and cultural inequalities, in: J Eggleston (ed), *Contemporary Research in the Sociology of Education*. London: Methuen.

DIS – Dutch International Schools (2011): *Annual Report 2010*. Voorburg/Hilversum.

EK (2006): 28 277, *Brief van de Minister van Onderwijs, Cultuur en Wetenschap aan de Eerste Kamer der Staten-Generaal*, pp1-7.

Fruhauf, G, Coyle D, and Christ I (eds) (1996): *Practice and perspectives in European bilingual education*. Alkmaar: Stichting Europdes Platform voor het Nederlandse Onderwijs.

IGO Archives, Postbus 700, 1200 AS Hilversum, The Netherlands: Appendix II: *Growth IGO in The Netherlands 1984-1988*; Speech by Mr M J Cohen at the Congress 'Global Education for a Smaller World', 11 July 1994 Rijnlands Lyceum Oegstgeest; uncorrected stenographic report of a meeting between the Minister of Education and members of the Education Committee, 26 March 1992, pp25, 16-25, 54; letter from Mrs Van Bijstervelt-Vliegenthart to DISS, 23 March 2011.

Innovatie Platform (2009a): *International Schools in The Netherlands: Preliminary Report.* The Hague, The Netherlands.

Innovatie Platform (2009b): *Deuren open! Advies internationale scholen.* The Hague, The Netherlands.

Jackson, M (2005): The role of the host culture as a resource for developing intercultural understanding in a Dutch international secondary school, in *Journal of Research in International Education*, 4 (2), pp193-209.

Keersemaker, C (2009a): *Evaluation of the IBDP Pilot for Dutch students: interviews with school leaders.* Apeldoorn: E&S publications.

Keersemaker, C (2009b): *Evaluation of the IBDP Pilot for Dutch students: student questionnaires.* Apeldoorn: E&S publications.

Lucardie, P, Noomen I, and Voerman G (eds) (1992): *Kroniek. Overzicht van de partijpolitieke gebeurtenissen van het jaar*, pp1-52.

Onderwijsraad (2006): *Advies internationale leerwegen en het internationale bacalaureaat, uitgebracht aan de minister van Onderwijs, Cultuur en Wetenschap.* The Hague. Online: www.onderwijsraad.nl/.../internationale_leerwegen_en_het_internationale_baccalaureaat,_uitgebracht_aan_de_minister_van_Onderwijs_Cultuur_en_Wetenschap (last accessed 4 September 2011).

Oonk, G H (2004): *European integration as a source of innovation in education. A study of the meaning of internationalisation and its results in secondary education in the Netherlands.* University of Amsterdam: doctoral thesis.

Prickarts, B J A (2010): Equality or equity, player or guardian? The Dutch government and its role in providing access opportunities for government sponsored international secondary education, 1979–2009, in *Journal of Research in International Education*, 9 (3), pp227-244.

TK (1988-1989): 21 113, nr. 2, *Brief van de Staatssecretaris van Onderwijs en Wetenschappen aan de Tweede Kamer der Staten-Generaal.*

TK (1991-1992): 22 452, nr. 2, *Nota 'Grenzen Verleggen' van de Minister van Onderwijs en Wetenschappen aan de Tweede Kamer der Staten-Generaal.*

Van Elderen, J J M, Fruhauf, G and van Haren, N J (eds) (1996): *Internationally Oriented Education in the Netherlands. An introduction.* Alkmaar: European Platform.

Weenink, D (2005): *Upper Middle-Class Resources of Power in the Educational Arena. Dutch Elite Schools in an Age of Globalisation.* University of Amsterdam: PhD thesis.

Chapter 15

Higher education and the IB diploma: a UK perspective

Leslie Currie

This chapter is written from the perspective of someone who studied in Scotland, who has worked in international and UK recruitment and admissions in an English university, and who now works in a role that deals with university admissions across the UK. As a university admissions officer it was my role to bring qualifications to the attention of academic staff, to understand their views and to reflect these in the requirements for their courses. I will not comment on the educational value of the International Baccalaureate (IB); that is the domain of teachers and academic staff. But of course I discussed qualifications with teachers, with academic colleagues, with admissions staff in other institutions and with IB specialists throughout the world; my thoughts following these discussions are reflected here. My own perspective is thus to a large extent a 'practical' one. In the past I have referred to a definition by Jim Cambridge of the then IB Research Unit at the University of Bath who identified two aspects of the IB: the 'internationalist' – 'a transformative discourse', and the 'globalist' – concerned with 'educational certification that is portable between schools and transferable between different educational systems' (Cambridge, 2003: 54-58). From the point of view of higher education admissions both are necessary, but to the admissions officer the latter is of particular importance.

In the UK, higher education programmes may be delivered by universities, by specialist institutions such as music conservatoires, in further education colleges and by some private providers. I shall describe them all here as 'higher education institutions' (HEIs) and will generally refer to them as 'institutions'. In this chapter I will first give a general introduction to undergraduate admissions to UK higher education and the many changes taking place. I shall then look at particular aspects of some policies and processes as they relate to the IB diploma, including the flow of information to institutions, the way IB diploma offers are made, and some issues around perceptions of IB diploma students, before looking briefly to the future.

Admission to higher education in the UK

Admission to higher education in the UK today is in a state of flux. Of course for higher education to be in a state of change is nothing new – this has been the reality of its existence throughout the ages – but at the time of writing there are particular questions that prospective students, their families and advisers, higher education staff and civil servants are all having to face. Readers may not be familiar with all of these issues – at least not from a higher education perspective – so I will take a little time to outline some of them. Education in the UK is now a devolved matter: that is, it is the responsibility of the four administrations in England, Scotland, Northern Ireland and Wales, rather than being centrally controlled by London. A useful general introduction to the organisation of higher education in the UK is given on the websites of Eurydice, an initiative of the Education, Audiovisual and Culture Agency of the European Union (Eurydice, 2011), and the Scottish Government (Scottish Government, 2011).

In higher education, different policies are beginning to emerge. Some of the most dramatic changes are to be seen in the area of higher education funding, including tuition fees charged to undergraduate students. Readers familiar with the world of international education will probably be aware of the distinction between 'home (UK)/European Union (EU)' and 'international (non-EU)' tuition fees currently made by UK universities, where the 'international' fee is usually substantially higher than the 'home/EU' fee and fee status is based on complex relationships between nationality and residence: the best general introduction to this area is from the UK Council for International Student Affairs (UKCISA, 2011). While the distinction between 'home/EU' and 'international' fees may well remain, the most dramatic changes are in the level of the 'home/EU' fee itself. Following its recent higher education White Paper (Department for Business, Innovation and Skills, 2011), the government in England proposes to allow institutions to charge tuition fees of between £6000 and £9000 per annum to UK and EU students, subject to various conditions and with a complex loan and support scheme, linked to a substantial cut in government funding to higher education. In Wales a similar level of fee may be charged, though Welsh students will effectively receive a substantial subsidy – wherever in the UK they study. In Scotland, by contrast, the government is committed to charging no 'up-front' fees at all to Scottish students, although it seems likely that students from elsewhere in the UK will pay amounts up to £9000. In Northern Ireland this issue is still under consideration. An added complication is that the four UK nations have to charge EU students from outside their own nation the same fees as their own residents, while being able to charge students from other parts of the UK higher fees! So while for a non-EU student it will still be a matter of seeing what an individual higher education provider charges, for a UK or EU student the part of the UK in which undergraduate study takes place will now have major implications for the cost of that study.

Widening inclusion continues to be a central concern for all the UK governments. In England, the previous Labour Government's focus on increasing participation has been taken up by the Conservative/Liberal Democrat coalition with a wide range of initiatives to increase social mobility (see, for instance, Cabinet Office 2011) while similar programmes are in force in all of the other administrations. Governments want higher education institutions to play a significant part in these initiatives and institutions and, indeed, in England and Wales institutions are only allowed to charge higher fees if a range of widening inclusion policies are in place. Institutions are responding by not only offering a wide range of outreach and aspiration-building activity for disadvantaged groups, but also by considering wider 'contextual factors' (such as school performance or social disadvantage) when applications are received, and by an increased awareness of 'vocational' qualifications (*ie* qualifications other than A levels and Scottish Highers).

Most undergraduate courses at UK universities and colleges admit students through a centralised system, the Universities and Colleges Admissions System (UCAS, 2011a) and related systems for specialist courses (such as CUKAS for the *conservatoires*). The UCAS system is currently under review. The 'Admissions Process Review' is looking at every aspect of the system, from how many applications a person may make, to when the application can be made (before or after the results of the qualifications are received by the institution) (UCAS, 2011b). The UCAS tariff, a system that allocates points to qualifications to aid comparison and to allow offers to be made, is being considered by the Qualifications Information Review, which is considering issues around the tariff and its constituent qualifications – including, of course, the IB diploma. When to these are added issues such as changes to the school curriculum in England, Scotland and Wales, and new immigration regulations, it is easy to understand that higher education admissions staff can sometimes seem dazed by the challenges they face.

'Selling' the IB to higher education

In the UK, admission to higher education institutions is, by law, entirely a matter for those institutions themselves. Consequently it is not enough for a qualification to establish itself with government, or an education ministry, or to show it is equivalent to a local qualification – issues which the IB diploma has encountered elsewhere. Instead the key constituency that qualifications for higher education entry have to satisfy are the higher education institutions themselves. As a then new qualification, for the IB diploma to succeed, and for schools to adopt it, it was vital that students were easily accepted by higher education institutions – otherwise the point of the qualification was lost. The IB and its member schools have been aware from the beginning of the need to sell the IB diploma to higher education institutions worldwide. Good information has been provided for higher education (first through publications and, now, through the website and electronic communications), while staff such as the university liaison officer employed by the IB Schools and Colleges Association (IBSCA)/International Baccalaureate Africa, Europe, Middle East (IBAEM) have been available to answer questions. It seems to me that there has been a recognition that higher education is as important a client as the schools, students and families themselves and that this view has been a key part of the diploma's success.

By contrast, the main focus recently of the A level awarding bodies has been on schools as their key customers, and until recently there has been no formal structure to encourage dialogue between the awarding bodies and the higher education sector as a whole. To quote Cambridge Assessment: 'We have concerns that over recent decades the "users" of qualifications, *ie* HE and employers, have become divorced from the "producers" of qualifications, *ie* exam boards.' (Cambridge Assessment, 2011). In England the coalition government's concern that higher education must be involved in the setting of standards for A levels is an indication of a feeling that there is a problem in this area.

Interestingly, the need to obtain recognition from higher education has also been felt in some other areas. The Scottish Qualifications Authority has had a 'Manager – HEI Liaison' for some time, with a remit comparable in some ways to the IBSCA/IBAEM university liaison officer. It is also felt to be important to obtain recognition of new qualifications; when the Welsh Baccalaureate was introduced in Wales, for instance, the Welsh Joint Education Committee (WJEC) set up an advisory group of higher education institutions to ensure acceptance and recognition, and both the Welsh Baccalaureate and the English Advanced Diploma funded specialist liaison officers within UCAS to promote their qualifications.

The IB has, of course, considered its success in establishing the IB diploma with higher education in various parts of the world. Its 2003 enquiry into perceptions of the IB at UK higher education institutions (IB, 2003) was a valuable report, confirming positive views. It often seemed to me, though, that the use made of it was not as wide as it might have been; a report that could have been of value to schools and colleges in setting parents' minds at rest was difficult to find and apparently classified as a research publication, rather than being trumpeted as proof of success. No doubt such publications in the future will be treated differently.

An interesting question for the future may be how the IB ensures that its qualifications can meet the needs of many different higher education systems, in many different countries that have different expectations of the curriculum new undergraduates will have previously completed. An initial look at the IB website does not indicate what discussions take place with higher education or, as far as I can see, how decisions are made on what the curriculum should be.

Who makes the decisions in the institution?

When thinking about admission to higher education, applicants, their families and advisors understand that the processing is undertaken by clerical and administrative staff. They may assume, however, that the application is directly considered by an academic member of staff, probably a lecturer in that subject area (an 'admissions tutor'), who will make the decision her/himself. In an increasing number of higher education institutions, however, admissions decision-making is now undertaken by administrative staff, with admissions administrators applying criteria established by academic staff. This may be carried out by administrative staff in departments, schools or faculties or it may be centralised, with a central administrative team applying the criteria. Of course in subjects where interviews or auditions are conducted, or which have specialist professional requirements, the decision on individual applications is often still made directly by an academic member of staff, and unusual or particularly complex applications will often be passed to them. An academic staff member will usually be actively involved in promoting the subject and answering subject-specific questions.

This development in admissions practice is intended to ensure greater consistency in offers made, as well as freeing valuable academic time for research and teaching. However it does mean that often an application is initially considered against set criteria and prerequisites by a non-specialist in the subject. This point is significant in considering perceptions of the IB as it affects who needs to know about the diploma. While most higher education institutions now have policies on the IB diploma in place, it may be that the IB or a school feels that it needs to bring something to the attention of key staff in a higher education institution. While in a well-run admissions operation there will be an excellent flow of information between administrative admissions staff and academic colleagues, it may still be worth sending information to both groups, to make sure that policies and decisions are based on up-to-date information. In practical terms this might mean copying emails to both the central undergraduate admissions office (the address should be easy to find on a website) and the 'course director' or 'admissions tutor' in the specific department in which the course is offered (a key contact or point for enquiries should be identified on subject fact files or entry profiles, on the website or in the prospectus).

The offer of admission, and the 'granularity' of the IB

In UK higher education the offer of admission has a variety of purposes. Its central purpose is to ensure that appropriately qualified students are admitted to the institution and to each course. Usually it is necessary for an applicant first to meet a general academic standard for the institution as a whole. Some readers will remember that universities used to have 'matriculation requirements': a particular group of subjects, often including mathematics and language subjects at GCSE or equivalent and with grades at a minimum level, which had to be met in order to be admitted. Some institutions still have them. Such requirements often form a bare minimum and in reality the institution's minimum may be much higher; not only are well-qualified students thought to be more likely to succeed, but students with higher entrance qualifications will reflect well on the institution when compared to its competitors (and will give it an advantage in university league tables).

It is also necessary for applicants to fulfil the specific requirements of a course. In the case of some professional courses it may also be necessary to meet requirements set by the professional bodies or regulatory authorities. For example, a professional engineering body may have specific requirements both about the subjects that must be successfully completed in pre-higher education examinations and the grades that must be achieved. So someone who has applied to study mechanical engineering, for instance, might both have to meet a general requirement for admission to the institution and to show evidence of specific knowledge and ability in mathematics and physics. Interestingly, professional courses may also have specific GCSE or standard grade/intermediate requirements, such as particular grades in mathematics and English; this is the case with many teaching courses, for example. These requirements, and the way equivalencies are decided on, can pose problems for applicants from many other examination systems (including the holders of IB MYP qualifications, who may be told that their own qualifications do not meet these requirements). It may be that admissions offices have no option but to reject these applicants, frustrating though that is for all concerned.

Another purpose of the offer is its function as a way of managing numbers to meet a particular intake target. Although funding arrangements for home/EU students are changing, currently institutions across the UK are still seeking to admit an exact number of students. If they exceed this number they will face 'fines' from government funding bodies and if they fall below target their income will be reduced. The UCAS Chief Executive, Mary Curnock-Cook, has likened this process to landing an aircraft on a moving postage stamp. Although government agencies do not control numbers of international students, and while in the future student number controls for UK/EU students may be relaxed, universities and colleges will still need to plan for specific numbers to ensure, amongst other things, that classes are not too big for the facilities available and that there is enough accommodation.

At the time of 'confirmation' (the period before the start of the academic year when final intake numbers are decided) an institution needs to 'fine-tune' its intake to meet the exact intake target. It therefore has to be able to discriminate very finely between different applicants to decide who can, and cannot, be admitted. One way of doing this is to use discretion in deciding which applicants who have not met an offer should still be accepted. So, for example, if an A level offer is BBB and an applicant is awarded ABC, the institution can decide whether or not the applicant's place will be confirmed.

Crucial to both these functions of the offer is the precision with which the offer can be made: 'granularity' in the sense used by admissions staff. With usually only three subjects taken, and over 25% being awarded 'A' or 'A*' grades, A levels have been a somewhat imprecise measure and there has been widespread discussion about how effective they are in distinguishing between excellent candidates. In particular it is felt that 'selective' institutions (the more competitive universities and colleges that receive a very large number of applications for each place) are simply not able to get to the right number of students by using A level grades to distinguish between them. This is also an issue for some courses in 'recruiting' institutions (less competitive institutions that receive fewer applications per place) as increasingly they find they have some specialised courses that are in high demand.

The IB diploma, by contrast, is noteworthy in offering a very high degree of granularity. The possibility of, for example, asking for 32 points overall, including six in higher level history, five in higher level French A1 and six in standard level mathematical studies means that it is possible to specify very exactly what is wanted. By implication it gives institutions the capacity to exercise their discretion at confirmation – and to take the numbers they want.

In making offers, institutions also have to be aware of their position compared to their competitors. An institution will have to make offers in the light of those made by competitor institutions, both to 'signal' the kind of institution they are and to ensure that the applicants they want accept their offer in preference to others. Further information about this issue may be found in the advice for admissions officers on planning and managing admissions, which can be found on the Supporting Professionalism in Admissions website (SPA, 2011).

IB and 'unfair offers'

'You say that universities do not understand the IB. On the contrary, they *do* understand the IB and are asking for exactly what they want', was a comment by Connie Cullen, then Director of Admissions at the University of York, at the UCAS International Baccalaureate Forum held in Cheltenham on 1 May 2009. (Presentations from the Forum are available on the UCAS website: UCAS, 2011c)

IB schools often talk about the 'unfairness' of higher education's IB diploma offers. This generally refers to offers considered to be too high compared to A levels, or unreasonably high in themselves, or having an excessive number of specific requirements. Schools sometimes comment that these offers are made because HEIs do not 'understand' the IB. On what is this idea of 'unfairness' based? – and is it true that higher education institutions do not understand the IB?

One aspect of this perception of unfairness stems from the IB's relationship to the UCAS tariff (UCAS, 2011e). Following the standard tariff review process, the decision on the IB diploma's entry into the tariff was made in 2006, for applicants starting in 2008. Famously, when compared to A levels the IB was allocated very high tariff points. A good IB student, for example, who had received 34 points in the diploma, received 479 tariff points: effectively the equivalent of AAAA at A level – an exceptional score in A level terms. Many leading institutions felt that this relationship was unreasonable and continued to maintain their former offers. I remember attending Council of International Schools (CIS) and European Council of International Schools (ECIS) conferences in 2006, shortly after the announcement had been made, and being told by almost all the experienced IB teachers there that the tariff points as awarded did not reflect a true equivalence; that a student with 29 IB points was not the same as one with AAB at A level. Understandably, however, many schools – and students and their families – expected institutions to use the tariff and objected strongly when they did not.

There are various responses to the concern of schools. One is that many of the more 'selective' (competitive) institutions, to which IB diploma candidates often apply, do not normally use the tariff in offers (since each individual HEI can decide whether or not to use the tariff). There is no reason, therefore, why they should accept IB/tariff equivalence. In addition, in the context of the current admissions system, higher education institutions may need to match the offers of competitors and so will make the same demands of applicants so that they must make a choice. There also seems to be greater awareness of the diversity of practice in higher education and an understanding of the realities of current admissions practice. For example, the IBSCA website now notes when talking of the UCAS tariff that 'it is not used by most UK universities in making offers; they say that comparing the full IB diploma with three A levels is not practicable'. It is reasonable, however, that schools should question very high offers if they seem to be out of line with other non-IB offers. If institutions are to make high demands of IB diploma candidates then it is reasonable to expect that similar demands should be made of those holding other qualifications, including using the range of unit grade and 'A*' possibilities that now exist within A level. If institutions are not doing this it may be reasonable to ask what is the reason for that difference. As already noted, UCAS has recently announced a comprehensive review of the tariff: the 'Qualifications Information Review' (QIR) (UCAS, 2011d). It will be interesting to follow its progress and see what its effect will be.

Stability

Over the past 15 years the school curriculum throughout the UK has encountered an extraordinary degree of turbulence. England saw the reforms of Curriculum 2000 with the introduction of modules and the new AS, the rejection of the Tomlinson proposal for an overarching diploma, and the introduction of the advanced diplomas, while in Wales the introduction of the Welsh Baccalaureate and now in Scotland the Curriculum for Excellence and the Scottish Baccalaureate have all presented higher education institutions with an ongoing set of challenges. In addition, it is felt some of these reforms are 'politicised', in that they are initiated by governments, without clear ownership by or involvement of the education community (Hodgson *et al*, 2005). They also tend to be introduced very quickly – not allowing higher education institutions the needed time to adapt their curricula. By contrast the IB diploma has offered an extraordinary degree of continuity; free of the pressures that face a mass system such as A levels, there is a feeling that the IB today can be understood as being comparable to the IB yesterday.

There is also a continuing UK worry over grade inflation, particularly in the case of A levels. Each results period in August brings forth extensive media and political comment on increasing pass rates, particularly in the higher grades, with the associated assumption that higher pass rates must mean lower standards. While it is difficult to say whether or not these concerns are justified in the case of A levels, the feeling among many is that the IB does not encounter the same problem and the standard has not changed – and, by extension, that the same reliance can be placed on it.

The IB: a qualification for the elite?

I recall, in the past, a stereotypical IB student being described as someone who looks as if they have 'walked out of a Benetton ad': a student from an international background with a prosperous professional family. Is this true? Is the IB diploma just an academic qualification for international schools – and, in the UK, some independent schools who wish for a qualification free from government interference? Internationally an increasing number of schools in national systems are adopting the IB diploma, with recent estimates that only about 20 percent of schools offering the diploma are 'international' schools. In the UK context, of the 217 schools and colleges offering the Diploma Programme in 2011 only 36 percent were from the independent sector, while the other 64 percent were maintained schools or colleges (personal communication from the IB). So IB students studying in the UK are likely to be from a mix of different socio-economic backgrounds and from different areas and types of school.

But from the point of view of UK universities and colleges taking IB students the position is more complex. The IB recently commissioned from the UK's Higher Education Statistics Agency (HESA) a major study: *International Baccalaureate Students studying at UK Higher Education Institutions: How do they fare?* The report shows, for example, that of the total intake in 2008/9, irrespective of fee status, the percentage of IB students domiciled outside the UK is 64.5 percent (compared to 3.5 percent for A levels), they are significantly more likely to come from higher socio-economic groups and they are more likely to attend the more selective 'top' institutions. It also shows that IB diploma students do well – but then surely non-IB students from supportive backgrounds and well-resourced schools will also do well?

Does all of this matter? Well, it might. How the IB diploma is perceived by UK institutions will be affected by the students who present themselves at those institutions with the IB diploma. On the one hand the perception will be positive, given the students' academic skills and success, but at the same time will it seem that most of these students are from a privileged background? Institutions that are now taking special care to widen the base of their UK intake may wish to consider these matters carefully.

It will be interesting to see whether the introduction of the new IB career-related certificate leads to significant changes to the groups of students offering IB programmes, and to the types of courses and institutions to which they apply. And the number of schools offering the IB diploma that are neither 'international' nor 'independent' is changing, both in the UK and throughout the world.

The future

The IB and its member schools have worked hard to promote the IB diploma to UK higher education, not losing sight of the need to prove its worth for entry to higher education. This work continues. For example, the IB and IBSCA have worked with the Specialist Schools and Academies Trust (SSAT) to offer conferences for university admissions staff, and a new IBSCA/IBAEM university liaison officer will succeed Nick Lee (Lee, 2011).

The IB itself is changing; parts of the diploma are being renamed, the IB careers-related certificate is promising to take the IB into new areas, and the kind of schools that offer IB qualifications is changing. The IB has strong and well-recognised qualifications, established over a number of years. They are now facing many changes and the IB, and IB schools, will have to continue to work hard, and imaginatively, as they seek both to maintain the IB's current position and to build acceptance of different type of qualification – and possibly different types of student.

References

Cabinet Office (2011): *Opening Doors, Breaking Barriers: A Strategy for Social Mobility.* London: HM Government. Online: http://download.cabinetoffice.gov.uk/social-mobility/opening-doors-breaking-barriers.pdf (last accessed 21 August 2011).

Cambridge Assessment (2011): *A Better Approach To Higher Education/Exam Board Interaction For Post-16 Qualifications.* Cambridge: Cambridge Assessment. Online (accessed 21 August 2011): www.cambridgeassessment.org.uk/ca/digitalAssets/193735_Cambridge_Assessment_HE_engagement_June_2011.pdf

Cambridge, J (2003): Identifying the globalist and internationalist missions of international schools, in *International Schools Journal*, 22 (2), pp54-58.

Conservatoires UK Admissions Service (CUKAS) (2011): Online: www.cukas.ac.uk (last accessed 26 August 2011).

Department for Business, Innovation and Skills (BIS) (2011): Higher Education White Paper, 2011. *Students at the Heart of the System.* London: HMSO. Online (last accessed 21 August 2011): http://discuss.bis.gov.uk/hereform/white-paper/

Eurydice (2011): *Overview of education in England, Wales and Northern Ireland.* Online: www.nfer.ac.uk/nfer/index.cfm?9B1817FF-C29E-AD4D-0F94-7C84904BFE2E (last accessed 21 August 2011).

Higher Education Statistics Agency (HESA) (2011): *International Baccalaureate Students studying at UK Higher Education Institutions: How do they fare?* Online: www.ibo.org/research/programmevalidation/documents/ HESAUKPostsec_Final_Report.pdf (last accessed 21 August 2011).

Hodgson, A, Spours K and Waring, M (2005): Higher Education, Curriculum 2000 and the Future Reform of 14-19 Qualifications in England, in *Oxford Review of Education,* 31 (4), pp479-495.

IB Online: www.ibo.org/ (last accessed 21 August 2011).

IB (2003): *Perceptions of the International Baccalaureate Diploma Programme: A report of an inquiry carried out in 2003 at UK universities and institutions of higher education.* Online: www.ibo.org/diploma/recognition/perceptions.cfm (last accessed 23 June 2011).

International Baccalaureate Schools and Colleges Association (IBSCA) (2011): Universities and the IB. Online: www.ibsca.org.uk/index.php/universities-and-ib (last accessed 24 August 2011).

Lee, N (2011): Personal communication from Nick Lee.

Scottish Government (2011): Overview of education in Scotland. Online: www.scotland.gov.uk/Publications/2005/06/13112946/29559 (last accessed 21 August 2011).

Supporting Professionalism in Admissions Programme (SPA) (2011): *Good Practice: Planning and Managing Admissions.* Online: www.spa.ac.uk/good-practice/offer-making.html (last accessed 25 June 2011).

UK Council for International Student Affairs (UKCISA) (2011): *Home fees: who is eligible?* Online: www.ukcisa.org.uk/student/fees_student_support.php (last accessed 21 August 2011).

UCAS – Universities and Colleges Admissions Service (2011a): www.ucas.ac.uk (last accessed 25 August 2011.)

UCAS (2011b): *Admissions Process Review.* Online (last accessed 23 June 2011): www.ucas.ac.uk/reviews/admissionsprocessreview/

UCAS (2011c): International Baccalaureate Forum, 1 May 2009. Online (last accessed 25 August 2011): www.ucas.com/he_staff/quals/ib

UCAS (2011d): Qualifications Information Review. Online: hwww.ucas.co.uk/reviews/qireview/ (last accessed 23 June 2011).

UCAS (2011e): UCAS Tariff. Online: www.ucas.com/students/ucas_tariff/tarifftables/ (last accessed 25 June 2011).

Welsh Baccalaureate Qualification (2011): *What is the Welsh Baccalaureate?* Online: www.wbq.org.uk/eng/wbq-home-2010/wbq_2010_home.htm (last accessed 25 June 2011).

Chapter 16

Promoting understanding and tolerance in a post-conflict society: the role of the IB diploma at the United World College in Mostar

Paul Regan

Introduction

At a meeting in Swaziland in March 2006 the international board of the United World Colleges (UWC, 2011) agreed to the establishment of two new colleges, one of which was to be located in an area of recent ethnic and religious conflict where significant divisions within society still prevailed: the city of Mostar in Bosnia and Herzegovina. The decision was the culmination of several years of research and lobbying by a small group of Balkan experts from within and outside Bosnia and Herzegovina. During this period a number of interested parties, including the Sarajevo Embassies of the Netherlands, Norway and Germany, the Council of Europe Development Bank, the Organization for Security and Co-operation in Europe (OSCE) and the Ministry of Education responsible for the City of Mostar added their support, including substantial promises of financial sponsorship.

It is not surprising that the United World College (UWC) international board gave its decision, in spite of understandable misgivings from certain members that there was too little time to set up such a college, that the local political divisions would kill it at birth, and that the financial underpinning was not yet secure. Other problems relating to the location of the college, the likely interest in sending their students there of National Selection Committees (who have responsibility in different national contexts for raising and allocating the funding that allows students to attend UWCs on a scholarship basis (UWC, 2011)), and the probable reluctance to accept an international college in Bosnia and Herzegovina were all deemed to lend themselves to solutions. In spite of the political, financial and practical challenges, the decision was seen at the time to be an opportunity for the UWC movement to reaffirm its commitment to bringing peace through education. If this college could succeed in its principal aim to foster active tolerance between the ethno-religious groups; Serbs, Bosniaks (Bosnian Muslims) and Croats (Catholics), then maybe it could provide a model for a fresh initiative aimed at societies emerging from conflict or where future civil conflict was likely to break out. With wars raging in Iraq and Afghanistan, international terrorism on the rise, and the memories of genocide in both Rwanda and former Yugoslavia still recent, these colleges, in whatever form they might take, could become a key player in some future post-conflict scenario involving healing, forgiving, and uniting. Indeed, wherever schools were used to divide young people rather than unite them, the UWC template – underpinned by the International Baccalaureate (IB) programmes – could be invoked. The IB was represented on the proto board of the new school by its Director General, who saw in this marriage between the IB and the UWC an opportunity to use practical examples of implementation 'on the edge' to inform decisions for future expansion.

Why Mostar?

In 1993 Mostar itself had been the theatre for a vicious 'war within a war', in the middle of the larger conflict that raged across the regions of former Yugoslavia in the wake of the political disintegration of that country in 1992. Yugoslavia under Marshall Tito, who had himself faced down an early threat of Soviet invasion, has been regarded as a poster child for communism when Stalin and Kruschev were terrifying the West with threats of nuclear annihilation. After the Second World War the country acquired a measure of political stability, economic prosperity, and ethnic tolerance, which belied the patchwork of local rivalries and linguistic divisions and disparities in wealth and opportunities. Yugoslavs, officially at least, spoke the same language (Serbo-Croat), served in the same army, had one football team, and developed a thriving export industry. The West fell in love with Tito and, in time honoured way, turned a blind eye to the endemic corruption, occasional purge, judicial murders, and ideologically driven experiments in collective farming. Health care and education were free and generally good, and two whole generations grew up in peace, inter-married, and went to the same schools.

After Tito's death in 1983, this elegant contrivance started to fall apart; not immediately, but with gathering momentum over several years until the convulsions in other parts of Eastern and South Eastern Europe and Russia in 1989 created the conditions for national resurgence and economic independence. Unfortunately, unlike those countries to the north such as Hungary, Poland and Czechoslovakia, in Yugoslavia the scene was set for an opening of old wounds that had lain dormant since the Second World War and which also had deeper historical roots. During that War the Ustase, mainly from Croatia, had collaborated with the occupying Nazi forces to repress the Serbs, Muslims and others with a zeal that astonished the Nazis themselves. Serb Chetniks has fought with equal barbarity.

Although in 1991-1992 the leading actors were entering the stage (Milosevic in Belgrade, and Tudjman in Croatia), to this day many people will say that right up until the first days of hostilities, very few seriously expected that a war would rage – never mind one that cost at least 100,000 lives and displaced millions. The historian Niall Ferguson has written that catastrophe rather than inevitability drives historical events, citing the falls of the Roman and British

Empires, and the outbreak of the First World War, as examples (Ferguson, 2010). It is only after the events have taken place that historians then seek to prove meaning, cause and effect, and predictability. The catastrophe that overtook Bosnia and Herzegovina in 1992, after it had declared its independence from the rapidly disintegrating Yugoslavia (Croatia and Slovenia had already seceded) left that rump country ravaged by Serb forces to the east and north, by its own Bosnian Serb forces, and intermittently by Croatian forces. As with the horrors of Rwanda, happening simultaneously on another continent, the real tragedy lay with the initial inaction of the United Nations, NATO, and the European Union. A widespread doctrine that intervention in 'civil war' should be avoided meant that the Bosnian Muslim army was starved of arms whilst the Serbs were able to use the intact weaponry of the Yugoslav army, and that their capital city of Sarajevo had to suffer the longest siege of any capital city in modern history, during which 10,000 of its citizens lost their lives. The fear that Bosnia and Herzegovina was also being used as a base for Al Qaeda and other Jihadist groups lent support to that argument.

Mostar was hardly a sideshow. During 1993, when the Bosnian Muslims (Bosniaks) and Croats, both enemies of the Serbs, fell out briefly over the future political map of Bosnia and Herzegovina, a vicious little war erupted and played out over six months. In the process 1500 lives were lost, thousands departed to become refugees, and the city became literally split into two with the main boulevard becoming the front line. The iconic Mostar Bridge was destroyed by shelling, and the equally iconic Mostar Gymnasia became the front line headquarters of the Croatian militia, in the process sustaining repeated bomb damage. It is ironic that the construction of this original school building had been a fusion of two architectural traditions, Moorish and south European; a tribute to the more enlightened colonial policies of the late Austrian period. More deeply, the town laid down a map that divided itself in two. Never mind that before the war the town had the highest number of mixed marriages and a history of tolerance between communities. As soon as the conflict was over and the physical process of rebuilding had started (which even to date is by no means completed), the psychological separation was profound. Distrust, suspicion and misunderstanding were the norms, and relationships between Croats and Bosniaks – most of the Serbs having already departed in 1992 – were at their lowest ebb.

Education has certainly played a part in this situation. The Dayton Agreement, signed in 1995 to bring an end to the hostilities, had failed to prioritize schooling as an agent in reuniting the once warring communities and, when there was an opportunity to revise the agreement in 2000, failed again to make the point. One of my first meetings on taking up the post of founding head teacher of the UWC in Mostar in July 2006 was with the Ambassador of Norway in Sarajevo. He had painted a dismal picture for the future of Bosnia and Herzegovina as a possible failed state, unlikely in the near future to heal its divisions; a reality that could lead to further conflict. The Section Chief of the OSCE was promoting the new doctrine of education as a form and guarantor of future security. But the minority Croatian population, mainly based in western Herzegovina and Mostar, had other ideas. They now had their own language (Croatian), their own political party (HDZ), their own religion (Catholicism) and their own schools. An understandable fear that their history, culture, language, value system and even religion might be undermined by shared classes with Muslims had led to a grotesque situation of separate school buildings, or even separate entrances and classes in the same building ('two schools under one roof'). In their separate schools, students could study a different historical interpretation of the same events, could learn to differentiate themselves linguistically and culturally from their neighbours and, in some cases, to learn the dangers of peer association with someone from the wrong group. This situation further led to various collateral abuses such as students needing either to travel huge distances to be in a 'Croatian' or a 'Muslim' school, or to be submerged in a culture within their own country which was fundamentally alien. Bosnia and Herzegovina was further divided between no fewer than 11 Ministries of Education (within its various cantons) and, where Serbs still resided, the same principles applied. These cantons formed the political structure of local government within the Federation of Bosnia and Herzegovina, which is itself one of two 'entities' forming the state of Bosnia and Herzegovina, the other being the Serb Republic.

Impact of the college opening

From its opening in September 2006, the impact of the United World College in Mostar (UWCiM) was dramatic. It took up residence in the previously bombed and still only partly renovated building already mentioned, which it shared with the first experiment, brokered by the OSCE, to deepen cooperation between Croats and Bosniaks in the Mostar Gymnasia. Croat and Bosniak students in the gymnasia were still taught their own history, language, and social sciences, but in timetabling there was recognition that there was scope for integrated teaching in 'neutral' subjects such as mathematics, the sciences, and even the arts. The UWCiM was swiftly authorized to teach the International Baccalaureate (IB) Diploma Programme (DP) in spite of having no library, very few library books, insufficient classroom space, and half of its staff (the local teachers) having no prior experience in teaching the IB diploma curriculum. This could be seen as a courageous decision by the IB authorization team, which was able to recognize that enlightened self-interest would help the college to open up the landscape for educational reform in the country at large.

So in 2006 the college enrolled a hundred 16-19 year old students in its first IB diploma generation, of whom 85 percent came from Serbian, Bosniak and Croatian families, with the remainder from outside the former Yugoslavia, including the UK, The Netherlands, Finland, Germany, Palestine, Israel and

Italy. In subsequent years the ratio changed in favour of international students, and Hong Kong, the USA, Egypt, Lebanon, Norway, Austria, Belgium and Spain all sent students. Students were to share residences as well as classrooms and extracurricular activities. The college administration had a tough task to fulfil. On the one hand it hoped to promote educational reform. This would be pedagogical and political. On the other hand it sought to integrate students not only physically but also psychologically, and to sow the first seeds for future leadership of the country. But, paradoxically, it also wished to provide a normal environment for adolescent growth through learning, activities and competent and loving supervision and care. The teaching faculty meanwhile reflected the student composition. The local teachers were also recruited from all three ethno-religious groups, and were supported by a small group of non-local teachers already experienced in IB diploma teaching who would act as their mentors. The ultimate outcome would be a school with a local administration and primarily local staff, trained in IB teaching and standards, able to promote the values of the IB within their own country, and to help to bring about education reform and an end to divided schooling. The timescale for all this would be three years, an ambition later universally regarded as risibly naive and unattainable. The glue would be the IB diploma itself, with its emphases on the learner profile, international-mindedness, intercultural understanding, historical multiperspectivality and critical thinking.

The task of integration

The physical part of the task was relatively straightforward; if you put young people with different backgrounds in the same room for two years; if you teach them in the same classes; and if you ensure that they share the same activities, then you can let human nature do the rest. Eventually, some level of camaraderie and *esprit de corps* will prevail based on mutual interests. By and large this was successful. Over time, the students did learn to discuss the differences that defined their communities in a rational and critical way, and these discussions did change views and perceptions, and lessen prejudices. Research undertaken during 2008-2009, for instance, identified four main areas that were influential in promoting integration within the student body:

- learning together in class
- shared student residences
- interacting with others from different cultures
- shared extracurricular activities

(Hayden and Thompson, 2010; Hayden and Thompson, 2012)

In each of these areas, evidence was found of growing mutual understanding and respect across cultural groupings of students, consistent with the 'contact hypothesis' of Allport (1988) (and subsequent researchers including Dovidio *et al*, 2005), which suggests that prejudice between groups may be reduced where a number of key conditions are present: equal group status as perceived by members of each group; common goals, shared across and between groups; inter-group cooperation, involving collaboration rather than competition; and the support of authority.

Impact of the IB diploma on the wider aims of the college

The extent to which exposure to IB diploma methodology contributed to positive changes in attitude is difficult to measure. Was it possible that the requirement to treat knowledge claims with scepticism and to measure them against rigorous testing from the Aristotelian definition of knowledge as 'justified true belief' proved to be a factor in examining old prejudices? Could the search for international-mindedness, cultural understanding and global citizenship have encouraged a worldview in which the squabbles of the previous generation now seemed paranoid and petty? Could the examination of historical events through interpretation of sources and critical evaluation of evidence have dispelled myths or untruths about the past?

Theory of knowledge

The IB theory of knowledge (ToK) component seems at first sight to be the most practical medium in which to explore issues of cultural identity. Teaching ToK to international groups of students provides a practical laboratory to test out the efficacy of the course, which is intended after all to encourage students to reflect on the nature and essence of knowledge through the prism of their own experiences. A good ToK teacher sets out to initiate the personal examination of assumptions that can free students from the lazy bonds of common sense and prejudice. The student can then move on to becoming a lifetime devotee of practical philosophical judgement in the sense of being able to apply a critical lens to information, and action based on shared knowledge. The student from The Netherlands who objects strongly to child labour in any form might be challenged by her contemporary from Afghanistan who was himself a child labourer in order to feed his family. The student from the UK who agrees with the notion of global citizenship as a way to achieve world peace and understanding may be surprised to find that his classmate from China finds the concept to be a Judaeo/Christian concept refined through the enlightenment, colonialism and western economic dominance.

The Serb, Bosniak and Croatian students in the ToK classes invariably showed flair for philosophical speculation based on their own pre-IB learning in the state schools. Concepts such as free will, ethics, the nature of consciousness, Platonic ideals and Cartesian doubt were more clearly within their grasp than they were for most students from other countries who came to them without much prior learning. But invariably the exploration of the nature of historic knowledge, and the problem of knowledge itself as it is often defined through culture and language, were difficult for most of them. Many of them saw an opportunity in their ToK presentations to retell events such as the Srebrenica massacre, or the siege of Sarajevo. The knowledge issues detached themselves from the student who was setting aside rational claims to make an emotional appeal on behalf of the victims. It was difficult to address this in the classroom. As a ToK teacher I was sometimes left wondering if the critical examination of knowledge and prejudice is easier for those who are fortunate enough not to have been directly affected by violence and prejudice themselves.

ToK is sometimes criticized for its rigidity in assessment. The final ToK essay makes too little allowance for students who have little or no grounding in the western tradition of doubt, scepticism, and rational enquiry. The success of the ToK presentation relies on a mature understanding of knowledge issues, something that can lie beyond the grasp of even the most capable student. Nevertheless our results showed that, in spite of all the emotion that many of our local students brought into debate and discussion, they mostly performed well in the final assessments. One evening a Muslim student came to tell me that, for the first time in his life, he had felt able to discuss the recent war of 1992-1995 'in a spirit of enquiry' with his Serbian roommate. This might have been a victory for ToK, since for the first time these young men had established a framework for debate; a set of tools with which to extricate themselves from their respective knowledge boxes and into a shared space for discussion and understanding. This kind of opportunity would not have been afforded to their contemporaries in local state schools where rote learning was encouraged, questions and critical enquiry discouraged, and reflection upon learning considered to be irrelevant.

Other subjects

Other subjects also brought challenges. One teacher of economics in the college wrote:

> IB economics is very challenging for any student and given the rote system of learning in Bosnia I knew it would be an uphill struggle. I normally teach very little in class and instead assign work for students to do at their desks with two students at the board. That way they work on problem sets with lots of discussion amongst the students. If there is a problem with the theory I teach them 'on the fly'. However, in Bosnia I could see that system was not going to work so I reverted to the more standard way of teaching where I would present a lesson, answer any questions and then set exams at regular intervals. I found the international students such as the two young ladies from The Netherlands and the young lady from Finland did an excellent job of asking questions. But the Bosnian students sat in total silence.
>
> Because of the strictness of no discussion in Bosnian classes and their fear of being ridiculed if they asked questions, students were very reluctant to

participate in the learning process. What was a fascinating component was the 'secret language' Bosnian students had worked out. This consisted of constantly whispering to each other in such a low voice that it was hard for me to hear. It was also delivered in some sort of 'code' rather similar to the way they type messages to each other on their mobiles. The only way to break this habit was to stand at the back of the class and teach from there. This was so disturbing to them that they soon stopped whispering.

The economics teacher went on to explain that:

As the year progressed I had many students coming up to me and thanking me for the way the classes were being handled. They finally understood that learning requires participation on their part and not just nodding off while a teacher droned at the front of the class. By the second year the participation was excellent and students volunteered to do presentations which was almost unheard of in Bosnian schools.

I think it was this 'learning community' element which is so characteristic of the IB that really broke the ice and helped these young people go on to get scholarships and do really well in university both at home in Bosnia as well as overseas in the US.

One teacher of theatre in the college wrote:

A challenge for group 6 [the arts] is how one can reconcile objective knowledge with subjective experience, an opposition that was painfully relevant to Mostar and many of our students. Thus I came to see IB theatre as exemplary for a much larger approach to understanding the world and expressing one's experience of it. The theatre assessments rely on establishing an artist's voice, whilst developing and incorporating knowledge from around the world that may be unfamiliar to the learner in both time and place. So at the same time that the student grows in creative output, the depth of knowledge and ability to apply this must also evolve. Instead of becoming fixed in one's belief or idea, as can be the case when one narrative is taught or 'passed down', the range of IB core components (including explicitly *Theatre in the world*) require true breadth, allowing a larger surface of depth. The array of starting points that the syllabus encourages keep students shifting perspective and approach.

At the same time the IB requires independent practical work, in which the student experiences the processes that give birth to ideas and form; and so they look at an idea from *underneath*. In so doing they are *experiencing* ideas of an 'other', whilst formulating and expressing their own. Thereby, to return once more to the specifically difficult context of Mostar (yet one that is pertinent throughout the world), IB theatre required the understanding and appreciation of various truths. This learning model certainly corresponded if not contributed to a very significant process in the lives of our students in Mostar. My only frustration is that this continues to be the only subject group that is still optional in the IB diploma.

The learner profile

The IB learner profile is a wish list for the virtuous person that goes way beyond the normal requirements for learning itself. Critics might argue that no assessment authority has the right to make these demands, which hark back to the Socratic/Aristotelian ideal that ethics consist of a set of virtues that, when taken together, create the virtuous person and promote right behaviour and obedience to convention. The history of ethics would also include at least the notions of rights and obligations, sympathy and utility, and piety. The IB student is basically meant to be a good person. It is easy to find fault with such an arbitrary list drawn up by committee no doubt, but in fact, as a guide to teachers and students, it can be very effective. One good example is academic honesty.

Our local students mostly came from academic backgrounds where cheating was considered normal even though it could be occasionally be punished. The issue could be summed up as 'if you can get away with it then do it'. Cheating was generally assumed to be something that you probably should not do in examinations, but otherwise it was acceptable. Teachers and students were known to conspire together to raise marks, and students' achievements – to some extent – were dependent upon the goodwill of the teacher. Outside tuition was normal, and results were unreliable.

The IB insistence on academic honesty as an axiom from which all academic behaviour was derived was seen as a strange concept. There was felt to be nothing wrong with copying from a friend or from a book, and no difference between working as a group on a shared task and simply plagiarizing or failing to give references to borrowed ideas. Research was confined to copying from the internet, and teachers were there to raise the grades if they could be persuaded to do so. Clearly those students from local state schools had huge problems in coming to terms with these notions of academic honesty, and some of them up until the end were unable to grasp it. However, for the majority of students the expectation was also a revelation. Most impressive were those students who were able in their history lessons, for example, to work together on presentations about their own past, bringing their own perspective or, more impressively, assuming the perspective of the other side. Not only the expectation that history be interpreted through trawling through evidence and reliable sources, but also that knowledge itself is best approached from a position of independent thought and honest appraisal of facts, turned many of our local students into fine historians.

One aspect of the IB diploma, and to a certain extent the ideals of the UWCs, which can fail to impress is an apparent assumption that the notions of universal tolerance and understanding between cultures are taken as self evident and right. They may be right but they are certainly not obvious to many, and it must be the case that many students, including a greater proportion of our local students relative to their international contemporaries, were greatly challenged by the expectation that one should approach other belief systems with acceptance and understanding. I used to invite adult audiences to imagine that they had been required to spend a night in a hotel in the same room as someone from a different culture who was determined to persuade them that their cultural conventions and historical traditions were right. Imagine now that you have to spend two years with that person. In fact that is exactly what we were asking our students to do. I am not convinced that all teachers in international schools are aware of, or sensitive to, the pressure to which we expose students by failing to explain the nuances of cultural – not to mention ethical – relativism. The situation is best summed up thus: how can we be tolerant of something that is abhorrent (stoning women for adultery, for instance)? Often cited in this regard is the famous and apocryphal story of the King of Persia (an old favourite of ToK classes), who had to arbitrate an argument between one tribal group, which burned their dead, and another tribe, which ate their dead, but who did not see that he had the right to judge since he was himself relying on his own belief system and cultural convention. The example provided by our local students, who really were not so very far apart, showed that it could be done providing certain conditions are met. These relate mainly to the institution itself, and the extent to which it generates a sense of solidarity, common goals, and universal respect. But, given the priority assigned by the IB to the importance of understanding and tolerance, which are more of a theoretical challenge to those studying in a school whose catchment is drawn mainly from a predominant culture, should not a core course in ethics, culture and beliefs itself become a core component at least for students who study, as it were, on the front line? In other words, should the IB consider different programmes in different contexts and be more sensitive to location and situation?

How did the college realize its aims?

It may be wondered how one of our aims – that we should neither try to politicize our students nor do so by accident or neglect – was fulfilled, given all of the above. It was true that we were engaged in a degree of benign social engineering, albeit with willing participants, and that our aim was to bring about reform and greater integration by example. But how could we justify our treatment of those students on ethical grounds?

According to Kant's categorical imperative, which provides a universal precept for many of our social and legal interactions, all individuals must be treated as ends in themselves and not as a means to an end (Gregor, 1997). They must in effect be treated with equal dignity and be accorded equal rights as long as they in turn acknowledge and act upon their obligations. Was the Mostar College using the students as agents to realize broader political, social and educational objectives?

The answer to this question presented itself to me in the first term of the college opening, and again the IB framework provided at least a part of the answer. By giving the students opportunities for self discovery outside their comfort zones and away from home, by providing the tools for critical thinking through ToK and their other IB subjects, by bringing them together in exciting and humbling creativity, action, service (CAS) activities, and by also allowing them to discover and explore at their own pace without external pressure, we were treating the students only as we ourselves would wish to be treated. Furthermore, the issues that had separated many of these students before they came to the college were rarely if ever explicitly discussed unless the discussion was prompted by the students. The pace was never forced, and this in fact led to criticism early on that we were not fulfilling the terms of some of our agreements with our major donors. I believe this to be a fault of the terms of some donor aid, which may be attached too closely to short-term feel-good targets. The gradual approach meant that the college took some time to settle into a state where it could be supported by its own traditions and where elder students could encourage debate in the younger ones. In the meantime, through the hosting of Model United Nations (MUN) conferences, by leading inter-school political dialogues, and through championing grassroots support for education reform, our own students eventually needed no encouragement. The eventual flowering of their initiatives answered those critics who had wished to see more evidence of reform in other schools. To imagine, as some did, that one school on its own could bring about educational reform in three years was naive and dangerous. History shows that a hoped-for outcome can arise suddenly after years of waiting and preparation. The outcome in Bosnia and Herzegovina is yet to be demonstrated.

The most moving testimony to the experiences of many of our local students has been in the personal statements that they sent to support their applications to universities. Some spoke of a Damascene turning point in their lives, others of the unexpected insights that their unique and challenging environment and unusual activities had given them, and yet others of the opportunities for lifelong learning that the IB methodology has encouraged and nurtured.

Conclusion

Looking ahead, it is interesting to reflect on whether the UWC in Mostar's IB DP might have provided a blueprint for IB schools in other post-conflict societies and, indeed, in other local schools. Some work has been undertaken to see if the general principles of IB, its core components, its range of subjects, its learner profile and its emphasis on international-mindedness can be incorporated into divided national systems such as exist in Bosnia and Herzegovina, which need a cohesive framework to bring them together. Local students in Mostar still learned their own languages – Croatian, Serbian, and Bosnian – no matter how similar they were and, through language, a deeper understanding of their cultures and literary heritage. They could even study their own history, though from more than one perspective, and they were encouraged to take pride in their culture whilst striving to understand the cultures of others.

But perhaps the IB should consider new opportunities that could be opened up for studying a portfolio of topics that enhance understanding of local language, culture and history. Local providers would need to be given greater flexibility if such a hybrid were to work. For the Federation of Bosnia and Herzegovina, where education reform – so desperately needed if the country is to emerge from its dark past – is still struggling to get off the ground (and where, even now in 2011, divisions are still systematic), this model could provide a breakthrough with the right amount of political pressure.

In a broader context, wherever tribes, religions, cultures, belief systems and ethnicities collide, the IB can act as a cohesive educational force to achieve reconciliation and understanding through education. The problem of Bosnia and Herzegovina, whilst still extant, has been replaced in the public consciousness and in public discourse with images and debates concerning the 2011 'Arab Spring'. On the other hand it must be the case that some of the beloved concepts embedded in the IB's ideological armoury will be challenged, as it expands eastwards, by radically different world views, particularly in newly dominant India and China.

Given these two very different challenges, is the IB itself institutionally ready for change, and is it prepared to be more flexible in its approach to pioneer IB schools in similar circumstances? By presenting itself as an overarching framework to enable cohesiveness and outstanding pedagogical practice, the IB could make serious inroads into systems that are in need of reform, and which will be looking in the periods after conflict for something that will unite their schools and educational institutions. It is an opportunity not to be missed.

References

Allport, G (1988): *The Nature of Prejudice.* Reading: Addison-Wesley.

Dovidio, J F, Glick, P and Rudman, L A (eds) (2005): *On the Nature of Prejudice: fifty years after Allport.* Oxford: Blackwell Publishing.

Ferguson, N (2010): Complexity and Collapse: empires on the edge of chaos, in *Foreign Affairs*, March-April 2010, Online: www.foreignaffairs.com/articles/65987/niall-ferguson/complexity-and-collapse (last accessed 5 September 2011).

Gregor, M (ed) (1997): *Kant: Groundwork of the Metaphysics of Morals.* Cambridge: Cambridge University Press.

Hayden, M C and Thompson, J J (2010): *Student Integration in Bosnia and Herzegovina: a study of the United World College in Mostar.* Reading: CfBT Education Trust Online: www.cfbt.com/evidenceforeducation/pdf/06_Bosnia_Report.pdf (last accessed 27 August 2011).

Hayden, M C And Thompson, J J (2012): Improving Intercultural Understanding: a case study of the United World College in Mostar, in C Ellwood (ed), *Learning and Teaching About Islam: Essays in Understanding.* Woodbridge: John Catt Educational Ltd [in press]

UWC (2011): Online: www.uwc.org/ (last accessed 28 August 2011).